Linda Grant was born in Liverpool, the child of Russian and Polish Jewish immigrants. Her first novel, *The Cast Iron Shore*, won the David Higham Award and was shortlisted for the Guardian Fiction Prize. Her second novel, *When I Lived in Modern Times* (Granta Books) won the Orange Prize for Fiction and was shortlisted for the Jewish Quarterly Prize and the Encore Prize. Her other novels *Still Here* and *The Clothes on Their Backs* were longlisted and shortlisted for the Man Booker Prize respectively. Grant's non-fiction includes *Sexing the Millennium*, *The People on the Street*, which won the Lettre Ulysses Prize for Literary Reportage and *The Thoughtful Dresser*. *Remind Me Who I Am Again* won the MIND Book of the Year and the Age Concern Book of the Year Award.

From the Reviews of *Remind Me Who I Am Again*:

'Linda Grant's book is an honest inquiry into a family of Jewish immigrants for whom identity was a self-made construct even before memory loss began to chip away at the truth. We can't all identify with this struggle for assimilation but there is so much here I could identify with that I found the book gripping.' Lesley Garner, *Scotland on Sunday*

'A skilful, moving, even humorous book. It is more than an elegy for a lost mother or the charting of one human being's decline that might make you weep for us all. It is an investigation of memory, which concludes that "Memory, I have come to understand, is everything, it's life itself"'. Sher

'This is a book about memory, above all, the memory of a family, and an individual's place in it. It is about the pain of loss of memory, about the creation of it, about the manipulation of it. It is also an occasionally funny book, a sometimes happy book, a history book and a medical book.' Claire Rayner, *New Statesman & Society*

Remind Me Who I Am, Again

LINDA GRANT

GRANTA

Granta Publications, 12 Addison Avenue, London W11 4QR

First published in Great Britain by Granta Books 1998
First paperback edition published by Granta Books 1999
This edition published by Granta Books 2011

A CIP catalogue record for this book
is available from the British Library.

1 3 5 7 9 10 8 6 4 2

ISBN 978 1 84708 269 5

Typeset by M Rules

Printed and bound in Great Britain by CPI Bookmarque, Croydon

For Ben

'Every day is alone, by itself; whatever contentment I have had, whatever sorrow I have had.'

HM. Lobotomy patient, 1953

My mother and I are going shopping, as we have done all our lives. 'Now Mum,' I tell her. 'Don't start looking at the prices on everything. I'm paying. If you see something you like, try it on. You are the mother of the bride, after all.'

In recent years my mother has become a poverty shopper; she haunts jumble sales looking for other people's cast-offs. I don't like to think of her trying on someone else's shoes, which she does not because she is very poor but because footwear is fixed in her mind at 1970s prices. Everything she sees in the shops seems to cost a fortune. '*You paid £49.99 for a pair of shoes?*' she would cry. 'They saw you coming.'

'But Mu–um, that's how much shoes cost these days.'

'Yes, but where do you go looking?'

In my childhood, my mother had aspired far beyond her station to be a world-class shopper. Her role models were Grace Kelly and Princess Margaret, Ava Gardner and Elizabeth Taylor. She acquired crocodile shoes and mink stoles, an eternity ring encrusted with diamonds, handbags in burnished patent leather. In her shut-up flat in Bournemouth were three wardrobes full of beautiful, expensive garments all on wooden or satin hangers, many in their own protective linen bags – a little imitation Chanel suit from the sixties that came back into fashion every few years; her black Persian broadtail coat with its white mink collar and her initials, RG, sewn in blue silk thread in a curly-tailed italic script on to the hem of the black satin lining, surrounded by a sprig of embroidered roses; her brown mink hat for high days and holidays.

And so today I want the best for her, as she and my father had always wanted the best for us. 'The best that money can buy,' my father always boasted when he bought anything. 'Only show me the best,' he told shopkeepers.

'So we're looking for a dress?' A nice dress. The sales are still raging through the summer's heat, hot shoppers toiling up and down Oxford Street. We should, I think, find something for £60 or £70. 'John Lewis is full of them,' a friend has said. She has an idea of the kind of dress someone's mother would wear, an old biddy's frock, a shapeless floral sack.

'I don't think that's her kind of thing,' I had told her, doubtfully. But then who knew what was left? Could my mother's fashion sense be so far eroded that she would have lost altogether those modes of judgement that saw that something was classic and something else merely frumpy?

'I'm not having a dress, I want a suit,' my mother says as the doors part automatically to admit the three of us, for tagging along is my nephew, Ben, her grandson, who also likes to shop.

'Okay. A suit. Whatever you like.'

And now we're in the department store, our idea of a second home. My mother has never been much of a Nature lover, an outdoor girl. We used to leave the city once, years ago, when we motored out of town in the Humber Hawk, parked in a layby, ate cold roast chicken from silver foil, then drove home early so my father could watch the racing and my mother refold her clothes. By the sixties we considered a day out to be a drive to the new service station on the M6 where we enjoyed a cup of tea as the cars sped along to London below. My mother has never got her hands dirty in wellingtons, bending down among the flowerbeds to plant her summer perennials. Or put her hands to the oars of a boat or tramped across a ploughed field in the morning frost or breasted any icy waves. She shrinks in fear from sloppy-mouthed dogs and fawning kittens. But show her new improved tights with Lycra! 'They never had that in my day,' she says admiringly on an excursion to Sainsbury's looking at dose-ball washing liquid.

And no outing can offer more escape from the nightmare of her present reality than shopping for clothes, the easiest means we know of becoming our fantasies and generally cheering ourselves up all round. Who needs the psychiatrist's couch when you have shopping? Who needs Prozac?

Through the handbags, gloves and scarves and utilitarian umbrellas. Not a glance at fabrics and patterns for neither my mother nor I have ever run up our own frocks at the sewing machine, shop-bought *always* being superior to home-made in our book. Why do an amateur job when you could get in a professional?

Up the escalators to the first floor where the land of dreams lies all around us, suits and dresses and coats and skirts and jackets. And where to begin? How to start? But my mother has started already.

At once a sale rack has caught her eye with three or four short, navy wool-crêpe jackets with nipped-in waists, the lapels and slanted pockets edged in white, three mock mother-of-pearl buttons to do it up. My mother says she thinks she is a size twelve. She tries the jacket on right then and there and it takes fifty years off her. She stands in front of the mirror as Forties Miss, dashing about London in the Blitz, on her way to her job in Top Ops. She turns to us, radiant. 'What do you think?'

'Perfect.' The sleeves are too long, but this is a small matter. We will summon the seamstress and she will take them up, her mouth full of pins. As my mother folds the sleeves under I steal a covert look at the price-tag. The jacket is reduced to £49.99, and this, in anybody's book, is a bargain.

'Now I need a skirt and blouse. I've got to match the navy.'

She disappears between the rails and I am anxious for it is not hard to lose sight of her, she has shrunk so in recent years. Five feet two all my life but I doubt if she is that now; perhaps she is under five feet. Her grandson, at eleven, is taller than her. How long will it be before he can lean his chin on the top of her head?

She's back quickly with her selection. The navy of the skirt and blouse she has chosen match each other and the jacket exactly, which isn't the easiest thing in the world to do, so I know that her perception of colour is quite unaltered and whatever else is wrong with her, there is nothing the matter with her eyes. I take the garments from her as we walk to the changing rooms, for everything apart from the smallest and lightest of handbags is too heavy for her now. A full mug of tea is too heavy for her to pick up. In cafés where they serve coffee in those large green and gold cups from France, she is stymied, remains thirsty.

What she gives me to hold is a Karl Lagerfeld skirt and a Jaeger blouse both substantially reduced at £89.99 and

£69.99 but not within my £60 budget I had estimated when the old biddy dress was suggested (these hang from rails ignored by my mother). She has obeyed my instruction. Half submerged in whatever part of the brain that contains our capacity to make aesthetic judgements, her old good taste is buried and my injunction to ignore the prices had been the key that released it. A young woman of twenty-five could attend a job interview in the outfit she has put together.

In the changing room, she undresses. I remember the body I had seen in the bath when I was growing up, the convex belly from two Caesarean births that my sister used to think was like a washing-up bowl. The one that I have now, myself. She used to hold hers in under her clothes by that rubberized garment called a roll-on, a set of sturdy elasticized knickers. She had been six-and-a-half stone when she got married, which rose to ten stone after bearing her daughters, and she would spend twenty years adhering to the rules of Weight Watchers without ever noticeably losing a pound. Then she more or less stopped eating when my father died, apart from cakes and sweets and toast with low-calorie marge, on which regimen she shed two stone and twice was admitted to hospital suffering from dehydration.

As she removes her skirt, I turn my head away. It is enough to bear witness to the pornography of her left arm, a swollen sausage encased in a beige rubber bandage, the legacy of a pioneering mid-eighties operation for breast cancer which removed her lymph glands. The armpit is hollow.

The ensemble is in place when I look back. The pencil skirt, a size ten, is an exact fit but the blouse (also a ten) is a little too big, billowing round her hips, which is a shame for it is beautiful, in heavy matt silk with white over-stitching along the button closings.

And now my mother turns to me in rage, no longer placid and obedient, not the sweet little old age pensioner that shop assistants smile at seeing her delight in her new jacket.

Fury devours her. 'I *will* not wear this blouse, you will not *make* me wear this blouse.' She bangs her fist against the wall and (she is the only person I have ever seen do this) she stamps her foot, just like a character from one of my childhood comics or a bad actress in an amateur production.

'What's the matter with it?'

She points to the collar. 'I'm not having anyone see me in this. It shows up my neck.'

I understand for the first time why, on this warm July day as well as every other, she is wearing a scarf knotted beneath her chin. I had thought her old bones were cold, but it is vanity. My mother was seventy-eight the previous week. 'Go and see if they've got it in a smaller size,' she orders.

My patient nephew is sitting beneath a mannequin outside watching the women come and go. There are very few eleven-year-old boys in the world who would spend a day of the school holidays traipsing around John Lewis with their aunt and their senile gran looking for clothes but let's face it, he has inherited the shopping gene. He's quite happy there, sizing up the grown ladies coming out of the changing rooms to say to their friends, 'What do you think? Is it too dressy?' or 'I wonder what Ray's sister will be wearing. I'll kill her if it's cream.'

'Are you all right?' He gives me the thumbs-up sign.

There is no size eight on the rack and I return empty-handed. My mother is standing in front of the mirror regarding herself: her fine grey hair, her hazel eyes, her obstinate chin, the illusory remains of girlish prettiness not ruined or faded or decayed but withered. Some people never seem to look like grown-ups but retain their childish faces all their lives and just resemble elderly infants. My mother did become an adult once but then she went back to being young again; young with lines and grey hair. Yet when I look at her I don't see any of it. She's just my mother, unchanging, the person who tells you what to do.

'Where've you been?' she asks, turning to me. 'This blouse is too big round the neck. Go and see if they've got it in a smaller size.'

'That's what I've been doing. They haven't.'

'Oh.'

So we continue to admire the skirt and the jacket and wait for the seamstress to arrive, shut up together in our little cubicle where once, long ago, my mother would say to me: 'You're not having it and that's final. I wouldn't be seen dead with you wearing something like that. I don't care if it's all the rage. I don't care if everyone else has got one. You can't.'

My mother fingers the collar on the blouse. 'I'm not wearing this, you know. You can't make me wear it. I'm not going to the wedding if I've got to wear this blouse.'

'Nobody's going to make you wear it. We'll look for something else.'

'I've got an idea. Why don't you see if they have it in a smaller size?'

'I've looked already. There isn't one. This is the last . . .'

'No, I must interrupt you. I've just thought, do you think they've got it in a smaller size?'

'That's what I'm trying to tell you. They haven't got one.'

Her shoulders sag in disappointment. 'Anyway,' I say, to

7

distract her, 'the seamstress will be along in a minute to take up the sleeves.'

She glances down at her arms. 'Why? They aren't too long.'

'That's because you folded them up.'

She holds the cuffs between her fingers. 'Oh, that's right.' She looks back at herself in the mirror, smiling. 'I love this jacket. But I don't like the blouse. Well, I do like it but it's too big round the neck. Why don't you nip outside and see if they've got a bigger one?'

'I've been. They haven't. I've told you already.'

'Did you? I don't remember. Have I ever told you that I've been diagnosed as having a memory loss?'

'Yes.'

Now the seamstress has come. My mother shows her the blouse. 'It's too big round the neck,' she tells her. 'Can you take it in?'

'No, Mum, she's here to alter the jacket.'

'Why? There's nothing the matter with it.'

'Yes, there is. The sleeves are too long.'

'No, they aren't.'

'That's because you've turned them up.'

'Well, never mind that. Go and see if they've got this blouse in a smaller size.'

And so it goes, like Alice in the garden, on the path that, whatever she does, always leads straight back to where she started. We are through the looking-glass now, my mother and I, where we wander in that terrible wilderness without landmarks, nothing to tell you that you passed here only moments before. And you thought *Groundhog Day* was just a movie.

We pay for the jacket and the skirt which are wrapped, the jacket remaining, ready to be collected absolutely no later than the day before the wedding, which is cutting it a bit fine but what can you do? We leave John Lewis and walk a few yards to the next store which is D. H. Evans.

Up the escalator to the dress department and on a sale rack is the very Jaeger blouse! And there are plenty of them and right at the front what is there but a size eight.

'Look!' I cry. 'Look what they've got and in your size.'

My mother runs towards me, she really does pick up her legs and break into a trot. '*Well*, they didn't have *that* in John Lewis.'

'They did but it was too big and they didn't have a smaller one.'

'Did they? I don't remember.'

She tries the blouse on in the changing rooms. The fit is much better. She looks at the label. 'Jaguar. I've never heard of them.' Her eyes, which could match navy, sometimes jumbled up letters.

'Not jaguar, Jaeger.'

'*Jaeger!* I've never had Jaeger in my life before.'

'You must be joking. You've got a wardrobe full of it.'

'Have I? I don't remember. Have I told you I've been diagnosed with a memory loss?'

'Yes,' I say. 'You've told me.'

'And now,' my mother announces, 'I need a jacket and a skirt.'

'We've bought those already.'

'Where are they then?'

'The skirt is in this bag and the jacket is being altered.'

'Are you sure?'

'Positive.'

'What colour are they?'

'Navy.'

9

'Well, that's lucky,' she says pointing triumphantly to the blouse, 'because this is navy.'

My mother wants to take the tube home, a tube and a bus, for a taxi is an unnecessary extravagance. 'I'm fresh,' she says. But I am not. A moment always comes, towards the end of these outings, when I want to go into a bar and have a drink, when I wish I carried a hip flask of innocuous vodka to sip, sip, sip at throughout the day. Most of all I want it to stop, our excursion. I can't put up with any more and I fall into cruel, monosyllabic communication. Here is a taxi and do not think for a moment, Madam, that despite the many burdens of your shopping, however swollen your feet or fractious your child, you are going to take this cab before me.

'Get in,' I order. As we drive off up Portland Place I am calculating how much her old biddy outfit has cost. It has come to £209.97 which is more than I have paid for mine and has beaten all of us, including the bride herself, my sister Michele, on designer labels.

My mother holds on to her two purchases, from which floral prints have been rigorously excluded.

She looks at us both, her daughter and grandson. 'Just remind me,' she says. 'How am I related to you?'

My mother is the last. The rest are all dead. My father dead fourteen years, all his five brothers and sisters dead *and* all their husbands and wives. Of a generation which had once posed on a sunny afternoon in the summer of 1950 in my aunt's garden (myself in embryonic form concealed under my mother's blue suit and fur tippet), there was almost no one left. They live there still, on a small piece of photographer's paper, in all their glory, 'like the Mafia', my cousin Sefton remarked once – the men standing like mountains in double-breasted suits and Homburg hats, the women resting on chairs, their prodigious flesh enveloped in what used to be called tea gowns, all, extremely unusually for them, *en plein air* surrounded by flowers and other vegetation, the sun in their eyes. They who believed that only in cities can you breathe freedom's air away from the diurnal tyranny of the land and an ignorant, anti-Semitic peasantry. We used to take my grandfather for runs in the motor to the Lake District, a sort of vacuum between towns without bookshops or bookmakers. Among the low hills, in the dense loneliness of the still air, he would cry in Yiddish: 'Here they could build houses for the workers.'

They were all indoor people, my family. The men liked

11

their rooms blue with the smoke of cigars, the card table set up, a bottle of whisky and cut-glass tumblers on the sideboard while the women were in the kitchen loading what anyone else would describe as a banquet on to a hostess trolley, but which they considered to be no more than a light snack. They loved abundance. It was not an obscenity of over-consumption but rather a way of raising an obscene finger at a past in which men and women and children went to bed with their bellies crampingly empty. When they were finished in the kitchen the women would go upstairs to unwrap their latest purchase from its protective tissue paper, proudly displaying the designer's label. Showed off diamonds and furs and the accomplishments of their pampered, spoilt children. Restricted by the most rudimentary of educations, all the brothers had gone into business on their own account, dealing in lines such as dried eggs, chamois leather, cheap clothes and, in my father's case, the manufacture of shampoo and other chemical concoctions that permed and primped and artificially coloured the hair, and these he sold to hairdressers along with brushes, combs, pins, and the kind of hairdryer you don't see any more, which you parked your head under as if the device were a helmet, the controls in one hand and a copy of *Woman's Own* in the other.

They were all hypochondriacs, constantly kvetching about their lungs and their hearts and their feet, showing anyone who could stomach the sight a look at the greenish, blood-streaked phlegm in their handkerchiefs. And beneath the exuberance there was a slight, depressive morbidity about them, for my father, for one, was prone to falling into terrible rages, tissue-paper anger, my mother called it, followed by sullen brooding in a room on his own. Death terrified them. They didn't know the meaning of introversion or solitude, and certainly not solipsism. Saul Bellow has said that the unexamined life is meaningless but that the examined life can make you want to kill yourself.

Confronted by their interior silences, they panicked. I'm talking about the Ginsbergs here, my father's side. My mother's family was a very different kettle of fish, and one I usually overlooked, blinded by the bright dazzle of the overwhelming charisma of my large aunts and suave, expensively suited uncles, bearing ostentatious gifts.

It was nearly half a century ago, the photograph, and only my mother is still alive out of that opinionated, bombastic, overdressed and overfed clan. And she is also, as it happens, the last of her own line, of her six Haft brothers and sisters, those small unassuming people who left subtler traces behind them in the world. She is looking at me, my mother, from the picture, her hands curled possessively around the arm of the chair, gloveless, clutching a handkerchief and wearing a hat with a small veil, blown by a slight breeze away from her face. She is smirking, staring into the future with confidence. She had bagged what she considered a rich husband, fourteen years older than herself. She had married into a sister-in-law who had a maid. *Had* a maid instead of being one. This woman who a few months later was to become my mother had recently stopped being a back-street girl and had taken her place amongst the charmed tribe who lived in the suburbs where shopkeepers' vans would deliver goods on account. Was soon to move from her honeymoon flat to a semi-detached corner house built between the wars with holly bushes growing on each side of the front door and a garage for my father's motor. A house which cost £5250 and had 'an attractive appearance being brick-built with colour-washed stucco elevations and a two-storey side bay with tile-hung relief'. I know this because she never threw out the estate agent's details from 1950 and they lay there, amongst her papers, until my sister came to clear out her flat and assault the detritus of a life which doesn't have the capacity to tell anyone what it is any more.

I show my mother the photograph now and she looks at it. But she doesn't smirk any more, hasn't had anything to be pleased with herself about for years. If only she had known then what life had in store for her, what would her expression have been?

'Who's he?' she asks, pointing to her brother-in-law, Louis, the chamois leather king, known as the nice one of the family, the second best-looking but the best-dressed, who always had his initials blocked in gold in the leather sweatband of his hats. She's here, with me, but her memory is on a boat that has had its moorings cut and is gone beyond the horizon.

I tell her that I am going to Poland to track down the family's history, my search for roots.

'My parents came from Poland, you know,' she replies.

'No, they didn't. That was Dad's family.'

'Well, where did mine come from then?'

'From Russia, Kiev.'

'Did they? I don't remember. Your Auntie Millie will know. Ask her.'

'Mum, Auntie Millie died.'

She begins to cry. 'When? Nobody told me.'

'It was years ago, even before Dad died.'

'I don't know, I don't remember.'

I don't know if it is a tragedy or a blessing when Jews, who insist on forgiving and forgetting nothing, should end their lives remembering nothing. My mother, the last of her generation, was losing her memory. Only the deep past remained, which emerged at moments, in bits and pieces – the picture of her little bed in the house in Devon Street in Liverpool where she grew up, long since demolished; the fire over which they cooked their food in an iron pot 'and the soot fell in but it tasted better than food does nowadays'; her older sisters and brothers who, when she went to school, clubbed together to buy the spoilt youngest child a cardboard briefcase with her initials blocked on it in gilt, though it dissolved into a soggy mass when it rained. The family was poor but she always had more than they did. 'My brothers and sisters were all working by then,' she told me. 'So I wore *shoes* to school.' They lavished attention and what they could spare from their pay-packets on her, on Rose, their little sister who grew up expecting that unlike them, reared in poverty and trained for hardship, she would always have the best that life could offer.

This moment, the one she is really living in, is lost from sight as soon as it happens. And the long-ago memories are vanishing too. Only fragments remain. So nearly a century of private history with a cast if not of thousands then of dozens – enough to mount a Broadway musical – is reduced to a shrinking lump of meat weighing a pound or two through which electrical impulses pass. Certain areas of it are permanently turned off at the mains.

I run little tests, standing at the bus-stop with her.

'What work did you do before you got married, Mum?'

In her silence cars pass along the road, wind whips the litter, teenage girls do their shrieky number. After a long time she replies: 'Hairdressing.'

'That's right.'

But a couple of months later that is gone too.

'Have I told you I've been diagnosed with a memory loss?'

'Yes, you have mentioned it.'

When she stood in front of the camera that day so long ago, she could confidently guess what the years to come would hold: prosperity, motherhood, the satisfaction of her own home. Now she has no sense at all of the progress of her memory's ebb. I do. She does not know what lies ahead and I'm not going to tell her.

Soon, she will no longer recognize me, her own daughter, and if her disease progresses as Alzheimer's does, her muscles will eventually forget to stay closed against the involuntary release of waste products. She will forget to speak and one day even her heart will lose its memory and forget to beat and she will die. Memory, I have come to understand, is everything, it's life itself.

Sunday is the traditional visiting time at the home. They like to use photographs for reminiscence work and slides are shown of the old East End of London, the immigrant world the residents grew up in.

'Do you remember the Battle of Cable Street when Mosley's Fascists tried to march through our community?' the reminiscence worker asks.

'Yes, unfortunately,' one very old woman shouts.

That's public, collective memory. Everyone shares it. He shows more pictures. Who remembers this restaurant, that shop? A chorus of voices cries out, 'Me. I do. My mother used to take me there. That's where my father worked.'

People who labour with the old value the use of photographs as if they were a switch that can turn on a light in a darkened room. We could, if we wanted, remember everything. An experiment was conducted in 1963 by a Canadian scientist called Lionel Standing which demonstrates this. He showed a group of volunteers a series of slides or photographs for five seconds each at three-minute intervals. Two days later they were shown the pictures again, with others that they had never seen, and asked if they recognized them. Standing found that not only could his subjects remember what they had already looked at but the error rate did not increase with the number of items, even when 10,000 photographs passed before their eyes and he had to conclude that perhaps nothing is forgotten, as long as we know how to remember it.

But the problem for my mother with this photographic exercise was that she was not a Londoner. The pictures which the reminiscence worker showed meant nothing to her. The public memory of the Jewish East End did not abut on to any part of her private past. We didn't know what to do.

Then a woman who was visiting her mother-in-law passed my mother's room, its door left open, and saw, hanging on the wall next to the photos of my sister's wedding and every Jewish mother's pride and joy – my sister on her graduation day in cap and gown – her framed, signed portrait of Frankie Vaughan, Britain's answer to Frank Sinatra in the 1950s and 1960s.

'Are you a relative?' the woman asked wonderingly at my mother's proximity to this once-great singer who had starred in a film with Marilyn Monroe, and been the object of her sexual attentions.

'No,' my mother told the woman, 'but I lived next door to him and wheeled him in his pram when he was a baby.'

For Sunday nights were Frankie's night in our house when everything would stop for the weekly variety show on television direct from the London Palladium. There were kicking Tiller Girls, the troupe of midgets who played harmonicas, the gent in evening dress who pretended to be drunk, and Frankie, the crooner with his top hat and tails and smarmy grin. 'Give me the moonlight, Give me the girls and leave the rest to me,' he sang. Oh, how he waved at the end of the show when all the acts gathered on a revolving stage as the signature tune played out. And we waved back. He was indisputably the lead act, the star turn in the days before the Beatles – you could even buy a comic with his life-story in pictures.

But the history it narrated was a fabrication, a publicist's manipulation. We knew the *real* story. We knew that Vaughan was not his real name at all; he was Francis Abelson and he and his mother and sister and grandmother, who kept hens in her back yard for slaughter for the traditional Friday night Jewish meal, lived next door to my mother and her family on Devon Street in Liverpool. Bubba Abelson would look at Francis and say, in her Yiddish accent, 'Frankie, you're number von.' And that's how he came to be known as Vaughan.

With her own mother on Friday mornings my mother would go to the Abelsons' where the hens had got inside the house and were squawking on the horse-hair sofa and they would select from them the fowl which they would eat that night.

My mother made a pet of one of the hens, one time, and even gave it a name, Snowy, because it was white. One Friday the bird was gone. 'Where's Snowy?' she cried over her plate. 'You're eating her,' her mother said as the family laughed.

So the woman who came to see her mother-in-law cried out when she heard this story for her own mother had grown up on the very same street. Her older brother remembered my grandparents, she said when a week later she brought in her album of photographs, and now my mother had a private reminiscence worker.

'Who's this?' she asked, pointing at a wedding group.

And without hesitation, my mother told her the name and who her parents were and who she married.

'She was a beautiful girl, she could have any feller she wanted.'

Or, 'Her real name wasn't Shirley, you know. But she was mad about Shirley Temple so she made everyone call her Shirley.'

They spent an hour with the album, laughing and crying as the distant past flooded back in to fill the vacuum vacated by the present. But then the woman left and fifteen minutes later my mother no longer remembered that she had ever been there at all. 'Who did you say? Lived on Devon Street? I'd love to meet her. Will you introduce me? Don't forget, now.'

I have rummaged through the box of loose photographs that constitutes the main record of our family's history. Who were we before the invention of the camera which democratized the preservation of the human face? We were nothing, a void.

Now I show my mother another picture.

She looks at it for a long time.

'Who are they, Mum?'

She stares harder at the rectangle of pasteboard. A group is posed in a gracious room against a stone balustrade, behind them the Gothic panes of a window, stained with sylvan scenes, artistically draped with heavy curtains and along from it a carved and gilded French escritoire. Did these people live in such opulence? Of course not, it was the painted back-drop of the photographer's studio.

There are five adults and a child. Second on the left is a

21

black-bearded man in a long overcoat, a Russian peasant's cap on his head. He grips his fists on his lap, facing the new century. A thick-boned woman with a wide strong face stands to his left, her hand on his shoulder. She looks as though she could go a few rounds with Mike Tyson, were she alive now. On his right a younger woman, more plump than broad, wears her hair in braids, the pair evidently sisters. Her hand is on the shoulder of a strong, clean-shaven young man in tweed jacket and muffler who holds in turn a little boy in a sailor suit and buttoned trousers. At his other shoulder is a woman I think must be his wife, again plump, in a checked dress with a watch pinned to its collar.

'Well, that's my father-in-law,' my mother says, pointing to the old man. But I don't think she's right. I believe, though I have no means of proving this, that the black-bearded man is her grandfather, the young man her father and the woman next to him her mother, for in photographs taken of her in later years there is something of a resemblance. I think the child is my mother's brother, Abe.

Her parents came from Kiev in what is now the Ukraine but then was Russia and later the Soviet Union and now it's Ukraine again. They carried their two children Abe and Miriam with them, leaving their parents and brothers and sisters behind. My mother said recently how sad it was for her when she was growing up that she had no grandparents, no uncles and aunts and cousins. My father had cousins, the Kirwans and the Axelrods, which made his branch of the family even more enormous and unmanageable, but on my mother's side there was no one. They wrote, of course, to those left behind but the letters of reply stopped abruptly at the beginning of the war.

I show her another photograph. In a photographer's studio against the inevitable balustrade a little girl of around two years of age sits in a smock, with hair that shows evidence of the curling irons.

A long silence. Then she says, 'That's me.'

The second is a school photo, my mother in a white dress marked with an inky cross for identification on the second row, flanked by two boys. Thirty-eight children and their teacher, posed against a brick wall, one girl in the front row holding the sign, St Augustus Council School, Class 5. Another shows my mother a little later, in her gym-slip, her brown hair in a twenties bob, sitting on a chair smiling shyly.

Here she is again, aged around ten or twelve, in a gypsy outfit, rented, she told me for a fancy-dress party. My mother! A gypsy! Already she was taking on disguises.

It did not matter to my mother, but it did to me, that with her memory, that vast house, was passing away a whole world which when it was gone would be finally beyond any recall, the life that existed on one summer day in 1950 when she and her husband and brothers- and sisters-in-law sat on the lawn of the garden of my aunt's house in Leeds. Sometimes I dream of walking through the paper surface into that photograph, of sitting unseen among them and listening to what they say. Whispering in their ear that they tell me all their secrets. Feeling the good cloth of their clothes and eating the food they spread out on the table.

For as my mother's condition progressed it came to seem that the question that friends asked us so often, with that concerned sympathetic tone in their voices which we got to know so well – 'Does she know you?' – was the wrong one. I understand what they imagined: a vacant drooling wreck in a chair from whom the last vestiges of personality have fled, or perhaps a desolate wandering soul in house slippers condemned until death to walk the halls of the asylum, mumbling. Not a screaming harridan with eyes sharp for matching navy.

But it was not so much, as the old song went, 'Mother, you hardly know me' as 'Mother, we hardly know *you*.' As her short-term memory dropped away the distant past was flooding back in to replace it. Or was it that she finally lost those mechanisms of repression, of covering up, of not letting on or giving yourself away, telling other people your business – a lifetime's habits of secretiveness that to us were part of her unreliable personality?

Here's another photo, of her father, or at least I think it's him, that's what *she* says – walking along the street with another man who is in the process of putting on or taking off his hat.

'What did he do for a living, Mum?'

'He was a cobbler.'

I assumed he had a shop. I always thought that.

'And what did your father do?' the woman whose mother grew up on Devon Street asked her.

My mother replied at once: 'He went round the houses

where someone had died and bought their shoes then he did them up and my mother sold them on a stall at Bootle market.' She'd kept that quiet for nearly eighty years.

When I sent away for her birth certificate (because she had given her mother's maiden name as a password for a bank account and couldn't remember it any more) I saw that my grandfather signed his name with a cross. He lived, it seemed, the most scavenging of lives, a poor illiterate who in another country would have crawled across refuse dumps to find something he could sell.

And later that day, because she had been looking at old photographs she began to talk about how her mother and father had come from Russia and how her father had said he would have stayed if only he could have got his hands on a gun to defend himself and 'Your father told me that when he was a little boy he overheard *his* father talking – in Yiddish, you understand – and there was a girl and they came one night, and they came back every night and she went mad in the end and when it was born they killed it.'

'What are you talking about? Who came? Who was the girl?'

'What girl?'

'The one you were just talking about.'

'What was I saying? I can't remember.'

So I was enticed and maddened by these fragments of the secret past where my grandparents lived and someone had been raped over and over again and the family gathered round and committed infanticide on the child born of the atrocity. Or had it ever happened? Was it a game of Chinese whispers or even something from a film or a book that she had read and was jumbled up with what had really been? Two generations were as remote to each other as the lives of nomadic peoples of the Australian desert are to me.

I had had my chance and I hadn't taken it. When I was younger I was bored stiff with my parents' reminiscences. I had no curiosity. I was living in a time when the past was going to be abolished. Born in 1951, I was part of the first generation that was put on earth, we fatally imagined, to be young and stay young forever. With pity and scorn we condemned our parents' youth to oblivion.

'In my boyhood days during the Roaring Twenties,' my father would boast several times a week, 'I lived in New York, the greatest city on earth, and my protector was Harry Houdini, the greatest magician who has ever lived, and I stayed with him and his wife Bess in their house.'

'Oh, for God's sake, Dad. That is *so* boring.'

And I would drown him out with my Beatles records. 'The Beatles,' he would say. 'A nine-day wonder.'

Both of us were wrong.

★

It is my fate now, in the middle age we never believed was coming, with its own ailments and wrinkles and sagging stomachs, to scramble among the ruins of my mother's memory in search of my past, of who all of us are. To have grown up as a Jewish daughter into an insistence of the importance of memory, knowing that without it, we are animals. In a hundred years there will be no one left alive who remembers her, who can tell you who she was. Some of us are haunted by our memories, others abide in their comforting refuge. People say, 'I only lived for the present, *in* the present.' Or 'The future is what matters.' But without the past we're nothing, we belong to nobody.

What was wrong with her? It wasn't Alzheimer's Disease but something called Multi-Infarct Dementia or MID, a condition I had never heard of until we were given the diagnosis in 1993 when we thought she was behaving like that on purpose: to seek attention or to drive her two daughters mad. Not Alzheimer's but she would one day reach the same place, that far-off planet where those without memory live and the rest of us can't reach. Tiny, silent strokes had been occurring in her brain, mowing down her recollections of what she had said half a minute ago. They were not the kind of strokes that paralysed or blurred her speech, far from it. She was not confined to a chair but could walk for miles.

'Why do we have to go back now?' she would complain. 'I'm still fresh. You know I've always been a walker.'

Apart from the physical wasting, the diminution of her body to the size of a large doll, she looked normal – she looked like a sweet little old lady – and people would start up conversations with her which would proceed as they expected until a question answered a moment before would be asked again – 'No, I must interrupt, you haven't told me yet where you live.'

'As I just said, Birmingham.'

And then asked and asked and asked until you lost your patience because you thought you had been entering a dialogue which had its rules of exchange, and it turned out that what you were really talking to was an animate brick wall. Questions asked over and over again not because she couldn't remember the reply but because a very short tape playing in her head had reached its end and wound itself back to the beginning to start afresh. She knew the conventions of conversation – these had not deserted her – but she could not recall what she had said herself a few moments before.

Sometimes the question was repeated before the person she was asking had finished getting through their response. There were little holes in her brain, real holes in the grey matter, where the memory of her life used to be, and of what she had done half an hour or even a few minutes ago.

This is an account of how two grown-up daughters watched their mother decline into dementia, watched her memory disappear. It is the story of how we made the cruel decision to take away her freedom and put her in a home, whether she wanted to go or not, in defiance of every democratic instinct which demanded human rights, even for the old. It's not so unusual, thousands do the same thing every day. Seven hundred and fifty thousand people are known to be suffering from dementia in Britain alone. It's going to be a million by the time the baby-boom generation – *my* generation – reaches old age.

But my story is not the same as everyone else's. No story is the same. Cancer is cancer but when you lose your memory the whole family goes down with it and you must do what you can to reclaim yourselves from oblivion. If you lose your memory in Yorkshire, Yorkshire is all around you.

You can go to the parish church and there are the records of births and marriages and deaths. That's not to say your experiences are commonplace, it's just that they are easier to replicate, though not of course those family memories, the secrets that all parents keep from their children. And in the end all of us have to ask this of the mothers and fathers who brought us into the world: Who were you? For you can be sure that every one of them had *something* to hide. How well do any of us know our parents?

But what was particular in my mother's case was that in her brain resided the very last links with her generation. And what a generation it was – those children of immigrants who had in their heads two worlds, the one they lived in and a partial, incomplete place that their parents had handed on to them, the *Heim*, the land they came from, be it Poland or Russia or Lithuania or Hungary.

And it was precisely because she was so divided that we were never able to trust what she said in the first place and so memory, in our family, was always a tricky business.

Who is she? To the end of my days I don't believe I will ever have any idea, though there was nothing that you would call really mysterious about her. No one parachuted her behind enemy lines, during the war, she had no famous lovers (or at least I wouldn't have thought so). The secrets she carries were all the more infuriating for being, I'm sure, no different from anybody else's, the ones all of us hide. What are we going to tell our own children about ourselves? How will we edit and mythologize the past?

I like to have a document. Documents can't lie. 'Oh yes they can,' says my more street-wise cousin, Shaina. 'You don't believe they told the authorities the truth all their lives, do you?' I see her point. Our parents imbibed with their mother's milk a deep distrust of the bureaucrats, the representatives of power whom, with skill and cunning, they plotted to outwit, whether it was over a planning application or a record of a birth. To them, a town hall clerk fell into the same category as the agents of a cruel and oppressive Tsar.

If I believe the public account of my mother's beginnings, I find that she was born on 12 July 1918 in Liverpool. She was named Rose. No one knows the date her parents arrived in Britain but she said they came from Kiev. I've never been there, put off by the brooding, right-wing Ukrainian nationalists I met in Canada in the 1970s, stalwarts against communism, still whiffing of the stench of instinctive anti-Semitism.

Always in our minds was the consciousness of what would have happened if they had not emigrated. It's odd that while there is such confusion about what *was*, there is absolute certainty about what might have been. I have only to pick up a book. On 27 and 28 September 1941, posters went up throughout Kiev demanding that all Jews assemble for 'resettlement'. Thirty thousand optimistically turned up. They were then marched to Babi Yar, a ravine just outside the city. They were stripped naked, made to walk in columns of 100 to the ravine's edge where they were shot by machine-gun fire and fell down into the Yar. In the evening, an eye witness reports, 'The Germans undermined the walls of the ravine and buried the people under the thick layers of earth. But the earth was moving long after, because wounded and still alive Jews were still moving.' It took two days of murder at Babi Yar, enthusiastically aided by Ukrainian militiamen, to get rid of 33,771 Jews. In 1943, 400 Jews and Soviet prisoners-of-war were set to work to remove the earth from the top of the grave, cover the bodies with inflammable material and burn them. The Jews who did this work were addressed by their German overseers as 'corpses'.

In the pit at Babi Yar lie the remains, I assume, of my Haft relatives, perhaps of the two young women in the photograph, and their children and grandchildren. That history breathed down our necks as we were growing up, a constant reminder that where there were suburbs and houses and trees and allotments and W. H. Smith and Tesco and Marks and Spencer, a kind of mental chasm yawned beneath our feet into which we were always fearful that we could fall. It was a habit of thinking, a trick of being in two places and realities at once, which conditioned the way we saw the world, hell-bent on shops and cinemas and walking in public parks in our finery but acknowledging that there was more to life than this, that there was a darkness in us we couldn't be rid of.

My grandparents, however, escaped their fate by leaving. The name wasn't Haft in Russia but something else no one could remember. Like thousands of others, they were awarded a new name by a careless immigration officer who, unable to spell whatever it was he heard, wrote down the easiest word that sounded like it.

I know, too, because Frankie Vaughan told me, that Devon Street was partly populated by Jews from Kiev. Each one, when he or she got off the boat, must have had an address of a friend or relative and so that one road in the centre of Liverpool became a home from home, as there used to be a pub in Brixton called the Atlantic where every immigrant from the West Indies could drop in at any time and find a friend or leave a message.

Frankie remembered three-storey houses with eight scrubbed steps up to the front door, an attic and a cellar, the lavatory in a shed at the end of the yard. In his house, there was a door leading into the hall with a coloured glass window in it. The Abelsons – and I don't suppose the Hafts were any different – kept salt herrings and cucumbers in the yard and made the Sabbath wine from grapes they bought cheap from the market; they made soup out of fish heads and the women went without so their children could have the best of everything. Frankie Vaughan's idea of a day out when he was a child was to go down to the docks and feed sugar to the dray horses. There was a little Jewish store on the corner that sold everything, but half the street was Catholic or Protestant. During the war, Frankie told me, when the cellars of the houses were used as air-raid shelters, 'Devon Street was bombed, but not entirely. It was the Corporation made it look like a bomb site later.' It exists still, though only on the map. John Moores University has taken over the whole area.

The Hafts who arrived in Devon Street were smaller, quieter, poorer and not so intelligent as the Ginsbergs. They had neither their vitality nor their chutzpah. Their jobs were tailors and cutters, seamstresses, cabinet makers, but that did not really put them in a different *class* from the Ginsbergs. The difference was essentially financial. What class were they? It's hard to tell. They arrived from Russia as peasants, part of the *shtetl* culture of Eastern Europe, those impoverished Jewish townships where poor Jews scratched a living in menial trades, neither part of the great proletariat organized in factories nor of a peasantry tied to the land.

In Liverpool they lived alongside the working class but didn't share any of the same cultural references that made the working class what it was. Only in the Irish could they recognize a people who looked back to another country and to political repression. Otherwise, they ate different food, worshipped in different places and never, ever thought that education meant getting above oneself or that their sort should know their place. Why should they? They didn't have one, other than what they made for themselves. Money, and position, to all my grandparents, was an insulation device against persecution. They yearned, they aspired to something better because for the first time in centuries they felt the stranglehold of anti-Semitism lifted from round their necks. They breathed freedom's air. What their class really was was Immigrant, who sacrifice their own lives for the next generation.

Both my mother's parents were dead before she was thirty and so she subsumed herself into the grandeur of her in-laws. Gradually the Hafts faded out of her recollection as an innate snobbishness grew ashamed of their smallness, poor clothes and modest houses compared with the gilded splendour of the homes she now found herself invited into as a Ginsberg family member. As her condition worsened she often forgot that it was not her own family's history she was talking about, but her husband's. And because, as she said, she had no uncles or aunts or cousins, there were fewer of the Hafts, they took up less space in the world, and so I too tended to overlook them.

The Hafts gave me four living uncles and aunts and two dead uncles. My Uncle Abie lived in London and we did not see him so much, but we were in and out of the houses of Miriam and Gertie who had between them three sons a few years older than me. Auntie Milly – she dropped the name Miriam in the 1920s, Milly being more modern and up-to-date – remembered sleeping at night on the shelf around the stove in the middle of the house in Kiev, the fuel banked up against the coldness of the bitter streets. Gertie produced the Hafts' cleverest grandchild, my cousin Martin who became a science teacher and had set his sights on becoming an anaesthetist but was dead of leukaemia at twenty-six. I never met Lillian, or 'her over the water' as my mother always referred to her, for she had married a non-Jew and gone to live in the Wirral, across the Mersey, never, ever forgiven by her mother and consequently my mother too.

Then there was Hershel, or Harry, a cabinet-maker, who was killed in 1943 in Italy. The photograph of his temporary grave, the sole wooden star of David among a field of crosses, was often brought out for my mother to look at. Harry was the favourite, the nice one whom everybody liked. The pictures of him show a dreamy, mild-mannered man with a hint of sternness in his eyes above a small, blondish moustache.

We kept, too, the black-bordered letter announcing his death and his own evasive letters home in a pleasant copperplate script, full of inconsequential chit-chat about the food and when they would move off and to where. Perhaps he died from a quick German bullet, but who knows? There might be someone alive today who keeps shut away in a part of the mind that cannot be visited too often, for its tormenting memories, the recollection of the terrible death of Private Haft, who once joked and shared a cigarette and spoke of his girl back home, but who wound up with his face blown off and lingered for hours or even days in dreadful pain. Maybe he was even killed by 'friendly fire'? Who knows? Who remembers?

My mother always said that the shock of his death killed her mother, but something else was true about this woman I never met – don't even know the date or place of her birth, only that she was called Leah and my name, Linda, is an anglicized version of that. One day, three or four years

ago, when we were talking on the phone, apropos of nothing, my mother suddenly told me that when Harry died her
mother had received a letter from a young woman, not
Jewish, to whom he had been secretly engaged. 'She never
replied to the letter,' my mother told me. 'And I think that
was very wrong, don't you? Because she loved him, you
know. But my mother was hard-hearted. She wouldn't have
anything to do with her. I wanted to go and see the girl but
I didn't like to go behind my mother's back.' Why had she
never told me this before? And why now? Or was it that as
tracts of memory vanished, those that remained were high-
lighted in sharper relief, like a single tree in a barren
landscape after the soil has been eroded and the forest has
died?

There was one other Haft, mentioned only once by my
mother, a boy who died of meningitis in childhood. She
couldn't remember him, she was too young, she told me.
What was his name, I asked when I was a teenager. She
couldn't recall. Even then, her memory was bad. In her
deedbox of papers, long after she went into the home, I
found a frail document, a circumcision certificate issued in
1912 for a Morris Haft. And so, eighty-five years later, that
is all that remains of him, for his family are dead and I doubt
that anyone alive today who knew him at school, in their
eighties or nineties now, recalls an old playmate who did not
survive into adulthood, just as one day there will be no one
left who remembers the children who were murdered at
Dunblane. So we will exist, one day, only on paper and
writing will be all that's left of us.

At fourteen my mother left school and her older brothers
and sisters pooled their resources to buy her her indentures

which would apprentice her as a hairdresser – a glamorous, *modern* job in those days when Jewish girls went to work as seamstresses or behind the counter in a shop. Did this make her a rebel? I don't know. She met a friend of my sister's once who was not going to defer to the feelings of other people's mothers by keeping it in any way a secret that she was a lesbian.

My mother eagerly told her: 'There was a girl in our street who used to dress in men's clothes and she acted like a man as well, she was the talk of the town. Do you think she was a lesbian?'

We sat with our mouths open. Twelve years later that information is still being worked on in my mental digestive system.

She was a kind of a rebel but her rebelliousness was not the same sort as mine. I was up in arms against the whole of society – I was a feminist, I was a Marxist, I wanted the world turned inside out but principally I wanted more than anything else not to be like my mother: to marry, to have children, not to have a career or any kind of significant working life. I was all afire for equality for everyone, but mainly myself. She, on the other hand, wanted to better *herself* for the material advantages that this would bring her. She stood with her face pressed against shop windows and looked in. Given a choice between a wig for ritual obser-vance, as her mother wore, and shopping in suburbia, she knew which she would pick. She wanted modernity, lip-stick, permanent waves, dancing to Glen Miller, the pictures three times a week – not eviscerating a hen or keeping up with what seemed like the three million rules concerned with the maintenance of a kosher home. She personally slashed that number down to a mere million and a half. Yet still she managed to convince herself and indeed me that she was, as I was not, a dutiful daughter. For what had she done that was so terrible? She had got on in life.

This must have been her existence throughout the 1930s: at work in a salon during the day, going to the pictures at night or to dances at the Jewish youth club, visits at weekends to her married sisters, in and out of their houses. Then home to her own little room in Devon Street. I don't know how the Depression affected her family. I don't know if they read the Jewish papers and sat in the evenings talking about the situation in Germany. I don't know how she came to aspire to wealth or if she ever got on a tram which glided along its rails away from the centre of Liverpool to the suburbs where the emerging prosperous Jewish population had already implanted itself. I suppose she must have, for the road we were later to move to, one which was part of the post-war private housing developments, she would always describe this way: 'I remember when it was all fields round here.' Was this the period of her apprenticeship into good taste, reading her magazines, looking at what there was in the shops, though she couldn't afford to buy what she saw? Envy was her deadly sin, it was her engine. It drove her into the future.

When the war started she was assigned to work in the wages office of a munitions factory but after Harold was killed and her mother was alone, she was given leave to stay home and look after her. She had a boyfriend called, improbably, Bunny Skulnik, but he died, too. I think there was another boyfriend, who emigrated to Canada. There are no photographs of these young men, perhaps she had some but threw them away. She was reasonably pretty, lively and, she told me, always happy and gay.

At some point she went after a job at a hairdressing salon on London Road. It was owned by my father and, reader, she married him. She also said once that she went out with his younger brother Ralph first, but, at only two years older than herself, he wasn't rich enough yet, not established, she said. She was out for the main chance and she saw it in my father. She took life by the throat and in her own small way, she got what she wanted. And that is all I can tell you about my mother's youth and childhood. Still I don't know what she had to be so secretive about.

When I am old and I have the disease my mother has now, maybe I will retain these fragments: of how as much as she would like to have guests in for afternoon tea, the bridge rolls spread with Philadelphia cream cheese on a plate with a doily, wheeled in on a hostess trolley; as much as she saw herself in the fifties as a young suburban matron in a semi-detached house with a garden and a child's swing and my father motoring to the office in the mornings in his Humber Hawk, me waving goodbye through the window in my patent leather T-bar shoes – what my mother really enjoyed was catching the bus to Penny Lane to sit in a terraced house with Libby, the seamstress, and her friends Gertie, Dolly and Mamie and reminisce about the past when they were poor and had nothing but were happy.

There was a dressmaker they used to go to when they were teenagers who ran up their frocks. You took her your material but she only had one pattern. 'She could do it boat neck, square neck or round neck,' the ladies recalled. 'But when you got to the dance everyone was wearing the same dress.' Oh, the tedium for me of those long, long afternoons by Libby's somnolent coal fire while my mother and her cronies gossiped about sweethearts long gone or gone recently.

'He dropped down dead of a heart attack. A young man!'

'How young?' I demanded.

'Only forty.'

Forty! Young? A young man to me was a teenager in winklepicker shoes and Teddy boy draped jacket.

They slipped in and out of each other's maiden names and married names and what the name was before, before it was changed from something unpronounceable. I never knew what anyone was really, legally, called. But how they laughed and how I felt excluded from their shared past, wriggling on my mother's knee or crouched on a footstool at the outer edge of the circle.

What else do I know? That she was mad for the pictures, went three or four times a week and loved Ray Milland and James Stewart, 'the lean and hungry look'. She could walk through a room with the television set on showing an old Hollywood film and just by glancing at the screen she could tell you who was who and who they were married to and who they had been married to before and after and any juicy scandal she had gleaned from her copies of the film magazines she and millions of other teenagers devoured in the 1930s.

She was touched by tragedy of course. Her father, she said, died sometime in that decade of cancer and she stayed up all night to sit with his body before the funeral the next day.

'Weren't you frightened?' I asked her, recoiling in horror, having lived a whole equivalent life cocooned from death.

'Why should I be frightened?' she replied. 'He never hurt me when I was alive so why should he hurt me now he was dead?'

★

41

In the early eighties a great fuss justifiably began to be made about the conditions of carers, those isolated and forgotten individuals who selflessly looked after their ageing relatives. They needed respite care, they needed counselling, they needed someone to acknowledge that often they had sacrificed their lives, their careers, their dreams of marriage or a busy retirement to change the soiled pyjamas of someone they loved. They were tied to infirmity day and night. And when we heard their voices at last, they all said the same thing: 'I could never put my mother in a home. I love her too much for that.' Or it was husband or wife or father but the point was that their love was greater than the inconvenience.

I have watched wonderful television programmes about people with Alzheimer's Disease. I saw a retired miner with the gentlest of hands brush his wife's hair and sing to her and stroke her face though she seemed as if the soul had gone ahead of the body into the grave and there was nothing left lying in bed but the shell of her. 'I married her for better or worse,' he said. And this was worse and so he kept, in honour, his wedding vows.

But my sister and I were not among the devoted.

I read Michael Ignatieff's novel, *Scar Tissue*, about a man who loves his mother so much that he abandons a professorship, abandons his wife and abandons his children to sit next to her every day and try to probe, through speech and touch, her darkness and silence. People with Alzheimer's, he told a conference of the Alzheimer's Disease Society a week or two before the shopping expedition for the wedding outfit, 'are on a voyage into deep space, sending back messages that it is our job to decipher'. 'There is a deep connection between compassion and curiosity,' my notes read.

What did I feel? Guilt is what I'm dealing with. Guilt and distance. Guilt that I had not become and was never going to be the daughter she wanted, who married young and gave her mother grandchildren and was there for her in her old age. Guilt that I had a career and a life and would never, ever give them up to sit with her and listen to her incessantly ask the same question over and over again until I could distract her and a few minutes would pass and she would find something else to ask. And then what would come later, the house like a fortress to prevent her wandering, the smell of piss and shit, like looking after a toddler with none of the hope and expectations.

Does my mother know me? Only too bloody well, some days, when she can recount a litany of my past misde-meanours, the sorrows I have brought her: 'I'm the only one whose daughters went away to university and never came back,' is an enduring complaint, which has seen a good twenty years' service.

Could I have devoted the second half of my life to caring for the very person whose values I had so violently rejected and overthrown when I was in wholesale rebellion against society, when everyone with short hair was a fascist and girls who married young and settled down were brain-dead nincompoops? Never. Selfish, selfish, selfish, yes. But my knowledge of how others behaved, of how it was possible to reach transcendence through sacrifice did not make it pos-sible for me to look after my own mother. Just as she did not re-create herself in the image of her mother, all selfless-ness and adherence to the rules, neither was I a carbon copy of mine.

The rules. Michele and I know what they are. You leave school at sixteen, do a secretarial course, take a position with a group of Jewish solicitors and marry one of them. You have children in your early twenties. You make your mother a grandmother and – when the hostess trolley is wheeled out, laden with coffee cake and honey cake and macaroons and the biscuits she makes during Passover when flour is prohibited, of coconut and whisked egg white dropped on to the baking sheet in conical mounds – now is the moment in which she can show off the photographs of her grandchildren. A Jewish stereotype, yes, but that was her. It was true.

When my mother was left with two unmarried daughters, no grandchildren and a dead husband, she felt that it wasn't what she had been led to expect. She had no abandoned hobbies to pursue, no thoughts of doing an Open University degree. She had signed up for marriage and motherhood along with millions of others of her generation, bought the gas cooker and the Bendix washing machine and the coaleffect electric fire and the Kenwood mixer and all the other labour-saving devices that freed her to go to coffee mornings organized by the Daughters of Zion. And was it her fault that the world and women had changed and feminism had undone her, given her girls who had not the slightest intention of following in her footsteps? 'A son's a son until he takes a wife but a daughter's a daughter for the rest of your life,' she used to say. She doesn't say it any more.

When I think about when it first started, this illness of my mother's, I sometimes felt that it had been going on all her life. When I overheard her talking to her friends on the phone she would often repeat herself, for emphasis or effect, I assumed. It was an easy habit to pick up, but hard to get rid of, I find.

So the faulty memory could always have been there, except that as we were growing up we understood that it was our parents' habit to conceal from their children, as it was our habit to be dishonest with them. They had a number of techniques for doing this. The easiest was for them to use Yiddish as a private language, so we wouldn't understand what they were saying. I picked up a few words by necessity. 'Zug ya,' my father would tell my mother when I was asking for something I could not have. 'Say yes.'

And the stories changed according to who was relating them and when and to whom and why, but no matter how much we children recognized the contradictions, they never let on. Why was there an eight-year gap between my sister and me, I wanted to know?

'After you were born I had my tubes tied but it didn't work.'

Or another time: 'I don't know, it just didn't happen.'

'But you said you had your tubes tied.'

'Rubbish.'

'You *did*. You told me.'

'Did I? I can't remember.'

Sometimes Michele and I discovered by accident that we had both held all our lives as fact quite contradictory versions of family history: 'No, it's true, Dad said.'

'Well, that's not what Mum told me.'

It was not a household which valued the truth. There was always the let-down, when you thought you knew, finally, what had really happened, and then, later, when my mother changed her story, she would admit, under duress, 'I just said that.' And when you asked why, she would walk out of the room to get on with some household chore and leave you stranded and gasping. In my teenage magazines the advice columns strongly recommended to its readers that if you had a problem you should discuss it with your parents who would respect and value your openness and honesty, for without trust you could not have a proper relationship with them. They were living in cloud cuckoo land. It didn't take me long to work that out.

I was never to understand completely why my parents were like this. I could only speculate, much later, that if we, as children, had much to conceal from them about our lives – our smoking of cigarettes and experiments with certain soft drugs, our insistence on sexual freedom, our plans to leave home and escape their grip, my truancy from school to sneak into one of the Cavern's lunchtime sessions in the era when the Beatles were just back from Hamburg and everyone at school was in love with them – well, however much we thought our parents to be dinosaurs from another age, the rift between their generation and their own parents would have withered away my self-important little differences.

When my father was a boy he won a children's painting competition in the *Liverpool Echo* and the prize was a paintbox. It arrived on a Saturday morning and at once he got out his jar of water and began to paint. When my grandfather saw him he took the paintbox and cracked it over his son's head for disobeying the Talmudic laws of the Sabbath which forbade anything that could be classified as work, including writing and, yes, wielding a paintbrush. My parents were twentieth-century people. But their parents were peasants, whose lives were the same as their parents' had been and their grandparents' and great-grandparents' before them, hundreds of years' worth of ancestors, all identical. My parents' parents belonged to another place and another time, marooned in an unknown country, in the machine age.

My mother plucked her eyebrows, wore lipstick and rouge and permed and dyed her hair. Her mother shaved hers off and wore a wig in ritual observance. Her growing children acted as interpreters with the new system. How honest were they going to be with the power of two languages at the tip of their tongues over their parents' ignorance and confusion?

Michele would later observe that she and I grew up astride the fault-line of our parents' great dilemma. For they struggled all their lives with two powerful obligations, the need to fit into the society and culture in which they would, after all, have to earn their living and whose laws they must obey, and the pressure from the demands of their religion and ancestry to remain different. Of course, as children, we didn't see it this way at all. We just thought they were hypocrites.

Inside their heads two realities were warring constantly. Out in the world they wore masks. Tell the truth? Which truth were we talking about exactly? The accuracy that they had a nice home in the suburbs, money in the bank, private health insurance and private education for their offspring? Or the reality always in the backs of their minds, that the rest of the world, they believed, was essentially anti-Semitic and that their children must be protected from what lay beyond the claustrophobic confinement of the small Jewish community in which they moved, in which the opinion of their neighbours counted for everything.

'Don't tell anyone our business,' they said. Not because they were reticent, private people, but because they were only just managing to control the contradictions themselves, never mind expose them to the 500-watt attention of others. All immigrant families are like this, whether they come from India or Jamaica or Mexico or the Philippines. All of them have to make a new identity out of a past they no longer have any access to and even if they go back, time has moved on. They can never return to the place they came from. The Russian-occupied Poland in which my father was born has not existed for so long that it is now just a collection of documents for historians to study, not a place at all. And if your personal history is inaccessible, is it surprising that all you can engage in is the manufacture of myths?

So I grew up knowing that I came from a long line of accomplished liars. Why was Ginsberg changed to Grant in the early 1950s?

'Well, you were starting school and when Dad was a boy they called him guinea pig and he didn't want to have the same happen to you.'

'Because we got a letter from Mosley's Fascists saying that

Dad was on a list and if we don't get you, we'll get your children.'

That was true. There was a letter. I saw it once, kept locked away in the black deedbox in the cupboard above the fitted wardrobes in my parents' bedroom. When Michele cleared out our mother's flat she found it, irrefutable proof of something, at last. Fifty years on, it survives, written, as letters from madmen always are, on lined paper, prompted by the appearance in the *London Gazette* of my father's application for naturalization as a British citizen in 1948:

> 'Ginsberg'
>
> I have *every* reason why you should be denied naturalization. As your name infers – you are a JEW. We don't want any more parasites in this country.
>
> Get out!!! Otherwise your address will be entered on our list for destroying. We, the Anti-Jewish Organization, have, and still are, compiling a list of all Jewish property to be destroyed.
>
> Take warning!!!
>
> This is no idle threat.
>
> > Signed
> > 'Anti-Jew'

I grew up in a family where the past was shifting and untrustworthy, where people's memories and what they said they couldn't remember were not necessarily to be trusted. My family had simply re-invented itself for the twentieth century and a new land, shedding the past which like a skin was left to decompose and die. And whenever they said, 'I can't remember' I always assumed they had something interesting to hide.

The one thing I was sure of was that I grew up amidst a conspiracy of liars, show-offs and story-tellers, but with a past without documentation who was I to prove them wrong?

I had told my mother that I was going to Poland and I was. I went because I wanted to visit Lomza, the small, insignificant town in the north of the country between Warsaw and Byalistock where my father's papers said he was born and had briefly lived for a few months as a baby until, wrapped in shawls and carried in his mother's arms, with his older brothers Louis and Issy beside him, he set sail for New York. Or so they thought. Blessed with the greenhorn ignorance of the hopeful immigrant who has just made landfall in a place he knows nothing of, my grandfather had walked round Liverpool for many days admiring what he believed to be the architecture of the New World, until someone put him right.

How could he have recognized the catastrophe that had befallen him? He spoke no English. He wouldn't have known an American accent from Scouse if they served it up backed by a symphony orchestra and fifty-strong chorus with lyrics by Irving Berlin. What did *he* know from the Flatiron Building? He saw docks and wharves and warehouses, felt the salt sea wind in his nostrils, tickling his beard, heard the screaming anguish of the seagulls, circling over the estuary. And beyond the sea, the Atlantic Ocean. Except he was on the wrong side of it, a stranger on the wrong shore.

There was a feminist twist to this tale. For it was my forceful grandmother, a mill-owner's daughter, who was the one who had been inadvertently educated for modernity, under the tutelage of a governess who taught her not only embroidery but also English. One by one her brothers had left for America and all did extravagantly well, fulfilling the American dream to become doctors, surgeons, consultants – one even had a hospital named after him. But she, the real brains of the whole outfit, had been married off to a *yeshiva bocher*, a student of the Talmud, a religious man. It was what the Irish would have done if the chastity rule had not prevented them marrying *their* daughters off to priests.

My grandfather was a world-class prayer. He did it morning, noon and night, a small leather box tied to his forehead with leather thongs. I only knew him in extreme old age (he died at the age of ninety-two from a fall out of bed), talking to him through the interpretative intervention of my father, for my *Zaidie* (as I was taught to call him in Yiddish), after the first knock-back never learned English. To study, to pray, to drink a glass of whisky and place a bet was enough of a life to him. Once only did he assert himself as a man, when he rejected my grandmother's help and insisted that he take on the responsibility for the future, and so he dressed in his best clothes and bought the tickets, the paper proof that after centuries of oppression and bloody pogroms and keeping one's head down, there was a route to freedom and self-determination. An end to slavery.

So it was that my grandfather, Wolfe Ginsberg, was

swindled. Some long-dead con-artist who sized him up and saw him coming made me English rather than American, a Liverpudlian, not a New Yorker. A European tied to this curious polyglot continent with its wars of trade and religion, on which the past continues to matter, instead of the United States where it is the future that counts.

My grandfather – until the end of his days in the Jewish old age home where the brave immigrants of his generation found their last but one rest – gathered all the phlegm in his throat and spat on the ground when the name of the Tsar was mentioned. The distant furore of the Russian Revolution, one of the most important events of the twentieth century, had some personal meaning for him. But I didn't care. I wasn't interested in those ignorant, misguided, above all *unimportant* people I had dismissed for so long as only being my own family.

Can I confirm that everything I have told you is true? I can't. I only know what lives and sings in the oral tradition that is the history of every family. For all I know it could be a pack of falsehoods, fairy tales to send the children and grandchildren to sleep at nights. So we all lie, staring into the darkness, trying to conjure up the dead.

If there was a single story that summed us up it was the one about how my father's oldest brother, my Uncle Louis, the one with the gold initials on his hat-bands, the chamois leather king, came to marry his wife, my Aunt Dinah, and have six children and live on Windy Harbour Road in Southport, where the Liverpool middle classes went when they aspired to be 'naice'. So 'naice' was it that I cannot remember a single thing about it. Blackpool, now that was a different story. But Blackpool was not naice at all, even though it sold sticks of pink and white striped rock in the shape of walking sticks and the size of a walking stick too, and I know, because there's a picture of me with one.

At any family occasion such as a wedding or bar-mitzvah my Uncle Louis' brother-in-law would be up on his hind legs with the time-worn story of how Louis and Dinah met, an automatic signal for me to turn off and crawl around under the table in my sticky-out party dress and annoy people. So it was not until the oldest son of the six, my cousin Sefton, the main recipient of the male Ginsbergs' wolfish good looks, told it to me again years and years later when he was almost as old as his father had been when he died, that I understood its relevance.

Uncle Louis had been born in the last year or two of the nineteenth century and as a teenager he ran away from home to join the army during the First World War. He did not go to France, to the trenches, but went with the Palestine Brigade which was fighting the Turks in the Middle East, and here he palled up with another Jewish soldier, Private Rosenberg. One day my Uncle Louis was wounded and the very moment that he took the hit, Private Rosenberg next to him stumbled over a tree root, possibly by accident or possibly not. At any rate the effect of his injury was the swelling up of his knee to the size of a football. Private Rosenberg went to his commanding officer and put the following proposition to him: 'Private Ginsberg is badly wounded and may die, sir,' he explained. 'My injury is slight but if you permit me to accompany Private Ginsberg back to the field hospital I could take care of him and who knows? Instead of one fit man being sent back to the Front, there might be two.'

As this was narrated to me by Sefton, in a burger restaurant in Hampstead one summer evening in 1995, the suggestion seemed dripping with guile and craftiness, but perhaps English officers were more gullible in those days. Anyway, the two men moved away from the Front and proceeded to medical attention. The surgeon examined my uncle. 'This man is seriously injured,' he told Private Rosenberg. 'The only chance of him surviving is if he doesn't lose consciousness. You have to keep him awake by talking to him. Do you think you can do that?'

Saul Rosenberg pulled himself up to his full height (which can't have been much), looked the doctor in the eye and said, 'Sir, in the whole of the British army you could not have picked a better man.'

For the next twelve hours Saul Rosenberg talked non-stop. I suppose he talked about the terrible food, the state of the war and the generals and politicians that led it, the prettiness of the nurses, the scratchiness of the uniforms and perhaps about religious matters and dietary laws and anything else that came into his head. At any rate there was never any doubt that talking for a whole night was going to present any sort of problem to him. But by dawn he had begun to flag, run out of things to say, his tongue feeling his dry mouth for words. He began to search through his pockets and bring out the things he found there and talk about them.

He showed my uncle photographs of his family. 'Here is my sixteen-year-old sister,' he said. 'Is she not pretty? I'm going to write down my address and when the war is over you must come and visit us and meet her and maybe you will marry her.'

My Uncle Louis did, of course, recover or he would now be only a lost photograph and an unfamiliar name on a document; the two boys went back to the Front and fought on, both surviving until Armistice Day *and* through the world-wide flu epidemic that followed, the era of the song my father loved to sing, 'Brother Can You Spare a Dime?' ('Once in khaki suits, gee we looked swell . . .') and which, having learned from him, I performed at a kindergarten talent contest around 1955, to the startled surprise of the teachers who had expected a little nursery rhyme about flowers or pets, not a world-weary tale of American down-and-out doughboys.

Some years later, at the beginning of the 1920s, Saul Rosenberg answered a knock at the door of his parents' house in Manchester. On the step stood a stained and weary figure with a pack on his back. He was selling chamois leather from house to house and had walked across the Pennines from Sheffield.

'Don't you remember me?' he asked Saul Rosenberg. Saul shook his head.

'I am Private Ginsberg and I have walked all the way from Sheffield to come and marry your sister Dinah.' And so he did.

Now it was instantly apparent to me, when Sefton had stopped speaking, that the moral of this story was as follows: *Never let anyone tell you that you talk too much.* For where would my uncle have been had he been nursed by a laconic Englishman prone to meaningful silences? Dead.

Ours was a family that talked all the time, it never shut up. It admired oratory and the rhetorical arts, while quite uneducated in these skills, and it seemed only natural for me to try to block out much of the noise by turning up my record-player and tuning out the old family tales of the past.

There are no photographs of my father as a child, I don't know why. Perhaps the family was too poor to visit the studio and have some taken. Or maybe they are just lost. He never spoke of childhood, except as hardship, never mentioned school or whether he had shoes to carry him there. Who was the first girl he ever kissed or made love to? Where is she now? Long dead, I guess. His youth vanished as if a conjuror waved his magic wand and made it dissolve into smoke.

He is seen first in Central Park in Prohibition America, wearing the long jacket of a barber and a bow-tie, a cigarette between his fingers, slim, dark, handsome, smiling and confident. He is in his twenties and has been out of school more than half his life for he finished his education at ten. In my mother's flat there is a scrap of paper on which she had written, Dad Could Have Got a Scholarship But He Wasn't Born Here. I'm not sure that this is true as plenty of Jewish immigrants obtained scholarships to grammar schools and went on to become doctors and lawyers. He was clever enough to get one, but perhaps that lie is what his father told him, wanting his third son to be out at work and bringing in a wage-packet.

There are no parish records. No family bible handed down. No genealogical tree. A single document exists. I have it. It is my paternal grandfather's alien registration book, issued in 1916. It shows that he was born in May 1874 in a town called Ostrova in a part of Eastern Poland then subsumed into the Russian Empire. It notes that between 1896 and 1899 he served as a private in the 4th Infantry of the Russian Army. His parents are named as Morris Ginsberg and his mother Rachel Berman, his wife, Janey Walman. He is five feet four-and-a-half inches (an inch smaller than me), his build is proportionate and his hair is black.

Asked to state whether he has any male relatives in arms for or against Great Britain and the Allies during the present war, he lists his son, Lewis (Louis) Ginsberg, For. His other children are Israel (called by his family Issy but the more urbane and sophisticated Leslie by himself), born in 1901; Benny, my father, born 1904; Gertrude, born 1906; Tilly, born 1907; and, a late afterthought, Gilday (who preferred to be known by that golf-club name, Ralph), born 1916. The document was impressively witnessed by J. Smith, Sergeant, at the Town Hall, Salford, near Manchester, where my grandparents and their children were then living. My grandfather's signature appears below, the uncertain letters of an unfamiliar alphabet as painfully joined up as a child's. J. Smith's signature is that of a snorting stallion, all muscle and sinew and thrusting nose; my grandfather's looks like a snail's track. One of my aunts claimed that the dates were all wrong, falsified by my grandfather to ensure that the younger boys avoided conscription. Conscription was one of the dirtiest words my grandfather could use.

'The name used to be something else,' my mother tells me.

'What?'

'I don't know, I can't remember.'

'Why was it changed?'

'Because your grandfather was a deserter and he took another name when they were escaping from Poland.'

My cousin Shaina insists, 'That's not true. When they came to England they moved into a house and took over the rent book from a family called Ginsberg so they went by that from then on.'

In the early 1970s some of the children of those who anglicized their surnames for assimilation into their new lives, to keep their heads down, began to revert to the Bermans and Greenbaums and Rosenbergs that their parents had abandoned long ago. I always thought Grant a very bland name, though we laughed when my mother was sent a letter from the Clan Grant Society asking her if she knew that her ancestors were mighty warriors on the shores of Loch Spey. 'Stand Fast' was our family motto, apparently. In our part of Eastern Poland it was 'Run Away'. I had thought once or twice of reverting to Ginsberg, but it had turned out to be no more authentic than Grant.

In our family papers is a letter from the Polish Embassy, dated 1959, responding to my father's request for a birth certificate, but the document itself isn't there. I don't know how to find one now. How could I when I lack the most basic information – his name when he was born and the real date, complicated even further by the use then of the old Russian calendar? And the place, Lomza, which after many years I bothered to look up on the map, is a town even Poles had not heard of. Unlike Lodz or Lublin, it was not one of the great centres of the obliterated pre-war Jewish world, just a hick burgh in the middle of a flat agrarian plain, as I found out when I went there and saw the site where the synagogue had been and the plaque on the wall that told the story of the town's Jews, rounded up and marched to the forest to be shot and buried in a mass, unmarked grave.

My father remembered heaving sacks of flour up Brownlow Hill in Liverpool, the ghetto where the Jewish community had settled at the turn of the century. He remembered being sent out after school to lather faces in a barber's shop at a halfpenny a time which led to his lifelong involvement with the hairdressing business.

His mother, the miller's daughter, didn't like him, he said, though he loved her and would cry out her name and shake his fist at the ceiling, thirty years after she died – 'Mother, mother, where are you now?' But she made him go to sea to work in his father's trade, as a ship's baker. In Liverpool the Atlantic was where you sent the people you didn't need or want or it was where you went when you longed for an escape or just an adventure, only a step away when the Liverpool docks were teeming with ocean-going traffic and the city had a cosmopolitan air, the streets filled with sailors home from far-off ports with the curious gifts they had found there. My father sailed round the world, he boasted continuously. But I didn't believe him.

Which of these two stories is right? Was my father, at the age of seventeen, given a one-way ticket to America by his

mother, despatched to make good in the USA, to find the
fortune which my grandfather had accidentally missed out
on, a remittance man without the remittance? Or was he a
wet-back, an illegal immigrant who jumped ship at New
York from his berth as a baker? If he was born in 1904 he
must have reached America in 1921. It was the Manhattan of
Dorothy Parker and Damon Runyan (his favourite author),
the heyday of Lindy's Delicatessan and Meyer Lansky – all
the Jewish gangsters who were his heroes. Whenever I go to
New York I remind myself that the skyline looked utterly
different to him, before the Empire State and Chrysler
Buildings reared up above the city. But the Manhattan of its
apotheosis as the greatest city in the world was under con-
struction, being dug and excavated and hammered and
drilled and sawn into shape, built brick by brick into a
metropolis of skyscrapers, bridges, tunnels and speedways, as
it shed the nineteenth century and fulfilled its dream of
modernity, fit for the immigrants who, like my father, had
shucked off the past.

On the Upper West Side I can glimpse for a moment the
New York my father must have inhabited, the Gothic apartment buildings, the low brownstones and the steps on which
families sometimes still sit out on summer evenings at the
end of the working day. My father lived in the New York
where the Jewish and Italian Lower East Side were still
immigrant neighbourhoods, before Ellis Island closed its
doors and quotas were imposed. He was there during the
Harlem Renaissance and Langston Hughes's New York was
his too. He told me he marched to save the condemned
anarchists, Sacco and Vanzetti, who went to the electric
chair despite a world-wide protest. Once, when I had been
forced to admit that I had been using drugs, he calmed me

down with stories of the opium fiends in Greenwich Village he had known in his 'boyhood days', for whatever British Industry could produce, whatever antics our tame hippies got up to, my father could always reply, 'In America they had that forty years ago.'

I walk round New York now, *his* New York, and remember how I asked him nothing. Nothing. I don't know where he lived or worked, or who his friends were. He said he learned to drive in America but never took a test because there were no driving tests in those days. He said he drove beer trucks over the Canadian border into Upper New York State during prohibition.

He said that when he first arrived in America he went to visit his relatives on his mother's side, the miller's sons. They asked him if he would like to join them for a meal, and half-trained to the politeness of English manners, he refused, expecting to be asked a second time and persuaded. But being newly minted Americans, hell-bent on adopting the new manners, they took his no at face value and he was forced to sit, hungry, watching them as they ate. The lesson from this was, he said, always take what you need out of life. If you see an apple and you want to eat, grab it, eat the apple. Don't spend your life on the sidelines. Go for what you want. Sell yourself to get what you want. It was such a very un-English philosophy and one which I had much trouble later on concealing, growing up in a country where decorum, modesty, self-deprecation, not putting yourself forward or getting above yourself, minding your own business, were the order of the day. Mustn't grumble, can't complain, the English said, actually *telling* you their orders from the ruling class. My father made scenes in restaurants, roaring for the waiter. 'You call this spaghetti bolognese? Tell your chef I've eaten in the finest restaurants in Little Italy, Manhattan Island, New York, United States of America and they cook spaghetti bolognese *nothing* like this garbage? Take it back.'

Then there was Harry Houdini, who saw my father starving outside Lindy's and took him in, bought him a meal and brought him home to stay with him and his wife Bess. My father was clumsy with his hands but when I was growing up he always kept books of magic tricks by his bed which he occasionally practised and performed badly. We always saw the card pass up his sleeve. More successful was the telepathy game he played with my mother which relied on how many fingers rested round the door one of them held. He had Houdini's biography and saw the biopic they made of him with Tony Curtis, my father loudly disputing the facts of the magician's life as portrayed on screen. 'It didn't happen like that,' he bellowed in the cinema until he was shushed down. When he and my mother revisited New York in the 1960s, they went and paid their respects at Houdini's grave.

But as I say, I asked him nothing about all this. Who cared about Houdini when you had Gerry and the Pacemakers on your own doorstep?

My father returned to England a few months before the stock-market crash of 1929. His brother Issy had been sent out to join him but was refused entry to America when he failed the medical. He was too ill to return alone and so my father accompanied him. He sold up and arrived back at the beginning of the Depression with capital, cash in hand. When I was growing up people said they remembered seeing him walking round Liverpool in a white Panama beach suit, whatever that was. He cut a striking figure, apparently. People turned to look at him in the street.

In his wallet was the formula for cold wave, a kind of

perm lotion, which, it was rumoured, he had stolen from Toni, the American hair product corporation for whom he had worked, climbing the ladder from the barber's shop. My father went into hairdressing in Liverpool at the beginning of the 1930s when a decent hairdo was about all there was to cheer you up, apart from the pictures.

That's what they told us but who could believe it and who gave a shit, anyway? Houdini, Greenwich Village, Harlem, Prohibition, so what? If my father had not returned to Liverpool and married my mother then the very worst thing in the world would have happened, I would not have been born and would have missed the most important event in the history of civilization, the Mersey Sound. I would later have a chance to see my father through other eyes, when I went to America for the first time in 1975 and had with me the address of his cousins in Connecticut who knew him when he lived in New York way back when. But I was headed for San Francisco and the very last thing that interested me, having at last found my freedom, was the decrepit reminiscences of relatives.

When you are a child you can't imagine that people really were alive before you were born, that they walked about in the world and ate and drank and worked, oblivious to your own monstrous absence. I entered this life in the second year of the new decade, so the 1940s to me seemed like a nightmare. I could not accept that my parents had really lived through the Blitz, had hidden in air-raid shelters at night, eaten the meagre contents of what their ration cards could supply and dressed so oddly. I assumed that life was in black and white before I was born because that is what the films depicted. I asked why it was that in the old days people walked in such a strange fast jerky way, meaning the silent films they showed on television, played on projectors at the wrong speed.

I was very frightened of our annual Christmas visits to London because whenever they showed you footage of bombing it was always the capital, not Liverpool, which had had, of course, more than its own fair share of destruction from the air. Once, on Oxford Street, on the way to the theatre to see a musical – *South Pacific* or *My Fair Lady*, perhaps – I saw a newspaper placard on which was scrawled 'Big Fight Tonight'. I began to scream and cry to be taken home. I thought the war had started again and no one was telling me, that there was going to be a dogfight over London, bombers clashing in the skies. I never told my parents what I feared, not even after I was sick and sick again in the hotel toilet. Years later I realized it was a boxing match.

My father was thirty-five when war was declared and a combination of his age and chronic bronchitis kept him out of active service. He had no scruples whatsoever about obtaining and even selling whatever he could on the Black Market. It was childish not to. He did his military service in the Home Guard which was nothing at all like the pleasant antics of *Dads Army*, a bunch of old buffers pottering around the High Street and sand dunes of a South Coast town. The Home Guard in Liverpool defended the docks against the Luftwaffe and searched amongst rubble for survivors. Once he spoke of pulling a child's limb from a destroyed house. But then, uncharacteristically, he said, 'I'll never tell a living soul what we went through during the war.' Whatever my father found there he kept locked away in the most silent part of his memory.

In the 1980s Hackney Council made a great public show of

demolishing some tower blocks erected as part of the ill-advised rush to build low-cost housing to replace the war-damaged slums. My sister was the Council's press officer at the time and we had privileged seats to watch the spectacle.

There was a pause, then a rumble and roar and the building collapsed into the great cloud of smoke made of its own dust and debris. In the silence that followed I heard my mother crying like a child along with all the babies who had been brought with their parents for this exciting morning out.

'I don't like it, I don't like it. It's horrible. It reminds me of the war and all the lovely buildings that were destroyed.'

Buried in the hearts of the parents of all my generation are untold traumas of destruction and loss. They are damaged people. When they began their families after the war was over they thought they were beginning the world, but the world they knew was over, finished. The people of the 1950s were aliens among the washing machines and jukeboxes and vacuum cleaners. They were mutilated, bits of them scattered across the battlefields of the world or sunk in the deepest oceans with the dead of planes and ships.

The war cast the longest shadow over my childhood, influencing and defining it. Not because my parents talked incessantly about the great japes they got up to, the prangs in their planes and all the gay parties held under cover of the black-out. The Germans terrified the living daylights out of them.

According to them you were never too young to learn about the Holocaust. What did Michele and I know about country childhoods and the names of flowers and shapes of leaves and texture of bark, who did not have parents who turned the television off in distaste when the mountains of corpses and skeletal survivors appeared on the screen?

'That could have been us if Hitler had got across the Channel.' My Mummy and Daddy in that unidentifiable mound. What could you tell me about Auschwitz that I didn't know already, even at seven blasé, old for my years, precocious with worldly knowledge?

My parents had lived through the war as British people did, sharing the rationing and the Blitz, writing hopeful letters to brothers serving overseas and mourning them along with a million others when they did not return. But the war, which made them like everyone else, also made them feel different.

Fifty years later, during the anniversary of VE Day, in the closing months of my mother's freedom before we put her in the home, she cried her eyes out for the beloved brother she had lost so long ago. The Queen Mother and her daughters were good people, 'for they never deserted us in our hour of need, you know'.

Yet they did not weep when two British soldiers died at the hands of Zionist terrorists during the years of the Mandate. Far from it: my father attended secret meetings to raise money to buy arms with which the British would be driven out and the state of Israel re-established after 2000 years. The long dream was fulfilled. When we said, in our Passover prayers, 'Next year, please God, in Jerusalem', they knew that they had only to catch a boat or even a plane to get there, the metaphor made real. It was the place that made them feel they could stand proud in the world, that took their victimhood and fear away from them, the country that turned their eyes away from the past towards the future for the first time in two millennia. All my childhood the blue and white collecting box for the Jewish National Fund stood on our mantelpiece amongst the ornaments. On our walls were framed certificates declaring that we had planted trees in a forest to reclaim the desert. Yet my father voted for Winston Churchill in 1945 and 1951. Patriots, they were, with divided hearts.

They wanted to protect us, to give us everything poverty and persecution had denied them. They did and didn't want us to know what they knew – about the dodging and diving to make a living, the phoney names, not to mention rape and infanticide before they were even born themselves.

They wanted to hide all this from us yet they also wanted us to be tough, to know how to survive, for survival was everything. At the end of the war simply being alive, a living mockery to fascism, was the victory itself.

Of course they had something to conceal. Of course when they said, 'I can't remember', they remembered all too bloody well.

The photographs of my family from the 1950s show us hell-bent on pleasure. They were prosperous days. My father had made the move from owning hairdressing shops to selling hairdressers their paraphernalia – their rollers and clips, scissors, combs, brushes and hood hairdryers. Stuck behind the mantelpiece clock there were always a few cards with sample curls of artificial hair coloured in one of L'Oreal's tempting shades of blonde or brunette or auburn or blue-black, each with its own glamorous name. But principally he 'manufactured' in the back yard of his premises: shampoo, conditioner and his famous cold wave, stolen from Toni, in the days when every woman had her hair shampooed and set once a week, if she could afford it, and permed every three months.

Between the slim young man posed in Central Park in the Roaring Twenties and the Daddy I knew, some urge to consume had taken hold. He was a compulsive eater and drinker who never walked when he could drive and never stood when he could sit. My father was loud, gregarious, bombastic and, as I got older, increasingly embarrassing. In the wardrobe of my mother's flat in Bournemouth after we'd taken her away was a square pale turquoise box from George Henry Lee's, the Liverpool branch of John Lewis. Whatever the box contained – a dress or a hat, perhaps – it had been sent to her on 10 September 1964 and once divested of its contents it had been used to store loose photographs that had not found their way into any album. So here are my parents at a succession of dinner dances, my father with his trademark cigar in his large evening suit, my mother in a low-cut, strapless gown; on New Year's Eve both of them with little conical party hats on their heads. My parents scowling at the camera after a row. My father in a heavy semblance of dancing. Where was I? At home, tucked up in bed with a baby-sitter, willing myself to stay awake, hearing the car pull up in the drive, the key turn in the lock, hoping for the paper napkin of *petits fours* they always brought me, the most curious sweetmeats in the world which existed only in a particular sphere which involved night-time and evening dress and my parents' absence.

Because our house was on a corner our garden was beside it, separated from the street by a high fence. Once, when I was playing on my swing, a rich kid's toy in those days, a man passed with his child and he held her high up above his head so she could see how the other half lived.

My father showered me with presents – an ottoman, colouring books and pencils and paintboxes and dolls and gollywogs and spyrographs and a red tricycle with its own trunk in which I could keep my toys and books about horses and ballet and anything else an astute toy department assistant could convince him to part with his money for, essential for the well-being of a growing girl. In my comics, *Bunty* and *Judy*, the heroines were always poor but honest girls dreaming of becoming champion skaters or ballet dancers or horse-riders, their parents scrimping and scraping to afford their lessons or their shoes or their skates. And in every story there was a snooty rich girl, the villainess, who had the best of everything but would not hesitate to lower herself to cheating or putting a sharp stone in her rival's point shoes. I was that rich girl and this was how, my comics taught me, rich girls behaved.

The values of post-war, post-Austerity Britain were sneered at by my parents and especially by my father who had once seen how the Americans lived. Discipline, self-restraint, modesty, respect for authority, introspection and even artistic sensitivity were values my father had no use for. These were the standards adhered to by the world beyond our front door and while slavishly trying to imitate *them* – the English – I secretly despised these self-same attitudes. Like my parents, I became a self divided. On the one hand I wanted a dry, mild, laconic father with a name like James or Charles or Timothy, and a distinguished war record. On the other I did not wish to have to do without the vulgar luxuries we took for granted. The one aspect of my parents' values I wholly endorsed without criticism was their utter indifference to any form of physical exercise as being somehow bestial, an abdication of one's humanity. Any half-hearted attempt to bounce a tennis ball against the wall of our house was greeted by my father with a roar: 'Why don't you come indoors and improve your mind with a book?' When I puff away on the treadmill now or lift weights at the gym, I try to imagine what my father would say if he could see me: 'What are you, a work-horse? Haven't you got anything better to do with your time?'

His own mind was, he thought, improved, in the manner of the autodidact. He tended to read declarative Great Thinkers of the American nineteenth century such as Ralph Waldo Emerson, whose name was never spoken by him in surname shorthand but always with the three orotund designations from the frontispiece of his works. My mother exclusively read Harold Robbins, an American author of thumping sexually salacious epics which charted the rise of a boy from the ghetto to handsome, two-fisted executive.

Comparing my parents' handwriting, it would later occur to me that in my mother's variegated words in which capital and lower case letters interspersed themselves at random, there were strong signs of illiteracy. Or today, middle-class parents would call it dyslexia. Whatever it was, something in my mother's brain seemed not to be wired up properly for writing.

My father and I drew apart as I grew older because he embarrassed me. I was embarrassed by his weight, by his loudness and ostentation, by the habitual lies he told, trying to pass himself off as a celebrity in order to get a better room at a hotel. For some reason he was particularly fond of pretending that he was the artist who drew the Gambols cartoon in the *Daily Express*, making unconvincing drawings to impress receptionists and waitresses. I was embarrassed by his constant showing off and boasting about his daughters' minor achievements. I was embarrassed about his age, for he was forty-seven when I was born and in his sixties when I was a teenager. Later, in the long years of his illness, I could not stay in the room at mealtimes to see him fall asleep over the dinner table, his mouth hanging open with food still in it. He more than embarrassed me, he disgusted me. I hated the years of his decline, his petty addictions to food and alcohol and gambling, putting the whole of the money set aside to pay the wages of his staff on a horse. Towards the end of his life I could not spend more than a few minutes with my father without us tearing into each other. I don't know what happened to our relationship. Perhaps we were too alike. Or maybe it was that psychosexual thing that always exists between fathers and daughters and from which both of us ran a mile when I reached puberty. When I was seven I was in love with him, demanding that he take me to the theatre and treat me as his date, buy me a box of chocolates as once he had sent me little posies of anemones, tucked into my mother's larger bouquets. But when I grew up, I wanted a thin, young, long-haired boyfriend. Not a fat, bald, sixty-year-old.

Perhaps too I had learned to stand up to my father's powerful ego, to pit my will against his. Authority – I can't handle it. I still hate other people telling me what to do. Always have the last word in an argument, never give in, were the lessons I learned from him. Something in me is still trying to defeat my father and rebel against him when I haven't been an adolescent for a quarter of a century. What is between a father and a daughter is always a love affair, but with me it was also a rivalry – for what? I don't know.

And yet now I feel nothing for him but love, having forgiven him everything. He did not allow me to have a bicycle. He had once been involved in a minor road accident and knocked over a cyclist, though it was the bike-rider's fault. Bicycles, he declared, were a menace on the roads. I kept up a six-month-long harangue with no result and to this day I cannot ride one because although it is possible to learn as an adult, when you fall off it hurts more. I felt dreadfully disabled when I was younger because in black-and-white war films people are always escaping from the Gestapo by grabbing a two-wheeler that happens to be leaning against the wall and riding off on it, furiously pedalling like hell while the impotent Nazis dance about on the road. And for years I thought that it would all be my father's fault if I was sent to a concentration camp because when my compatriots cycled away, I would be left behind. Of course today, if any bike was handy, it would be padlocked to the railings.

Yet I have forgiven him because whatever my father's many, many failings until the last, worst, years he was always a father to me, seeing his job as my protection and his life's work the winning of bread to support us in the most luxurious manner he could muster. Nothing but the best, for us. I see now, fourteen years after his death, how his life was defined by disappointment and the loss of freedom, how he had once roamed the world and lived with Harry Houdini and mixed with mobsters and hoodlums and girls that were no better than they oughta and that he had lost the world and replaced it with the confines of suburban domesticity. And how much of his bombast was a heart that yearned for bigger and better things. He was born for America, my

74

father, for its vastness. He was just the size for America. All his faults would have seemed like virtues there. In a child's book of the Gulliver story there is a picture of the adventurer in Lilliput, prone on the ground while scurrying little men and women enslave him with tiny ropes and pins. Me, my mother and sister and his business did that to my father.

It was always my father's lap I crawled on to and squirmed around on. That stopped, of course, at the right time. When I was around thirteen and entering puberty I was lounging around the house in a dressing-gown and my father looked at me and said in a tight voice, 'Cover yourself up.' He was doing what so many abusive fathers fail at, protecting me from adult sexual desire. Later, I spent some years interviewing the victims of child sexual abuse and after every one I dreamed of my father and they were always happy, innocent dreams.

Until I die or senile dementia gets me first, as I am so sure it will, I'll remember the chemical stench of his premises on Mount Pleasant, between the Adelphi Hotel and the Mardi Gras Club where so many of the Mersey Beat groups got their start, the smell of peroxide which stripped all the colour from the hair and the huge vats in the yard in which he stirred up his terrible potions, his tie falling into the concoction. When herbal shampoo became fashionable in the 1960s I watched him make his own brand – the usual stuff with green dye in it. And I learned that beauty and appearances were all mixed up with dirt and sweat and that you could not separate them, for if it was true that when you scratched away at the gilded exterior of things, you'd find the iron beneath, then from my father I learned another verity – that you can't have depths without surfaces.

The yard and the shop were his domain, which like Houdini he had conjured out of nothing. He had taught himself chemistry from books in the public library during the 1930s. Primo Levi was also, of course, a chemist, engaged all his working life in the paint industry. Both men used their knowledge of the mysteries of inorganic matter to dedicate themselves to enhancing the surfaces of things. Both were in the beauty business one way or another. Night after night my father had spent in the library learning the Periodic Table, the formulae in his mind – the deepest structure of the universe – which he manipulated into bouffant hairdos to pay for an education which taught me to read George Eliot and Virginia Woolf.

So now I remember the best of him and nothing can soothe me as much as the voice of Peter O'Sullevan, the BBC racing commentator, whose voice gathering pace and excitement sums up our Saturday afternoons together in front of the telly, my father making regular trips to the telephone in the hall to place a bet with his bookmaker. In the balance sheet of wins and losses he came out further and further behind as his life went on, but of one thing I felt quite sure, that he openly and sentimentally loved my mother to whom he sent bouquets on birthdays and anniversaries always with that small posy tucked in for me so I would not be forgotten.

When my father went out in the evenings, to play cards at the Jewish golf club, the house seemed cold and empty and dark. It probably *was* colder because my mother would not feel it necessary to turn on the heat just for the two of us. And it was emptier because his bodily bulk took up more space. When my father was home the lights in every room blazed and there were gargantuan meals of at least four courses. When my mother and I were alone together she would only prepare what she wanted for herself, which was usually just a bowl of soup, over which I cried once, for it seemed even then like orphanage fare.

In our family, as in every Jewish family, food was part of our ancestral memory. In her kitchen my mother cooked recipes for cheese blintzes and *matzoh brei* that her own mother had brought with her from Kiev, and the dishes that came to the table were our link to the vanished communities of earlier times; they traced the wanderings of the Jewish people across the earth. In the 1990s when I went to Poland to find my roots I pointed out that the meals they gave me were not Polish, but Jewish – the *cholent*, the *borscht*, the *kreplach* soup – or maybe it was that what I thought of as Jewish was also Polish, for the falafels and pitta bread of the Middle Eastern Sephardi tradition which they serve in Israel today are as unfamiliar to me as bacon was in our house when I was growing up.

Our religion was embodied in our cooking, like the Passover meal on *Seder* night where everything we put in our mouths symbolizes the slavery of the Children of Israel under the terrible rule of the Egyptians, and their flight to freedom: the hardboiled eggs in salt water representing the hardness of our labours and the salt of our tears as we bent our backs under the yoke that tied us to the stones of the Pyramids we built; the *chorozeth* – a mixture of nuts and cinnamon that was the mortar; the *matzhot* that showed that in our haste to flee with Moses across the Red Sea that God parted for us, we had no time to allow our bread to rise. 'In Judaism you don't study theology, you eat it,' Rabbi Lionel Blue has noted. The holiest place in our religion may be the kitchen table, where countless blessings are said, the table from which some medieval rabbis asked that the boards of their coffin be taken.

I was not a happy child, not because my parents made me miserable but because childhood did not suit me, it was not my ideal time of life. And this may have been because motherhood – at least of young children – was not one of my mother's talents. I grew up assuming that my mother did not particularly like children. When she heard a baby cry she did not rush to comfort it but said under her breath, 'Is someone going to shut that brat up?' Our relationship wasn't physical. I don't know why. My sister remembers being cuddled but I don't, so perhaps it was me and I just wasn't the cuddly kind.

I do not think she would have chosen motherhood if there had been any realistic alternative. She would, I think, have preferred to maintain her position as beloved child bride to a man fourteen years older than her. But then what else would she have done with the rest of her life? It was not, after all, as if she was a frustrated bluestocking, doomed to change nappies when she would rather have been reading Charlotte Brontë.

What galled me in childhood was that she was not *capable*. She did not sew or mend or make things or have hobbies. She did not have a work-basket out of which I could steal scraps to make useless objects as seen on *Blue Peter*. She cooked well, but only if someone was there to cook for. Otherwise, she didn't bother.

'I can't be bothered' was one of the great themes of my mother's life. There was, in those days, a habit among better-off schools to celebrate Harvest Festival by demanding that parents give their children some offering of fruit and flowers to bring in. Most children's mothers ordered elaborate gift baskets from the greengrocers wrapped in cellophane and decorated with a lavish bow which would be displayed on a platform in the assembly hall. A few mothers of an artistic bent even baked loaves in the shape of wheatsheaves. But my mother who 'couldn't be bothered with that nonsense' sent me to school with a pound of apples in a brown paper bag. Or sometimes nothing.

We all have childhood memories of humiliation, which can still today prick hot tears. In my last year at primary school, needlework class was dedicated to the making of a skirt. Letters were sent home to our mothers instructing them to purchase a length of material and matching thread which was to be brought in so this dress-making enterprise could get underway. As the weeks passed each girl produced her fabric, pretty in pink, sprigged with flowers, and every-one gathered round to ooh and aah our admiration, with discussions going on in the corners of the classroom concerning whose was the nicest.

My mother did nothing to acquire my fabric. Day after day I went to school empty-handed. When I begged her, she said that making a skirt was nonsense, why bother when you could buy one? But I *have* to, I told her. Grudgingly, when I was the very last girl in the class not to have produced her floral length, my mother greeted me with a bag. 'There it is,' she said.

Inside was a piece of material in large brown checks. It was hideous. Perhaps it wasn't hideous and now I would find it smart but in 1961 it was utterly unsuitable for a child. She had given no thought at all to the purchase.

When I took it to school I saw everyone's faces and heard their whispers. Of all the material of the thirty or so girls, mine was voted the ugliest.

I did not forget. I didn't forgive. It's absurd to say this, but I have not forgiven now. For my mother's ongoing demeanour of couldn't-be-bothered-with-that-nonsense summed up her mothering.

If she had been hard pressed with a job outside the home or coping with a large family or engaged in some great enterprise or charitable work I could have excused her, but she had established that her status was to be gained by being a wife and mother and I thought she could have given a bit more of herself to the job. She had, after all, all kinds of domestic help, including at one stage a live-in Spanish maid called Maria, a brutal peasant woman who spoke no English whatsoever and whose forearms gripped the iron as if it were a farm implement pressed into service as a murder weapon. If you mentioned the name of Franco she drew her finger across her throat. She adored my mother who somehow managed to convince her that she was 'a lady'.

And this, to her children, was the paradox of our mother,

the knot we can't undo. For people liked her. She had many, many friends. Perhaps she was someone different with them, another person altogether. People willingly gave her their secrets, they called on her to go with them to hospital when they had to have a test that would tell them if a cancer was growing in their body. She could be bothered then. Sometimes I felt that her friends protected her not only from the world but from her family. 'Does she know you?' Did we know her?

But we saw another side to her, or rather many sides. In the home she runs and takes the arm of her care worker. 'This is my Florence Nightingale,' she says, smiling at her. Then the woman goes and she turns away, the smile wiped from her face. 'You have to keep in with them,' she tells me, coldly.

'Your mother came and told me how happy she was here,' the head of the home tells me.

When I put this to my mother she replies, 'I only said that.'

My mother wanted what went with motherhood, the prestige, but none of the work. So out of touch was she with her own reproductive system that she did not notice she was pregnant with my sister until she was five months gone, having been convinced by the family GP that she was suffering from a cyst. My baby sister was often referred to as 'a mistake'. What my mother really wanted to be was not a wife nor a mother but a daughter. She carried with her from her earliest years all the tricks she learned as the spoilt youngest child. She had junked the past, discarded her own mother as a role model for married life, that peasant woman from another century and another land. So it wasn't surprising that her mothering sometimes felt like a vacuum.

Sunday morning. I was ten years old. My parents had unaccountably taken to locking their bedroom door with instructions that they were not, under any circumstances, to be disturbed. From inside I could hear muffled giggles and groans, leaking out through the keyhole. My father would then have been in his early sixties and my mother in her mid-forties so of course they *couldn't possibly have been having sex*.

If the phone rang I was to answer it, being responsible enough to reply, 'Who's speaking please' and 'My parents are unavailable at the moment, can I take a message?' My baby sister was gurgling pleasantly in her pram out in the garden, in the sunshine. I was doing what I did with most of my time: lying on my stomach on the bed, reading a book, improving my mind with *Jill Has Two Ponies* or *A Dream of Sadler's Wells*.

There were three phones in the house. One was where every decent Englishman had his equipment, in the cold hall, the chill of which we had moderated with central heating – central heating! In 1961! Spoilt rotten, we girls were, living in imitation of Sir Bernard and Lady Docker, rich and common. Another was in the kitchen and a third by my mother's bed.

I was standing in the hall listening to what was being said to me down the receiver in a grown-up woman's voice: 'Can I speak to Daddy, please?'

I said, 'I'm awfully sorry, but you've got the wrong number.'

'Is that Linda?'

'Yes.'

'This is Sonia.'

'Who?'

'I'm your sister. Haven't they told you about me?'

A little thing like that slipping their minds, it was easily done.

So when my father had finished speaking to her, I was told. The white Panama beach suit had done its sexy work when he came back from America at the beginning of the Depression. He had pulled a teenage girl called Bessie Cohen and instead of escorting her respectfully to her parents' door, instead of treating her as he demanded that his daughters should be treated, he had not just had sex with her but got her pregnant. They married, briefly, at the beginning of the 1930s and quickly separated. Do I believe that they were together for so little a time? Or had my mother insisted that Bessie was airbrushed out of the bigger picture?

After the war Bessie married an engineer in the Dutch merchant navy and went to live with him in Rotterdam. He wasn't Jewish. Among the family papers which Michele found when we cleared my mother's flat was a copy of their marriage certificate showing that on 19 September 1946 Walter Schaaij, son of Wonter Schaaij (deceased), occupation stevedore, married Bessie Ginsberg, formerly Cohen, daughter of Benjamin Cohen, tailor. They were living at the same address at the time of the wedding. All this made her, to my mother, not much more than a prostitute.

'You know your mother was pregnant when they got married?' my cousin Shaina said to me on the phone recently.

'Oh no she wasn't,' I replied, very firmly.

It was out of the question that my mother had had sex before she got married, *out of the question*. This was the mother who advised me, during the sexual revolution, 'No one wants a cake with a piece cut out.'

'Yes they do,' I countered. 'It shows it's a good cake.'

'Well, he'll never marry you.'

'I don't care. Marriage is an outdated bourgeois institution. No one gets married these days.'

'You mean they live in sin?'

'What's sinful about it?'

'Don't think you're going to bring a baby into this house.'

'Why should I? We have the Pill now, you know.' And we had, just, I had slipped under the wire.

My mother's sexual values were what we were in revolt against. It was not possible, in fact entirely out of the question, that *my* mother could turn out to have been no better than she should be, that she harboured erotic desires and acted on them in defiance of convention.

But Shaina, who was old enough to have been at the wedding, insisted. She rang another cousin, Joy, in Birmingham and she concurred. It was definite, they said. How can this be, I argued. My parents got married in 1946 and I was born in 1951. 'Is that what they told you?' Shaina replied, pityingly. What was this? Was I suddenly five years older than I thought I was?

If I were to ask my mother, did you have sex before you got married, the words would turn to ash in my mouth before I uttered them and what could possibly make me think that I would be told the truth, anyway?

But there was another witness. My mother's oldest brother, Abie, had moved to London and married in the 1930s, but his wife died young and when she was fourteen his daughter Marina was sent back to live with her grandmother in Liverpool. My mother, the youngest daughter whose nearest sibling was away fighting in Italy, was still living at home when Marina arrived. As she grew up, Marina, her niece, was to become her closest friend until they fell out in the early 1980s when my mother felt she was not treated with proper distinction at a family event.

Marina still lived in Liverpool. Her eldest son, Jonathan, a photographer, had married the girl of every man's dreams – Britain's only female managing director of a brewery. The younger one was a limo driver in Los Angeles. That line of the family made a bit of a specialization of transport. Marina's late husband had been a car worker at the Ford plant at Halewood in Liverpool and her half-brother, Betty's son, is a London cabbie.

'Is it possible,' I suggested tentatively on the phone, 'that Mum was pregnant when I was born?'

'No, she wasn't,' Marina said, a gallon of cold water in her voice. 'I was at your mother's wedding and you didn't come along until five years later.' Thank God, I hadn't passed the half-century after all, though now my complexion no longer bore a miraculously youthful appearance.

'I didn't know you were at the wedding, I thought it was just the Ginsbergs, at Auntie Tilly's house.'

'That was the second wedding, the Jewish one. Auntie

Rose got married from Devon Street. I always remember her standing in a striped dress in the yard and your Auntie Gertie from Birmingham arrived and I said, "Who's that posh lady?"'

I recalled that my mother had also spoken of a reception at Reece's Ballroom, where, coincidentally, John Lennon was to have his desultory wedding lunch after he married Cynthia. For years these two events had coexisted in my mind without me ever noticing that there was a contradiction.

'So there were two weddings?'

'That's right, one in the registry office, and then the Jewish one in Leeds, years later. She could have been pregnant with you at the time.'

There was a photograph of my mother in a back yard in the 1940s in a striped dress and a hat with a feather in it, linking arms with my father and holding a decorative horse-

shoe. It had never been referred to as a wedding photograph. My mother had eliminated it from history. The Ginsberg wedding, in a garden with an embroidered Madeira tablecloth, a suit and fur round her neck, had become the real and one and only wedding when she discarded the Hafts and annexed herself to the Ginsbergs.

'Mum always told me

that she wouldn't get married until her own mother died because she had to look after her.'

'Well, that's not true because Bubba was there.'

I said to my mother: 'Why did you have two weddings, Mum?'

'Because that bitch, your father's ex, wouldn't give him a religious divorce.'

I reported this back to Shaina. 'That can't be right,' she said 'because in Jewish law a woman can't grant a divorce, only the man can.'

So my parents' marriage will remain a persistent mystery, one that can't be cleared up.

I suppose my father had not told me about Sonia because divorce, in those days, was a stigma, and looking back I was perhaps the only girl I knew at school with a divorced father. I didn't mind. I thought it was interesting.

After Sonia outed herself to me, my father decided to do the decent thing as far as Michele was concerned. When she was sixteen, at a bar-mitzvah, he told her, 'There's someone I want you to meet.' Then he took her to another table and said, 'This is your sister.'

I only saw her twice. The first time, when I was about thirteen, was at my father's office when she dropped in unannounced and I realized that he had had, all these years, a continuous other existence that Sonia was a part of and I wasn't and that when he told us he was going, say, to the races at Uttoxeter or to the golf club, he could not always be believed. In that other place Sonia was his eldest daughter, not me, and they had lunch together, he visited her house, wrote her letters and received her replies, was privy to her secrets.

A sophisticated woman in her early thirties walked in, a beauty with blue-black hair and blue eyes and pale skin. She made us stand together in front of the mirror. 'Do we look alike?' she asked. And that is all I can remember about her, nothing more, not her clothes nor her scent nor anything else that was said, other than the promise I made to myself, that when I grew up I was going to be just like her.

The second time was at my grandfather's funeral in 1965. My mother would not be in the same room as Sonia. She thought she had some nerve, coming to the house.

I never saw or spoke to her again.

It was my cousins who filled in Sonia's history for me. She grew up with her mother but when Bessie moved to Holland she was sent to live with her maternal grandmother. What sort of stepmother did my mother turn out to be? Marina got to know Sonia at a youth club in the 1940s until she was warned off by an aunt. 'Rose will kill you if she finds out you've been seeing her. She's Uncle Ben's daughter, you know.'

Many years later my mother told me that when Sonia had got married she had 'made the wedding'. But somehow Sonia was not grateful enough, or had said the wrong thing or had in some other way offended my mother's vast sense of *amour propre* because she at once fell into the large category of women defined by my mother as 'that bitch'. (Men were designated as 'that swine', which could bracket together Adolph Hitler and the husband of a friend who she believed had made a disparaging remark about her mink stole.)

How did Sonia get on without her stepmother? She moved to London and became South East area manager for

the cosmetics company, Revlon and married, then separated.
The telephone call that surprised me with her existence was
to find out my father's Hebrew name for the Jewish divorce.
She married again – a pharmacist whose first love was play-
ing the piano on ocean-going liners – and went to live in
Leeds but had no children.

We never talked about her. She was like our family's amputated limb which still causes phantom pain in the body. We
tried to forget her but that did not mean she did not exist.

Still the name Sonia haunts me. It is *her* name as if no
one else ever born had the right to it. Like everything that
went on in my family, I didn't get interested in her until it
was too late and now however hard I pump my mother for
information, she always says, 'I can't remember' and I don't
know if it's true: whether she can't because disease has
eliminated a portion of her memory which contained
things that she never wanted to think about anyway; or if
she has, at long last, found an excuse not to talk about the
girl who reminded her that my father was not entirely
hers.

The revelation of Sonia inspired a brief burst of honesty and
authenticity. A few years after that phone call, when I was in
my late teens, on another Sunday morning, my father came
downstairs and histrionically announced that he had something on his conscience. Around the time I was born,
perhaps a few months before or after, he and my mother had
gone for their only visit to Paris. In the hotel lift, my father
confessed, he had been accosted by a prostitute and had paid
her for her services.

My mother smiled at this scandal. In Paris he had bought

her a pair of earrings which, while they were only diamanté, were exquisitely fashioned, and I had them myself for a while until I lost them.

'I knew you had something on your conscience because of those earrings,' she said.

My father begged her for her forgiveness which my mother easily granted. She did not appear to care either way about the prostitute. She had suspected something. What she had got was the earrings which easily outweighed a sexual infidelity with someone he would never see again. This still seems to be an implausible explanation for the easy sang-froid with which she greeted my father's revelation, but I do not know of any other. It was just another facet of her mad-dening personality. Recently she accused one of her oldest friends of being a prude. I don't know what that could mean at all. It wasn't as if she had a pre-marital sex life.

I clearly remember that my father said that he had learned a few tricks from that prostitute but to be honest I can't

believe he could possibly have uttered such a thing, at least in my presence, though I knew he kept a small amount of tame pornogra-phy like a typed-out copy of *Eskimo Nell* hidden in the bookcase by his bed along with his collected Damon Runyan and Jack London stories. So that must be a false memory. It just has to be.

Never believe that fashion is trivial, materialistic, shallow and of no consequence. Fashion, which had made my family's prosperity, destroyed it, too.

The late 1950s and early 1960s, the heyday of the beehive hairdo, were years of exceptionally heavy use of rollers, hairspray (which in those days was still called lacquer and had the consistency of it, both hard and sticky at the same time), perm and setting lotion, clips, pins and hood hairdryers. There was a more limited call for conditioner, for the health of the hair mattered less than its ability to stand up by itself, several inches away from the head.

The beehive kept my father's business roaring for a while, enough to buy us, in 1959, our detached house backing on to allotments which extended the view, though they caused us many puzzled hours as we examined the goings-on of the men with spades and hoes and trowels who for no apparent reason chose to spend their leisure hours in old clothes, growing things they could have easily bought. Our garden was attended to by a firm of contractors who arrived once a fortnight with a lawn-mower and looked after the mainly evergreen low-maintenance shrubs.

The beehive gave my father private medical insurance on which he had treatment for such minor complaints as

ulcers and hernias and it bought my mother the basis of
what was to become her fabulous wardrobe with its mink
stoles and coats and jackets, diamond-encrusted eternity
ring, Charles Jourdain shoes and handbags and Jaeger suits.
My mother's wardrobe was a fairy kingdom for my sister
and me, painted white with gilded curlicues and inside
smelling not of mothballs but of mysterious little scented
packets which hung from the hangers of her clothes. A
place in which you could lose yourself in fantasies of what
it was like to be a grown woman. And in the drawers of her
kidney-shaped dressing-table with its three-way mirror in
which you could see yourself reflected to infinity (and more
startlingly, what you looked like when you were not looking yourself in the eye) there was her more limited
collection of cosmetics which she applied with a light
hand – her blue Revlon eye-shadow (which she still has,
surviving thirty years into the future, a museum item now
and still not finished up), her face powder, her lipsticks, her
bottle of Elizabeth Arden Blue Grass perfume and the
squeezy bottle of lacquer with its pump (the aerosol had not
yet been invented). In the bathroom were her jars of cold
cream and cotton wool for, as she boasted, she had never let
soap and water touch her face since she was a girl and her
marvellous complexion was a testimony to her skin-care
programme. She retired to bed at night in a nylon lace
diaphanous nightie with rollers firmly anchored to her head
by hairpins and the whole works held in place by a pair of
nylon knickers which were more capacious and aerated than
a hairnet and gave her bouffant room to breathe, so to
speak.

The beehive paid for an interior designer to come and
decorate the rooms of our new home in pale *eau-de-Nil*

and gold. It sent my mother and father to the East End of
London where master craftsmen knocked up resplendent
new copies of eighteenth-century furniture fit for the
Palace of Versailles. Haunt antique shops and buy the real
thing? You must be joking, my father would *never* have
contemplated having secondhand goods in his house.
Everything had to be new, nothing but the best. We lived
in a style I still think of as Jewish Rococo: ormolu clocks
that didn't work, an 'eighteenth-century' coffee table,
nests of gold tables and the pride of the house, our blond
walnut 'eighteenth-century' cocktail cabinet which lit up
when you opened it and in which my father kept his
stocks of Noilly Prat vermouth, Haig and Haig whisky in
its triangular bottle covered in gold wire mesh, and various
kosher wines for the Sabbath made in Israel and of a med-
icinal sweetness. My father, unusually for a Jew, was a
drinker. He would go out to the local pub, the Greenhills,
at the far end of our road where the detached and semi-
detached houses petered out into post-war council estates,
and there he would drink pints and pick a fight; he was the
verbal version of the fist-happy bruiser. 'Let's have an argument,' he would say to visitors, 'pick a subject – politics,
religion?'

My mother did not drink apart from the occasional snow-
ball, which had advocaat and soda water in it, or something
called a gin fizz which you don't hear much of any more.
She thought the consumption of alcohol was common. I
doubt if she has had a dozen alcoholic drinks in her life. I
tried her on Pina Coladas once which she enjoyed but
preferably without the alcohol.

The evil genius who stole our wealth away from us was
Vidal Sassoon who invented the geometric cut in which

everything depended on the hairdresser's scissors and the skill that manipulated them. The shampoo and set was out. The blow-wave was in. Perm lotion was the dinosaur of the hairdressing trade. Young women no longer went to the hairdresser's once a week but only occasionally, for a trim, leaving their long curtains of hair to drop down dead on either side of their face. Which is what I did myself, a permanent taunt to my father.

Besides, he was old now, in his sixties, struggling to run a business in a new age of trade union militancy and a belief in technological progress. He should have retired but it wasn't his way to save money, to put it by for pensions. He lived for the moment; my mother kept him youthful, dressing him in modish pink shirts and running Grecian Formula through what was left of his hair. When he had money he spent it lavishly, on suits for himself and dresses for my mother and gadgets for his children.

But suddenly he was old and it was all going wrong and the central heating was hardly ever turned on and my mother's voice grew bitter and resentful as she spoke of what others had and she didn't. A loggia, for example, which I believe was a form of conservatory. A mink jacket rather than a stole which she considered dated. She wanted an ankle-length velvet skirt for evening wear and in the end she borrowed one from a friend.

She said to someone who admired it: 'Oh, this old thing. I've worn it so often that this is going to be its last outing.' These were lies that grown-ups told. I thought all forms of lying were normal.

My father spent more and more time in the betting shop and fewer of his horses seemed to come in. He drank more and ate more, growing larger in front of our eyes. 'God help me in this house full of women,' he would cry out, shaking his fist heavenwards, shaking his fist at God. And 'Why didn't the Almighty grant me sons to take over the business?'

In the spring of 1969 when my father was sixty-five and I was eighteen I came home one evening to find the house shut up and dark. It seemed so odd that home should not be, even for a moment, the place where my parents always were, laying down rules, trying to trap me in the closed ghetto of their expectations. For it was all-out guerrilla war now, no compromise, no surrender. The life that I presented to them was a tissue of lies. I never told them a single truth about what I was up to. I did not share with them the sex and the drugs and the cigarettes. I never brought a boyfriend back. I'd have been ashamed to take anyone there. Just as they had double lives, I'd now entered mine.

After a while a neighbour, seeing the chandeliers lit, came over to break the news to me that my father had had three heart attacks, one after the other. 'It's touch and go,' she said. There was hope but that was all there was. I felt the sun go out on the world and that we were doomed to live forever in darkness and despair, like primitive peoples at the sight of an eclipse.

For thirteen years my father went on living, in a way. Ordered not to smoke or drink, put on strict diets, they cut the pleasure out of him, surgically removed all his sensuality. My mother went to work in the business. Just when she had expected that the rest of her life would be spent as a lady of leisure, attending coffee mornings and shopping, designating which children of the pogrom immigrants could be designated as 'top drawer' and which others, 'toe-rags'. She'd come to this, no better than her sister Miriam who still turned a hand as a seamstress. There was no private medical insurance for my father any more – he couldn't afford the premiums. There was no money to send my sister to the school I had attended so she went to the local comprehensive. She spent the summer holidays sitting in the office with a colouring book, hour after dismal hour. For her, the fabulous fifties and sixties, the years of dinner dances and *petits fours* and furs and cars with leather upholstery and the lights blazing in the house were as mythical a time as the lives of our grandparents, and all I have described no more than oral history.

'You're going to give me another coronary,' my father would shout, if anyone disagreed with him. 'You want to kill me.'

And he would actually take a knife from the table and point it at his neck and shout, 'Look what my family have driven me to. I'm going to cut my throat.'

My mother would ask him in the morning what he wanted for dinner and he would reply, 'Give me fish.'

When the meal was served in the evening he would look at it and say, 'I don't want fish. Take it away. Give me something else,' as if he was in a hotel.

My mother would scream and cry real tears and tell him that she wasn't his slave or his skivvy and she had been out at work all day while he had been in the betting shop and this was what she had to come home to.

Maria, our Spanish maid, left, suddenly announcing she was getting married, to a man from the Salvation Army. Then she got cancer and died young. Without her, the house was slovenly and cold. They'd bought oil-fired central heating in 1959 and now it was 1973, the oil crisis, the three-day week when we sat in darkness at tea-time staring at the lifeless TV set in the gloom. Without illumination, you could disguise the way the interior decor had cracked and peeled. Only the brand-new antiques attracted no patina of age. Each car we bought to replace the old one was smaller and smaller and the last one was secondhand.

Every expectation she had was confounded. Having hoisted herself above her small, poor Haft sisters and brother now she was back at their level, more or less.

Now my mother who had once bestowed her custom on the best shops in town, became the poverty-shop shopper I was to know so well in later years, the hunter for bargains, for marked-down goods. 'This is horrible, Mum,' we cried. 'Why did you buy it?'

'It was on offer.'

Michele wanted a Cindy doll, the kind whose hair 'grew' when you pushed a button on its plastic back. My mother bought a cheap imitation at Garston market where the poor people shopped. We were so ashamed. Bitterness and anger were her condition now, she who had been brought up to expect that others – first her sisters and brothers, then her husband – would provide her with the best of everything, was rooting around on stalls, picking things up, putting them down when she saw the prices.

In these years I very much took my mother's side against my father, who became a domestic tyrant. There had always been something of the bully in him, but looking back perhaps they bullied each other. I constructed for her and me a Sisterhood, a feminist solidarity. I gave her *Spare Rib* to read and delivered sanctimonious lectures. I told her about the theory of the double work day, how women who went out to work had to come home and do their time all over again, cooking and cleaning, while the men did nothing. 'That's me,' she said.

Most of my affection for my mother derives from this period in our lives, when we had a semblance of closeness and our relationship seemed uncomplicated. I was away from home, at university, and she was always happy to see me when I returned, always burdened me with gifts to bring back to my flatmates: half a dozen thin frozen steaks, a rather clumsy but satisfyingly large chocolate cake, half a gallon of my father's shampoo. Now that I had my own life, the rules didn't matter so much any more because I'd broken them. I'd got away. There had never been the possibility of compromise, with my parents. Either I was a dutiful daughter, then wife, then mother or I was a student revolutionary, sexual revolutionary, all those isms that were how you defined your cool in those days. And my mother seemed to accept that she had lost the battle. Their reverence for education, for getting on in the world, for making something of yourself contradicted their rooted sense of tradition and continuity. They shrugged their shoulders. 'She's a clever girl. What can you do?'

But during all these years I didn't actually ask my mother anything or really listen because I was too enthralled with the sound of my own political voice.

In 1976, I went even further away, to Canada to do an MA, leaving Michele behind. While, like me, she was never able to recall a time when she first noticed what was going wrong with our mother, she remembered that she seemed to change when she went through the menopause though she didn't realize at the time what was happening. She had a memory of walking into the bathroom and finding our mother lying in the bath crying and it upset her because there wasn't any particular reason for it. She thought she was depressed. This incident became fixed in her mind as a watershed after which our mother became grumpy and unpleasant. She had a foul temper throughout Michele's teens.

The thing Michele always found perplexing about our parents' relationship was that she believed that our father really loved our mother and she couldn't understand why. She didn't think our mother loved him. She doesn't think of her as being capable of loving anybody really. 'But there was something about Mum,' she thought. 'People who knew her way back when saw her as someone you wanted to marry, someone you wanted to be your friend. She had some status somewhere down the line and from what was that derived? And there's her secrecy. My feeling is that there isn't a big secret that we could find out if we tried hard enough, but there is a reason why she's secretive. Or maybe it's just to do with the importance of appearances.'

In front of her three-way mirror, my mother practised showing her different faces to the world.

My father had died and I was 6000 miles away hearing the news at two o'clock in the morning, at the end of the telephone which rang into another world, the one I had made for myself, which didn't include my parents, for like them I had edited and re-created my own history. I stayed up all night, dry-eyed. Jews bury their dead within two days of the life leaving them and there was no time for me to come back for the funeral. I returned a year later when the tombstone was erected on his grave. My cousin Marina offered me a tissue before we left the house to go to the cemetery. I said, 'It's okay, I won't cry.' But then a stone broke in my chest and I was sobbing uncontrollably, as blinded by tears as if I was in a rainstorm.

The move to Bournemouth had been on account of my father. The sea air was supposed to be good for his lungs and anyway, he longed to get out of Liverpool. He was full of restlessness and travel fever after all those years, or perhaps it was that Liverpool was a prison to him, the place which had trapped him so long ago when he got Bessie Cohen pregnant. Most of the mock eighteenth-century furniture went to the sale room where it did not fetch much in the first years of Merseyside's nose-dive into rack and ruin, the docks closed down, the ships of the world gone, the heroin dealers and gun merchants moving in, the city marooned on the wrong side of the country as Britain turned its back on the Atlantic and its trade with America and towards Europe.

My father lasted eighteen months down there. It wasn't his heart that got him but emphysema, the smoker's disease, where you fight for every breath. He died like an Aids victim, like a victim of famine or a concentration camp inmate, death devouring his flesh, blind and skeletal, he became. The last photograph of him is so terrible I have only looked at it twice.

While my father was dying, his eldest daughter was dying also. Still only in her early fifties, she had discovered a mark on her forehead, visited the doctor and was told she had cancer of the brain. She lasted three terrible weeks after the diagnosis. Michele thinks there was a letter telling us that Sonia wanted to see her father. She did not know his own condition.

'I wanted to get some kind of message from Dad to Sonia. He couldn't have visited her because he was very ill by that stage. I said to Mum that she and I should go and see her but Mum did what she always does in these situations, which was change the subject. Then Sonia died, really quickly before any of it could be resolved. And Mum decided not to tell Dad. So each died not knowing about the other. It haunts me. I deeply regret not taking the matter into my own hands.'

Beautiful Sonia was gone, the last link with my father's youth. If she were alive now, what could she have told us? I wish I'd known her, defied the silence to go and meet her. I have nothing of her except a photograph and a torn corner of her birth certificate. In a way it was as if my father took her with him, to make sure. She was childless too. He died without grandchildren.

The last time Michele saw our father was a week or so before the Angel of Death came to call. As she got in the lift to leave, the doors closing, she saw the tears streaming down his face, the image indelible in her mind. He had gone on living months longer than he should have because he was so frightened of dying, that great ego extinguished. He died in his sleep, in the night, death caught him when he wasn't looking, a few days before his seventy-ninth birthday. Or maybe if he had lied about his age to avoid conscription, he was older than that. My mother had seen him the day before. The very last thing he had done, his final communication with his family, was to give her some money to take to the betting shop and put on a horse. No one can remember if it won or not.

103

When did it all start, this business with my mother? What are the signs and symptoms of diseases of memory?

But it isn't just about what she can or can't remember for I have to ask myself, which bit was the illness and which her own real personality? And how could you tell them apart? And my own self, the one that grew out of my relationship with my parents – was it partly formed out of the slow composition of blood that ceased to be liquid and flowing but clumped itself into clots which made their silent way into her head?

It is 1983, a couple of months after my father died. One by one the Ginsberg boys and girls had been felled by diseases of the modern era and their husbands and wives went too.

I am living in Canada, on the far side of that vast continent, which some might say is as far as I can possibly get from my parents. I believe that I have begun a new life for myself but actually my mother is about to begin a new one for me. We talk on the phone in the weeks after my father's death. I think I detect in her voice a new confidence.

After nearly forty years of marriage she appears to have started becoming her own person, as the Americans say. She is a volunteer with the League of Jewish Women, affiliated to the WRVS; indeed she is the treasurer of her local branch in Bournemouth. She sits holding the hands of those she calls her 'old dears' at a day centre for the elderly. Never in a million years does she think that one day she might end up in such a place herself. Or at least not until she is so frail, so incapacitated that she would need constant nursing care. 'And I hope I drop dead before it comes to that,' she always says. 'I'll kill myself first.'

When I make my duty calls home, often she is out or away. She goes to the pictures every Sunday afternoon with some 'girls' from the League. Or they walk to Boscombe for lunch at a hotel. Once, she went to London to attend the League's annual general meeting at the Albert Hall. If you looked in her diary, there were things in it.

I have a fantasy that at long last – after failing my mother by not being the dutiful daughter she thought she had contracted for by getting married and having children as her mother had done before her – she and I are going to become friends. Mates. Bosom buddies.

'I'm still a young woman, you know,' she says to me, matily, on the phone.

'Yes, I know. You're only sixty-five. Come and stay with me in Vancouver. I'll send you the ticket.'

'Well, if I'm going such a long way there's no point in it being for a short time.'

'How long would you like to come for?'

'At least a month. Six weeks.'

'Okay.' I have misgivings about this long stretch. But then on the day she arrives I am excited, as my boyfriend and I drive to the airport to meet her.

My mother gets on a plane at Gatwick Airport and travels a distance of 6000 miles. She eats her in-flight meals and drinks many cups of tea. Because drinks are free she consumes some unaccustomed alcohol. She looks down and below her she sees the Atlantic Ocean, makes landfall across the Maritime provinces, passes across the flat monotony of the prairies until her craft reaches mountains and a bay. She sees the Pacific Ocean for the first time in her life. She has holidayed in the South of France, Mallorca, Italy, Israel and New York. She has never been to Scotland, though she'd like to. She remembers that when my father worked on the ships he docked in Vancouver and pronounced it one of the most beautiful cities in the world. I do not think, then, of the enormity of this enterprise for her, going so very far from home, alone, for I am young and callow and confident and do not recognize difficulties.

She talks non-stop on the drive home from the airport,

then sleeps for twelve hours. Things go badly wrong at once and as far as she's concerned it's all my fault.

She says: 'You leave me alone like a dog all day.'

'But I told you before I came I wouldn't be able to take more than a week off work while you were here.'

She says: 'What sort of daughter allows a man to stay overnight in the same house as her mother?'

'But you can't expect me not to see my own boyfriend for six weeks.'

'What sort of daughter has sex with a man she isn't married to?'

Still, I want to make her happy, I do. I tell her: 'We're going to Vancouver Island overnight. We get there by boat. I've booked a room but I'll take you for afternoon tea at the Empress Hotel. It's like having tea at the Ritz, you'll love it.'

In our hotel she cries: 'Why did you have to take me there and then bring me back to this dump? Why can't I stay at the Empress? I'm sorry I went now. If I hadn't gone, I wouldn't have known what I could have had. I deserve to be treated better than this.'

We go to a restaurant where she orders salmon wrapped in puff pastry. Beneath its crusty blanket she finds some prawns, strictly forbidden by Jewish dietary laws. She pushes the plate away in disgust. We ride back on the ferry and there is a photograph she took of me, the wind in my hair and eyes, still surprised by the ferocity of her hostility and unhappiness.

So I insist on an open and honest talk, as recommended by the new cult of psychotherapy which is sweeping North America and its religion, the authentic, honest, open human relationship.

'You've given me nothing since I've been here. Nothing,' she says.

'What did you want?'

'I wanted love.'

'What do you mean?'

'Why do you never hug me and hold my hand like other daughters?'

'What you've never had you can't give.' For someone has noticed that in the photos I show them of my mother and me, we are always standing apart and under the influence of this observation I have recalled that I have only one childhood memory of sitting on her knee in the kitchen while she read to me from my Rupert Bear annual, when I was at an age when I could only look at the enchanted pictures in my books, unable to decipher a word for myself. My bunny rabbit was hanging by its ears on two pegs from the old-fashioned clothes

pulley suspended from the ceiling, having endured a good wash in our pre-automatic machine with the mangle which we kept in the garage. But then she pushed me off and I was expelled from that warm paradise. I am urged by my friends to seek therapy to deal with my cold, loveless child-hood which they conjure up out of some stereotype of English reticence and reserve.

My mother says: 'Isn't the pattern on that carpet lovely.'
'Why can't we talk?'
'Talk to you? A daughter who leaves her mother all alone, who's never given her grandchildren?'

'You're depressed. You need bereavement counselling.'
'Why should I tell a stranger my business? I wouldn't be depressed if I could go and live with my daughters, if I was busy looking after my grandchildren. I told your father I would never get married while my mother was still alive. I *cared* for my mother.'

'I'm the only one whose daughters left home and never came back.'
'I'm the only one who doesn't have grandchildren.'
'I'm the only one who doesn't have a husband.'
'Dad, Dad, why did you leave me?'

At the airport, a side of frozen smoked salmon under her arm, she says: 'I'm sorry, I'm sorry, I'm sorry, I'm sorry. It was too soon. I came too soon.'
Someone says to me: 'You know what your problem is, don't you? Your mother has become your daughter.' And not an obedient daughter but a spoilt brat.

Had it begun then, the dissolution of her mind? Because before that she was this person who all my life had told me what do and whose approval I still secretly craved because – well, isn't that what the bond between mother and daughter is? They try to make you in their image and something inside you wants to be made, even while you are running like hell to get out of there, away from that terrible sphere of

109

influence, as fast as you can. I admired some things in my mother, her dress sense, for example. I have to admit now that the lulling tranquillity which falls upon me whenever I walk into a department store is entirely her doing. *She* instilled in me a sense of womanhood that derives from the instinct to turn plates and saucers and cups upside down to determine whether they are Royal Doulton or Wedgwood, to sample a lipstick by running it over the skin beneath my wrist, to know which perfume is heavy and harsh and how to match navy. My memories of childhood are not of running through fields or pinching apples from orchards or playing in the street. They are of trailing around after her while she tried on hats. Or having a sophisticated lunch of egg mayonnaise at the Kardomah Café. Or sitting in my patent leather T-bar shoes and short white socks on a footstool while she and her friends talked and ate cakes.

Who else was my mother? She was the person who had had to put up with the worst of looking after my father in his terrible old age: blind, incontinent, breathless, his lungs engaged in a futile attempt to fill themselves as emphysema took possession of his body, wasting his bulk down to the skeleton below.

A woman spends the whole of her life protected by others, first her parents, then her husband. My mother had never lived on her own until my father died. She had sacrificed no independence for marriage. And so she had not won freedom but loneliness and depression. 'You aren't the latest widow any more,' a friend advised her. 'There are newer widows than you now.'

'Should I go back to Liverpool?' she asks me on the phone, on her return.

I have just read an article in a magazine about bereavement. Never take a major decision in the first eighteen months, it warns. 'Now, Mum, you shouldn't take a major decision in the first eighteen months.'

I do not realize that she is not asking me for advice but for permission. She's always been like that. You have to read her mind. What she says is not usually what she means.

'The North holds nothing for me any more,' she announces.

That means she is afraid of returning, of admitting her failure, like people who crawl back to Britain after emigration. She can't bear to show others that she has made a mistake, that the move has been an error.

She sobs on the phone. 'I'm so depressed, so depressed. Who can rid me of this depression?'

I think, 'I can.' I am still trying to get her to go to bereavement counselling. She does in the end. Someone in the greengrocers gives her a leaflet about it. '*You* never told me about this,' she says.

Depression is an early symptom of Multi-Infarct Dementia. And in one of the standard works on Alzheimer's much later I will find these words:

Although it may sometimes appear to be precipitated by a stressful event, the most common example of this being the family who attribute the onset of dementia in one ageing parent to the strain of the bereavement and grief caused by the death of the other, this is not so. In these circumstances, careful inquiry will usually reveal that the intellectual changes had probably been present for some time before the bereavement occurred, but that the person who died was assisting the sufferer so that waning mental abilities were less noticeable. When the spouse dies, the surviving partner is suddenly left exposed to the world at large, and his or her failings become more obvious.

Was this true? Had my father been covering up for my mother all these years and if so, for how many? The characteristics of my mother, her lies and evasions and I-don't-remembers – what were they about?

I am sitting on the world's most uncomfortable sofa, mock Louis Quinze, knocked up by skilled cabinet-makers in the East End of London and upholstered in pale blue embroidered velvet. The venue is my mother's flat in Bournemouth from which a view of the sea can be obtained if you crane your head out of the kitchen window. My mother brings out a set of twelve silver-plated spoons for eating ice-cream sundaes which I have no recollection of ever having seen used. God knows why she bought them. Who makes ice-cream sundaes at home? Perhaps one of her friends had a set and she did not want to be 'the only one who doesn't have sundae spoons'.

'I've got no use for these,' she says, putting them on the marble-topped Louis Quinze coffee table with legs carved in the shape of lions' heads. 'Would you like them?'

'No, I don't think I've got any use for them either.'

'Would you like these sundae spoons?'

'No.'

'Would you like these sundae spoons?'

'No.'

'Would you like these sundae spoons?'

'I've already told you three times. No.'

'Are these sundae spoons any use to you?'

113

To shut her up, I say, 'Yes, okay.'

Two or three minutes later she's at it again: 'I'd like you to have these sundae spoons.'

'I've already said I'll have them.'

'Good.'

Then, 'These sundae spoons are something I'd like you to have.'

I put them in my bag and the demand ceases. Every time she sees the spoons in their cardboard box she remembers that she wants me to have them. Each time she asks, she forgets again. Only by taking them out of her sight can the recollection of them cease.

This is why I have a set of a dozen silver-plated sundae spoons in my kitchen drawer at home and perhaps one day I really will make knickerbocker glories for twelve. Though somehow I doubt it.

It's the autumn of 1992 and the 1980s have been a bad decade for her. Her husband dies. She's on her own in a South Coast town they had only moved to eighteen months before his death. She's lonely and bored. For all she begrudged going out to work after my father got ill, what she really wants now is a job. She applies to become a counsellor at the Citizens Advice Bureau, though nothing comes of it. I'd love to have heard the advice my mother would have dished out. Then, reverting to her poorer roots, she applies to become a shelf-packer at a local supermarket but they tell her the work is too hard. Finally, humiliatingly, as far as I'm concerned, she wants to follow up an ad in *The Lady* and become a live-in companion. Anything, she says, other than her own company. Mind you, none of this would be necessary if her daughters were living on her doorstep and she was busy with her grandchildren like every single other friend. For as we know, she is 'the only one whose daughters went away to university and never came back'. Which, I'm afraid, is what you end up with if you come from a culture which keeps its children out of the garden and indoors improving their minds with a book.

I'd thought we'd got over all this when I left home. I thought she'd accepted my life but deep down, it seems, she never had. Looking at the dismal landscape of her life after my father's death she wants to repopulate it with dutiful daughters. What would have happened if Michele and I really had got married to a pair of Jewish solicitors and moved round the corner to nice semi-detached suburban houses and started families young? Would all this grief and anger she now bears have been obliterated? Or is it that we are an easy target for her to vent her misery on? 'Why am I unhappy? Because my daughters are not like the daughters of my friends and if they were, I'd be all right. It's their fault that I'm depressed.' Like King Lear, she wanted Regan and Goneril who would say what she wanted to hear whether they meant it or not. What she wound up with was a pair of Cordelias.

She gets breast cancer. She's very frightened. She thinks she is going to die but she does not. They gave her a fifty-fifty chance of the cancer recurring within five years but the treatment is successful, she pulls through and remains healthy, apart from a permanently swollen arm. Going to see her in hospital was like visiting your daughter at boarding school. 'We have midnight feasts,' she said.

She adores the attention, the nurses fussing over her, the relief from her own company. She can tell you everyone's story – what ailment they have and the likely prognosis: 'She's a very sick girl,' she says of a middle-aged cancer victim in Marks and Spencer satin pyjamas. 'One night she got up and got dressed and tried to walk out and the nurses had to drag her back.'

As long as there's a satisfactory display of cards and flowers, she's happy. But if it falls below the level of what she considers she deserves, she falls into bitter outbursts: 'I'm the only one who doesn't have a quilted card.

'I'm the only one who doesn't get at least two visitors.'

Still, she goes round the beds, holding the hands of the sick. 'I'm needed here.'

We are not as much by her side throughout this ordeal as she would have liked for we are very preoccupied with certain matters in our own lives. I, for example, have returned to Britain after seven years abroad and am trying to find work and somewhere to live. Michele has resolved the grandchild business though in an unfortunate manner, setting up house with her boyfriend Mark who is not Jewish. They choose to live in a terraced house in Hackney, the old Jewish East End, near where they both work, at the town hall.

'People struggled hard all their lives to get out of Hackney and now you're going back,' my mother complains. 'Why can't you live in Mayfair or Hamsptead, I hear that's very nice.'

It is the beginning of the 1980s housing boom. We stand her in front of estate agents' windows.

'See? See how much houses cost these days?'

'You have to look around, you know. You don't buy the first place you look at.'

The baby is born at the end of 1984 and named Ben after his grandfather, *our* father. I wouldn't call her the best of grandmothers. In fact neither Michele nor I have the impression that she's very interested at all. She likes the *idea* of being a grandmother and photographs of her grandson are displayed in frames throughout her flat. But you wouldn't want her to look after him for too long.

She is, however, brilliant when her grandchild cries and cries at night and will not under any circumstances settle, despite lullabies and rattles and head-stroking. 'Don't go into him,' she says. 'Let him cry and it will break the habit.' Mark finds this so distressing he has to go to the pub. She's right. The habit is broken. But now she has habits of her own.

What we notice is the way in which she has fine-tuned her running-away routine which has become a predictable part of any visit. We offend her in some way and the next thing you know, she's screaming, 'I won't stay in this house a moment longer, after what you've done to me,' the door slams and she's off down the road, tears streaming down her face.

Our job is to go after her and beg her forgiveness and ask her to come back, which she always does, because she can't fall out with her own children without losing even more face with her friends than she feels she has already, and the apology and the attention are what she is actually after. Sometimes she's too successful in her escape attempt, a bus comes and she jumps on it and someone, usually Mark, has to go as far as Victoria Coach Station to search for her in the crowds and it is possible that he can't find her at all. She rings the next day. 'Why didn't you come after me?' she demands. Once, having run away from Michele, she gets as far as a cheap hotel near Victoria. She rings me from her room. 'It's horrible,' she sobs. 'I've just got a bed and a television and a chair. Come and get me.'

It is funny that she knows how to deal with a child's tantrums but cannot stop herself from having them.

Of *course* we should have known something was wrong.
But we put it down to attention-seeking and her lifelong
capacity for taking offence, bearing lengthy grudges against
those who, she believes, have slighted her, not treated her
with due respect, which by now is almost all her brothers
and sisters *and* brothers- and sisters-in-law. She can even
take offence on our behalf, no longer speaking to relatives
who do not invite us to a wedding, though she has been
invited herself. '*My* daughters are first cousins and *they* are
only second cousins.' No matter that these second cousins
have actually met the person getting married and Michele
and I haven't.

And because she directed so much of her unhappiness at
us, making us feel guilty that we were not the daughters she
wanted, that guilt came to blot out everything in the sky. If
she felt that it was our fault that she was unhappy and we felt
guilty about not being the daughters she wanted us to be,
then how could we have examined her condition in a
detached manner and looked for causes in anything other
than the dynamics of our lifelong relationship with her? The
guilt was bigger than anything else. We've heard of
Alzheimer's but we knew about people with that disease,
slumped in their chair. 'Does she know you?' Oh yes, she
knew us, all right.

Why don't we notice? We do but we fail to recognize
what it is that we have seen. Michele first starts to think that
something is wrong when she and Mark and Ben visit
Bournemouth for a weekend where Ben plays with a bucket
and spade on the sand, building castles in which he can
implant the flags of the world and eat ice-cream. He is a
lucky boy, brought up in Hackney, to have a grandma at the
seaside and another in the country. He loves his grandma

who makes chicken soup which he devours when he cannot be tempted with another morsel.

Our mother, who is not interested in eating anything but sweets and cakes (a child's taste), nevertheless has always prided herself that when it comes to entertaining she will put on a magnificent show. The Madeira tablecloth is unfolded on to the walnut dining-room table. Expensive dinner services, gilt-edged in floral patterns, come down from their boxes. Silver-plated cutlery is polished and arranged. Silver-plated cruet sets are lined up. Doilies and serviettes and placemats with hunting scenes on them battle for a place on the overloaded table.

This is her stage setting for sides of beef, roast turkeys, sliced tongue and brisket and fried fish and fish cakes and huge dishes of potato salad and coleslaw, plates of pickled cucumbers, sliced loaves of poppyseed bread, silver cruets of mustard and horseradish, cut-glass jugs of orange squash, all followed by her own masterpiece, the pavlova – a meringue shell filled with whipped cream and tinned fruit cocktail.

Now, when Michele, Mark and Ben arrive for the week-end, 'She'd not done anything and she started pulling things out of the freezer that didn't go together and putting it on the table,' Michele says.

Sometimes my sister or I are talking to our mother on the phone and the conversation develops into a row, bitter and accusatory, in which our failings as daughters are lashed at us like a whip. It reaches such a pitch that she cries out that she feels that her head is falling off, her speech becomes slurred and she puts down the phone. When you ring back, a few hours later, she says she's as right as rain and her mood is improved. Michele and I tell each other, 'It's just attention-seeking.'

Michele begins to notice that our mother is emotionally disengaging from her daughter and grandson, that she no longer seems to care about anyone or what is going on. They spend long stretches of time together when our mother comes to babysit during the school holidays while Michele is at work but it's always a continuous dirge of 'I'm hard done by, I've got to live all alone.' Michele thinks she's always been a bit like that but again maybe it was exacerbated by the start of the dementia. Now she seems only to be able to relate to Michele by enumerating the extent of the ways she is failing her.

What are the sensations in our mother's head? Can they have been the tiny strokes that cause Multi-Infarct Dementia?

One of the symptoms of this disease is called emotional incontinence. In most human beings there is an innate tendency for going for what we want even if that means becoming aggressive with others. Parents bring us up not to behave in that way. What may be eroded in MID is the capacity to dampen down or repress these primitive feelings, as getting drunk causes us to forget to inhibit our desire to tell our best mate that we love him or strip down to our underpants in the middle of the high street. Let's face it, we've all been there.

In the spring of 1990 Michele and I decide that to cheer up our miserable mother who has been through so much, I am to take her on a package holiday to Sorrento in Italy.

As our coach drives along the corniche past the umbrella pines and the blue, blue sea she begins to cry.

I ask her, 'Why are you crying?'

And she says, 'Because I'm happy.'

120

This is the dream of her girlhood. A grand hotel, excellent food which she packs away in large quantities, the ladies in proper dresses, a pianist in the evening tinkling melodies that she recognizes, her own small balcony where she can sit and sunbathe, the excursion to Capri where she drinks coffee in a café in the Piazzetta and buys the tackiest souvenir the island can offer, Italian men in perfectly pressed Armani suits who bring pink to her cheeks. 'Total success,' I succinctly write on a postcard to Michele.

I am surprised that she quickly finds the way from her room to the lobby and back again, so I suppose I must have known something was wrong that long ago.

She had to get a new passport for the holiday. It expires in 2000. She never used it again and I believe that the week in Italy was the last time that life was, for her, what it was supposed to be.

Now there is a chronology. A history of a disease begins to take shape.

Two weeks before the business with the spoons she's in bed with the hospital radio headphones on, talking very loudly. My mother adores hospitals after a first unfortunate visit when she went in as a child to have her tonsils removed and cried because it was the Passover and nobody brought her the prescribed unleavened bread. There were two visits to the Oxford Maternity Hospital in Liverpool at which, with her dead to the world, her daughters were surgically removed from her abdomen. When she came home with her second bundle of joy she brought with her a half-completed jumper suit in black wool flecked with silver which she had begun to knit but abandoned because she couldn't be bothered. It knocked around the house for years, ending up as dusters. I bet it's still somewhere in the world, indestructible though incomplete.

At Poole Hospital, this time, things aren't quite the same.

The GP says he is not convinced that she has had a heart attack at all. Michele thinks he sees the dramatic episode with the after-hours call and the ambulance and the rushed admission as another form of attention-seeking. She's always coming into the surgery, he complains.

I go to see him. He is a vain, shallow, good-looking man with a case-load which he feels to be heavily burdened by geriatric patients though if he had wanted to avoid them he should not have taken up practice in Bournemouth. None the less, he finds my mother particularly difficult. She thinks she has a hold on him, for when she contracted cancer he had wanted to put her straight into hospital for a mastectomy – an old woman like her, what did she need with two breasts or even any? But Michele manipulates the system to get her taken on as a temporary patient by her own doctor, which opens the door to a second opinion at Barts, and so she was saved from that grisly fate. Now she thinks that gives her the right to demand his attention at will. She has told me this herself.

I ask him about her memory. 'Old people forget things,' he says, dismissively. 'My own mother forgets things.'

So for the first week after she comes out of hospital I stay with her as she is still too weak to care for herself and though the hospital had suggested a few days in a nursing home, she has turned them down flat. 'Why do I need to go there,' she demands, 'when I have daughters to look after me?' I am told that she mustn't do any heavy cleaning, like hoovering or moving furniture. I ring Dorset Social Services and ask if she could be assigned a home help. The Welfare State exists only to a minimal extent in Bournemouth, I discover, with its Tory council and huge population of elderly residents. With £9000 invested in a unit trust and the ownership of her own home, my mother does not qualify for state assistance. I am given a list of private agencies but no recommendation. I select one at random.

The owner comes to the house. She wears high boots and

perches on the edge of my mother's gilded chairs, nodding furiously. She seems pleasant and sympathetic. My mother likes her and Ms Big Boots thinks she has just the woman to suit. I think so too, when I meet her, for she is Liverpool Black, one of that odd ethnic minority which did not come to Britain as immigrants from the Caribbean in the 1950s and 1960s but is descended from black American and African seamen who married or fathered children on the girls they met on shore leave. She had nursed her own mother in her own home until her death. The first thing she does is bring her husband over to fit a hand-rail into the tiled wall beside the bath. We think we have struck lucky.

'I'm determined I'm going to make a friend of her,' my mother says, 'so I can keep her.'

The bill is sent to my sister and me.

For two or three days my mother seems to be rallying fast, speaking of short coach trips to the surrounding countryside and taking up her old work holding the hands of her 'dears' at the day centre. I meet the neighbours who are in and out with cakes and biscuits and cold fried fish. Her friends from the League throng the house. Offers of kosher meals on wheels are made. She can come back to her old volunteer role as soon as she is well, her place will always be held for her.

I go out for a long walk along the front in the autumn sunshine, kicking sand amongst the dunes, watch the late holidaymakers on the beach and locals brewing tea in their beach huts. The funicular railway still toils between the promenade and the sand and the hotels are there as I remembered them from my childhood holidays when we booked rooms at a strictly kosher establishment where activities were organized for the teenagers. Here is the Cumberland Hotel where I had my first-ever cigarette and went green and was sick; where I kissed a boy on the avenues that are lined with pine trees, and I wonder what has become of him – a dad now, probably, with daughters of his own. I think of my father's oscillating path between flat, bookmakers, pub and promenade in the brief time he had had there, the incongruity of a pensioner's bus pass in his back pocket instead of the jangling keys to his Humber Hawk with its cream leather interior. When they first came my mother sat on the beach and closing her eyes, raised her face to the sun.

'It bores me,' she says, when I ask her why she doesn't do that any more.

When I get back the doctor's locum is there. The minute I'd gone she had felt pains in her chest. The locum gives her a spray to hiss into the roof of her mouth. 'You've had an angina attack but if you use this spray whenever you feel it coming on, the pain will pass,' she said. It's a shame I don't look at the clock because it would have told me the precise time she became an invalid.

She will not eat the meals on wheels. 'Horrible.'

She will not go back to the League. 'I'm not ready.'

She does not want to see visitors. 'I can't be bothered with them.'

I send off for brochures for sheltered housing thinking that this might be a solution to her problems. She looks at them and rejects them. 'Too far out,' she says. 'No shops. Here I've got everything on my doorstep.' She's quite right. Those places are designed for people who like a garden, who want to be just a hop away from fields and hills and rivers, and those pleasures bore her stiff, or rather she likes nature in the same way that I do: it's scenery, exterior decor for the motorway.

During that week I injure my back helping her into the bath. I had had back trouble for years but I am to notice increasingly that the bouts recur every time I visit my mother. The physiotherapist says it's stress. It *is* stressful, swallowing down my irritation at what I see as her malingering and her bored repetitions, due, I believe, to her not having much to talk about.

A few months later she tells me, 'I've sacked the home help, you know. She was useless.'

'I don't see how you can sack her,' I say, 'since it's Michele and I who are paying for her.'

The agency finds someone else.

My mother also mentions that the hospital has diagnosed mild diabetes. Her own mother had had the same thing. It is to be controlled by diet. After a lifetime's consumption of sweets, cakes and biscuits she is now forbidden all sugar.

Diabetes is one of the many factors that increases the amount of arteriosclerosis in blood vessels. Most diabetics, if they have badly controlled diabetes, are more likely to get heart attacks, strokes, blood-vessel damage in the eye, which is one of the reason they're more likely to go blind. They are more likely to have problems with their legs, which eventually lead to amputation. Diabetes aggravates or causes arteriosclerosis. And that is true of late-onset diabetes, to a lesser extent than early-onset but it is still a risk factor. Diabetes is an early-warning symptom of Multi-Infarct Dementia. I often wonder if a sweet tooth cost my mother her mind and if it will cost me mine.

27 April 1993

Dear Doctor ——

I wonder if you would consider seeing Rose Grant and taking over her care. ——, an old friend, recommended you as the person best able to deal with this problem. In brief she is a dementing lady with two distantly located daughters. I was asked to give an opinion by a mutual third party. I enclose correspondence from her daughter Linda.

Mrs Rose Grant and her husband retired to Bournemouth but unfortunately he died two years later leaving her somewhat isolated. As Linda says, her mother is rather resentful that they do not live in an extended family environment in Liverpool. Medically she has a history of diabetes (mainly diet-controlled), ischaemic heart disease, and carcinoma of the breast. She may have had a cardiac infarct eighteen months ago and went to Oxford for further tests. She certainly seems to suffer from angina but I suspect some of her pain is muscular-skeletal and in part related to her lymphoedema following axillary node dissection. Her medication includes Nitro, Isosorbide,

Tenormin 100 mg a day, Diltiazem 60mg t.d.s.,
Aspirin 75mg a day, Prednisolone 5mg (?why), Zantac
150mg b.d., and Gaviscon prescribed since the infarct.

The major problem is of short-term memory loss.
This predated her cardiac trouble by two or three
years but has been worse since then. The family
report a stepwise deterioration consistent with
vascular disease. The patient herself retains insight
into the difficulty. Self-care seems to be reasonable
and continence is preserved. She is still able to go out
of the house and does not feel lost. She claims to feel
depressed – her sleep is normal but she is occasionally
tearful. She has a home help but I suspect she does
not do much cooking.

On examination she is reasonably well orientated
and scores 24/34 in an extended MTS. I did not find
her overtly clinically depressed. The pulse was 80
suggesting she may not be using the Beta blocker.
The blood pressure was 150/90. There was no cardiac
failure and no abnormal signs in the chest or
abdomen. In the central nervous system the fundi
were normal but I thought there was a slight weakness
of the right arm and leg with increased reflexes.
There is lymphoedema of the left arm. Overall I feel
she has a dementing illness almost certainly on the
basis of vascular disease. I am not sure how many
clinics she is attending but feel she needs to be under
a single umbrella. Whether all the medication is
necessary (and indeed if she is taking it) is uncertain.
The Beta blocker may be contributing to her mental
state. She may benefit from an anti-depressant. I feel
she requires a district nurse to advise on medication

and to provide a daily drug dispenser, and to monitor
her dietary type and intake. She may require a health
visitor or a CPN to monitor her functional state. I
wonder if you would kindly consider taking her on
and seeing her. I am sure in the first instance the
family would be happy for you to see her on a private
basis although in the long term NHS care would be
more appropriate as they are not insured. Thank you
very much for your help.

With best wishes
Yours sincerely

----

cc GP
   Linda Grant

This is the time when people say to me, 'How's your
mum?' and I reply, 'For God's sake, don't ask.' The time of the
Hundred Years War when it's more the depression than the
memory loss that I notice. 'I'm so depressed, I'm so depressed.
Can't anyone take it away?' The slammed phones. The
aborted visits. People with Alzheimer's often do not know
what their own condition is. One of MID's cruellest tricks is
to preserve in its victim until quite a late stage, some insight
into what is going on in their mind, so they can observe
themselves lose their own sanity. Depression and emotional
instability is a marked characteristic of this disease and who
wouldn't be miserable, watching themselves going mad.

So Michele and I have consulted our friends in the caring
professions and the address of a Harley Street specialist has
been given, the expedition to Harley Street organized – only
the best for our mother and now we know what's the matter.

Sixty pounds has been well spent there. He has written to a colleague in Bournemouth assessing her health, suggesting that she be assigned to his care.

On the tube, after the appointment, I say to my mother, 'It isn't Alzheimer's, you know. It's something called Multi-Infarct Dementia, little strokes. But not Alzheimer's.'

She replies, 'Thank God you told me. Because that's what I've been so worried about.'

A moment later she asks: 'Did the consultant say what was wrong with me?'

I have suggested to him that he try to talk her into going into sheltered housing. 'I think it may be a bit late for that,' he replies.

At any rate, *we* now know that *she* knows. Michele later believed that this was why she had dropped her friends, couldn't be bothered, never went out, didn't return their calls. That she was perfectly well aware of what was happening to her and was ashamed, embarrassed and afraid of their response. She had cut herself off because she could no longer manage the skills she needed to be in company. It was a proud, brave thing to do, though of course counter-productive. 'I cringe inside when someone tells me I'm repeating myself,' she had said once, in a rare acknowledge-ment to others of what was happening to her, so that just for that moment she was not covering up, putting on an act. For a lifetime of keeping up appearances had only prepared her for her greatest role, dementia, in which she did everything she could to pretend to the world that she was right as rain and could not stop to talk if she saw someone in the street for really, she had to dash, she was meeting a friend for morning coffee. Her neighbours told me that, later. They

suspected that there was no date. Instead of cakes and gossip
she would return to her empty flat, bereft of husband or
children or grandchildren, to cry her eyes out. Yet she went
on presenting a bold facade, artifice instead of authenticity.

That letter from the specialist, when it came a few days later,
seemed to us like a visitation from another planet. A superior
life-form had turned its cool, wise, penetrating eyes on the
madness of our family and told us that the long-borne
grudges about grandchildren or bad daughters had nothing
to do with anything. The specialist had seen beyond our spe-
ciality, surfaces, or rather he read the signs and symptoms
that he saw there and detected that inside the bony helmet of
my mother's skull there was a strange state of affairs. That
phrase – 'a dementing illness'.

Until I was in my early thirties I had never heard of
Alzheimer's Disease and I thought it was a new form of suffering, like lung cancer which came in with cigarettes, as
Dandy Nichols once said in *Till Death Us Do Part*. We all
knew people who were senile, gone soft in the head, which
was not a medical complaint but an inevitable punishment
for living too long, and those that escaped from its personal
Alcatraz were heroes: 'He's ninety-one but he still has all his
faculties,' people say admiringly of their loved ones. 'She's
eighty-two but she's just run the London Marathon.'
Madame Jeanne Calment of Avignon, who until 1997 was
the oldest person alive in the world, kept all her marbles,
enough to cry aloud on her 121st birthday, 'Why has God
forgotten me?'

When Alois Alzheimer, who first identified the disease
and after whom it was named, was working in an asylum in
Frankfurt at the turn of the century, he also discovered

131

Multi-Infarct Dementia and published a short report describing arteriosclerotic changes in the brain which, he wrote, usually occurred in late middle age. There is less written on MID than Alzheimer's, less research. It is less mysterious, mechanical rather than chemical. Also it is preventable, we now know, by those bores of contemporary living, a low-fat, high-fibre diet and no cakes.

Diabetics are prone to vascular problems and hence to MID. A sweet tooth runs in the family. But none of us had ever had a stroke. We knew what they were, or so we thought – people who had lost all sensation in one half of the body, cripples, the slurred of tongue.

To have a stroke is to be struck down, felled like a tree. It's not an illness, just a figure of speech. The arteries in the brain are like a road map on which each highway is separate from every other and if there is an accident in one place you can't get round it by going a different route. It's like the rays in a child's drawing of the sun all leading to the centre, providing no means of hopping on to a different ray. All roads lead to Rome, but what if you want to go from Venice to Genoa?

If an artery is blocked, the blood can't get through and the part of the brain that is supplied by it is famished and starved of oxygen and dies. Sometimes the blockage affects part of the brain which appears to be redundant, because if you do a brain scan you find evidence of strokes but the patient hasn't noticed any deterioration in his or her health. Which makes me think of that old hippie lore about us only using 10 per cent of our brains and how if you took drugs you could access the wonders of the mind that you had never dreamed existed. And all the time it was just non-functioning meat.

Or the part of the brain that might be stopped is the one that affects movement so that part or all of the body is paralysed and you might wind up with the thing that terrifies me more than anything, including being tortured by Nazis – so-called 'shut-in syndrome' where the brain is working perfectly but the only way you can communicate is by blinking one eyelid and you're left to go stark raving mad in there, trapped alone with nothing and no one but your own thoughts. Or the blockage might cut off the function that allows you to recognize objects as three-dimensional, so you live in a world that resembles a Tom and Jerry cartoon. Or it might be syntactical memory so you can't remember how to speak. Or topographical memory so you can't find your way up the stairs to your own bedroom at night.

But the part of my mother's brain that had died was part of the hypocampus which is concerned with processing short-term memory, the kind that lasts for half an hour or so before its contents are transferred somewhere more permanent or dumped altogether, as almost everything we experience is. And this was not surprising because the hypocampus resides in a part of the brain that has a very delicate blood supply and is particularly susceptible to being damaged by a lack of oxygen. As simple as that. It could happen if you had a sudden drop in blood pressure or if you were in hospital being anaesthetized and the anaesthetist made a mess of it. Being a hypochondriac, like all the Ginsbergs, I was most interested in this theory for since my mother's illness my obsession has become my own failing memory which causes me to forget where I have left my keys, or what I came into the kitchen for or, more embarrassingly, people's names.

I had an operation once and my blood pressure sank so

low I could hear the panic in the surgeon's voice as I came round, and now I think, that's it, that's where my memory went, that night in the recovery room. But an expert told me I was wrong and everyone forgets things when they get to middle age.

In childhood I imagined my memory to be like the inner workings of a music-box. These were presents people were always giving children in those days, in the great silence before Nintendo, Walkmans and even transistor radios. When you attempted to lift up the red lace skirts of the Spanish doll which sat on top, a mechanism was revealed like a metal drum with short square prongs sticking out which were meant to catch as the device rotated and produce a tune as they struck a metal plate. I saw my mind as being like this, but instead, there were a number of slits in it and the memories that were thrown at it caught there until time or too much thinking or perhaps even running about dislodged them.

When I read of the work of the Open University biochemist, Professor Steven Rose, I discovered that I was not that far wrong, except the analogy was with fly-paper, not a music-box. To form a short-term memory a flood of glutamate rushes in to open the communications channels between neurons so that data about the experience, encoded in electrical and biochemical signals, can be transmitted through synapses. The second phase, making a memory which will stay put, is the production of a class of proteins called cell adhesion molecules which have 'sticky' ends, protrusions like Velcro that enable them to cling to the sticky bits of their partner molecules. So the memory is caught in a kind of lattice.

My mother's difficulty was the retaining of any new experience and the extremely limited transfer of any new memories into the long-term store. What was already in there, like the ability to shop and match navy or know who had been in love with Frankie Vaughan or how a young girl in the thirties called herself Shirley after Shirley Temple, was disappearing. Very little that was new arrived, like the extreme case cited by Dr Oliver Sacks of the hippie whose mind, damaged by a benign tumour, was unable to accept that it was no longer 1970 and that he had not seen the Grateful Dead six months before.

In Alzheimer's Disease, a protein called beta amyloid accumulates into tangled plaques that prevent communication between synapses and as they grow, neurons throughout the brain are gradually strangled to death, which is why sufferers of this disease decline continuously, with all functions affected.

In MID, the areas of the brain where the blood cannot get through are called watershed areas. Once, without us knowing, or even knowing herself, my mother had reached a watershed in her life. A silent, unnoticed death had taken place in her head. They liken Alzheimer's to a tree, the leaves of which gradually drop, but MID is more like lopping off a whole branch at once and all the leaves that go with it. Alzheimer's has an orderly progression like an army with a strategy, invading and occupying a foreign country and destroying everything in its path as it marches to the capital, but with MID the next vascular accident could strike anywhere – at speech or movement or topographical memory or the whole lot. I cut out an article from the *Daily Telegraph* by a woman whose mother also had MID. At Christmas she had helped her daughter choose a dress for the holidays and gossiped over coffee and cake; a few months later, having just celebrated her seventy-sixth birthday, 'she looks ninety-six, needs two people to dress and wash her, can hardly speak and has to be spoon-fed. But she is sufficiently aware to know what is happening to her; she wails day and night.'

I read in a book about Alzheimer's of a man who drove to a town a few miles away from his home, did his business but could not remember where he had parked his car. He could not remember his own phone number to ring his wife to pick him up. He could not remember the name of the place he lived in order to get a bus to it. So he walked all the way back for his topographical memory was unaffected, the part that had stored within it the map of his journey.

I notice an obituary of a novelist called Gerda Charles. She was born to an impoverished Jewish family in Liverpool and gave her date of birth as 1930, though some cruelly said she was many years older. She had changed her name and come to London and had quite a success in the 1960s until she had given up writing to care for her mother, a victim of Alzheimer's Disease, as it happened.

It occurs to me that if Gerda Charles really was older than she said she was, she would have been a contemporary of my mother and perhaps they had known each other. I give my mother the cutting. 'Did you ever know this woman, Mum?' I ask her.

She looks at the photograph and the name. 'Never heard of her.'

'Just have a look at it and see if there's anything you recognize.'

She reads it slowly. I notice that she moves her lips now, as her eyes pass down the column.

'Gerda Charles, no. No. I've never heard of her. No, no . . . *Gerda Charles!* Don't give me Gerda Charles! She was

Edna Lipson. Her mother ran a boarding house. SIXTY –
SIXTY! She was my age. The bleddy liar.'

'So what else can you remember about her?'

But just then the phone rings. My back is turned for six
or seven minutes. When I come back, my mother is still
reading the cutting. 'Gerda Charles? Who is this dame? It
says she came from Liverpool. *I've* never heard of her.'

Something in the obituary had triggered off my mother's
recollection of a girl known long, long ago. Perhaps the distant past that was slipping away into darkness was not gone
forever and if I knew how to look I could find it and it
would be there, if only for the moment it took to pass it
from one generation on to the next.

When I contact the geriatrician in Bournemouth to whom the Harley Street specialist has written the letter, he says he thinks that it's the job of the GP to co-ordinate all the services my mother needs. That is what care in the community means. He's not able to take her on. We are, in some senses, back where we started, except now we're heavy with knowledge. We fall into the role of badly armed guerrilla armies, taking on the might of the system.

The GP, for example, only vaguely remembers having received the Harley Street letter.

'Could she have a District Nurse?'

He supposes that's an idea.

'And someone to help with the pills?'

He'll look into it.

So now it's: 'Has a District Nurse been to see you, Mum?'

'Nobody's stepped foot over the door.'

True or false?

Michele buys our mother a contraption from Boots that should help her to remember which pills to take when. Each day of the week has a container and all seven fit into a smart blue case which she can carry in her handbag. But when she comes to stay she does not bring the case but individual pill boxes for random days. I can't make rhyme nor reason of her system.

Out comes a big plastic bag with bottles and packets of medication and the little boxes. With fierce concentration, each evening, the tablets are counted out into the box for whatever day of the week happens to take her fancy. I tell her that if she doesn't know what day it is she should go and look at the paper. Except she has to remember that she has this aid to memory. It becomes just another thing to forget.

The next morning she gets her glass of water and swallows her morning's course.

Half an hour later she asks: 'I haven't taken my pills, have I?' God knows what's happening at home, taking no medication at all one day, overdosing the next.

Picking up a biscuit from a plate and putting it in her mouth: 'I've never once broken my diabetic diet. I haven't touched sugar since the day I came out of hospital.'

Christmas 1993. Christmas Eve and Christmas Day at Michele's in Oxford. The actual festivities are a blank in my mind. Other Christmases have had their highlights like the one, years before, when Michele decided to go on a gourmet adventure and cook duck in orange sauce. The duck, basted with Cointreau, browned in the oven. When it was ready Michele removed it from its roasting tin to rest on a platter and went upstairs to the bathroom before coming back down to make the sauce from the pan juices, only to find that my mother had washed it up and it stood, clean and sparkling, an hour's worth of marinade down the sink.

This year we have a scheme which involves me taking her to Bath overnight, after the great success of her seventieth birthday in Cheltenham five years before. She was ordered to pack a night-bag, and then we drove her off through the Cotswolds to one of the best, most expensive hotels she had stayed at in her life. Nothing to complain about here. Her jaw dropped when she walked in, literally, showing what truth there is in these clichés. We had flowers placed in her room. It was a pity she had a feverish cold. Every five minutes she asked, 'Is it warm in here, or is it just me?' That was as long ago as 1988 and we thought nothing of those repetitions then.

We hope this trip will measure up to the previous one. Bath has much to offer: shops, museums with old costumes, the Pump Room where, with a tinkling piano in the background, afternoon tea is to be taken. The only downside is that because it is Christmas everything is shut. The wind on the open-top bus ride cuts us like knives. We sit on the twin beds in our room and watch a Rock Hudson/Doris Day film on TV. The afternoon after Boxing Day we stand on the station platform waiting for the train to arrive.

'Doing anything nice for Christmas?' she asks me.

The high-booted owner of the home help agency rings me and this is what she says: 'I think we've come to the end of the line with your mother. You know what she's done now? She's accused the home help of stealing her watch.'

My first response is: 'I'm sure she's done nothing of the sort. I expect she's just mislaid it.'

I soothe and placate her. I know what it is like, I tell her, these absent-minded old folk who, as my mother has done all her life, hide something because it's important and then can't remember where they have put it. Not that such a habit is restricted to the elderly. I do it every day. I beg her not to let my mother go. I tell her how depressed she is.

'I don't know what she's got to be depressed about,' she replies. 'If you ask me she has a very nice life.'

'Mum, the home help organizer rang, she said there was a problem about your watch. Which watch is it? Dad's Omega?' She has taken to wearing the timepiece he had bought in Cannes in 1963, a holiday which Michele claims my father won in a card tournament. When we got there my mother insisted that we upgrade to the five-star Martinez Hotel, where the celebrities stayed, from the charming little establishment we were booked into whose head waiter my father nightly abused for the restaurant's cooking. In the Martinez's night-club, a torch-singer came and sat on his lap in the mistaken belief that he was a sugar-daddy. I saw a handsome, gilded young man danc-ing with middle-aged women but when I got up close I saw, to my horror, that he was an old man, in make-up. 'The gigolo,' my mother whispered. I became, techni-cally, a woman in that hotel, my first period bloodying its sheets.

The Omega watch was everything to us; it represented wealth and happy memories and a taste of opulence we were always reaching for but never quite catching.

'I'm glad I've had a chance to talk to you about this,' my mother says. 'I haven't liked to say anything but I think I know who took the watch. My helper, she's got another job as a childminder and she brings them with her. There's a boy, he's a rough sort and I think he pinched it. You know I always keep it on the dressing-table when I'm not wearing it? Well, I think he's picked it up and sold it at school for sweets. I wish she wouldn't bring the children because I have to run around serving them lemonades.'

'Is this true?' I ask the home help organizer. 'That she brings children with her?'

I hear the defences build up around her voice. 'Okay, she does have another job as a childminder and she may have brought them with her once or twice but they're *little* children.'

I terminate the services of the home help. I search the flat for that watch. I look everywhere. Michele looks. To this day we have never found it. I go into a jeweller's and price the cheapest Omega watch. It's £900. 'But this would have been worth more if you bought it in 1963 because they increase in value,' the jeweller says.

There are other things that we never subsequently find, like her diamond-encrusted eternity ring. She thinks the window-cleaner might have stolen that. She's at everyone's mercy, the ideal target, old, alone, confused, so very far from that bright confident girl who sat in her fur on the lawns of her sister-in-law's house, her life ahead of her, the new Elizabethan Age and foreign travel and all mod cons lying in wait, hers for the taking. The war was behind them and sorrow was pushed down, cramped into small places. To my parents, the sun was always shining in the 1950s. But as muddled as she is, I think her assessment of the situation is quite correct. I think she got to the heart of it. I think the child did steal the watch. And this capacity to get to the bottom of important things will remain with her, long after her short-term memory has reduced to span only a few seconds. That immigrant's instinct for survival, for summing up human nature before it gets you, endures after so much else that is essentially trivial passes away.

Now I come to have my first dealings with Pat Tennuci, a care manager from Dorset Social Services who is our link to the System. We communicate by phone, fax and letter. She's our lifeline. It will turn out to be extremely lucky that she was the duty officer on the morning I phoned.

'I'm *very* concerned,' she says, 'about a home help bringing someone else's children with her. Your mother may have lost the watch but I don't think you should rule out that it was stolen.'

A small burst of activity takes place.

Another person from the Council rings me. 'I've been to see Mother,' she announces.

'Her name isn't Mother. She isn't your mother, she's mine. It's Mrs Grant to you.'

Two different kinds of home help are assigned, from another private agency which we pay for, one to come in and do the cleaning, another to take her out on excursions.

'My helper,' my mother says. 'She's a lady. I go to Christchurch, you know. I've been watching a sculpture being built. It's very interesting.'

When we look back now, we ask ourselves, how could we have left her so long in Bournemouth? But it wasn't that simple. For years after our father died Michele and I were continuously grappling with the question, where should Mum live? But there were many obstacles to her moving, some of her own volition, some caused by the System. Michele, for example, had taken her to see a new development of sheltered housing right across the road from her own house in Oxford. Our mother looked around and said she didn't want to live with old people. I don't know how to convey the extent of my mother's stubbornness, how difficult it is to get her to do something she has set her mind against. Pride made her block off many options, like going back to Liverpool or seeking help where she lived.

Michele rings the Help the Aged Helpline. The thinking on residential care for the elderly with dementia goes like this: they are best left to stay in familiar surroundings for as long as possible, where they are habitualized. It is moving that causes crises, since they will have to deal with unaccustomed rooms and will not have, secure in an undamaged portion of their minds, the routes to and from home. When they are taken away, like dogs they try to find their way back. Then they are shut in, the keys and the bolts get heavier until in the end only a locked ward of a mental institution can hold them. Better to keep her where she is. And anyway she has rights. *We* cannot put her away, just to suit us, we are told.

During that year a bar-mitzvah is held in Bournemouth to which many of my mother's friends and relatives from Liverpool are invited who see her for the first time in years.

My cousin Marina says to me, 'I can't believe what's happened to Auntie Rose, what she's like. We went to Beales for a cup of tea and she insisted on getting it. She went to the counter and got one cup and brought it back, then she went and got another cup, she was running backwards and forwards. Everyone was saying to me, "Do you think her daughters know?"' I feel humiliated by this, cast as such uncaring children. Do we know? What do *they* know?

Michele notices a new twist. Our mother is now going through a long phase of saying she'd met someone she hadn't seen for fifty years. The first time she told an amazing story about how she'd been in a café and who should walk in but . . . Michele thought it was extraordinary. But then new stories kept cropping up until it got to the point that she and Mark realized that you don't bump into three different people you haven't seen for fifty years on the trot. It had happened once and she was reliving it. The central story was there but the scene had changed each time. Or had it happened at all? Was it just wish-fulfilment, had loneliness conjured out of nowhere an old friend from the past to populate her diminished world?

She always liked to have an appointments diary. In her very last one, for 1995, I see that there is nothing but her painstaking ticks against each day, her last link with a clock which ticked out time in regular doses, the past always discarded, the future always in front. On 10 May she has written: Benny B'day. My father's birthday was 27 February. My nephew's is 12 November.

Whenever my mother has another stroke, she takes a further step down the stairs into the dark cellar of her life. The year which begins for us at Christmas 1994 and ends eleven months later when she will first walk, unwillingly, through the doors of the old people's home, is the one in which great tracts of memory start to disappear in quick succession and it is no longer a matter of sundae spoons, for the disease begins to turn its malign attention to the very heart of her self, as she struggles to hold her identity together.

On 15 December 1994 I move house, relocating from one end of London to the other, and in my reckless enthusiasm for all my new space – three bedrooms just for one person – I suggest that the whole family should spend Christmas there. 'Suits me,' Michele says. So I shop for smoked salmon and turkey and Christmas pudding and chocolates and cheeses and even crackers with proper presents inside them like pen-knives and key-rings, none of your useless bits of Taiwan-made plastic for us. Only the best. Totally conditioned by our upbringing, if it had the word luxury on it, we'd buy it. I get a tree and load it lopsidedly with balls and bells and tinsel. We have always regarded Christmas as an entirely commercial festival, editing out the Infant Jesus, the

146

manger, the carols and Midnight Mass. The Yuletide holiday is, to us, an excuse for shopping.

Everyone arrives on Christmas Eve and we go to a party at a friend's. 'She'll be all right,' Susan says, who has heard many tales of the person she robustly describes as 'Linda's mad mother'. 'I'll stick her in the corner with a glass of sweet sherry and a piece of cake.'

'She doesn't drink and she can't have cake because she's diabetic.' Nor will she be put in a corner. She surges towards centre stage. She adores it. She stands with a glass of orange juice in her hand, a smile on her face, eagerly butting into the conversations of complete strangers.

'What? What's that? Don't leave me out.'

'I'm sorry,' I say. 'It's my mother.'

'Oh, don't say that. She's so sweet.'

'Sweet?'

After I think the other guests have had enough of her I drag her home. 'But I want to stay,' she argues. 'I'm enjoying myself.'

I give her my bedroom. The woman I had bought the place from told me she was taking the carpets and I imagined that I would be moving in to fashionable bare floorboards. She had, however, left the brown rubber underlay tacked down along the walls by wooden batons with inverted nails sticking out of them.

'*Don't* walk on the floor in bare feet, Mum.'

The three-bedroom flat, which when I had viewed it the previous July had had such 'potential' (as estate agents say), now looks like a dingy assault course. It hasn't been painted for more than a decade and the cream colour scheme gathers in the corners as dark brown shadows above the darker brown rubber underlay. The whole place is heart-breakingly depressing. Just the sight of the walls makes me want to sob. It's an apartment for cutting your throat in. Two days after moving there, a kind of pustular growth has appeared on my abdomen, puzzling the doctor who forbids me from taking a bath or shower for a week.

Michele and Mark sleep in the spare room next to my mother, Ben on the couch in the living room, me on an inflatable mattress in the empty room that is going to become my office. Mark has been over-enthusiastic with the pump and the mattress is hard as a rock.

The firmness of the mattress and the continuous thumps above my head make for an uncomfortable and sleepless night, in which I drift from one half-dozing nightmare to another.

Michele says the next morning, 'I was up with Mum all night.'

'Why?'

'She kept getting up every five minutes and trying to leave because she thought she was in the wrong house. She didn't recognize the bedroom. I wrote out This is Linda's New House. You Are In The Right Room on a piece of paper and propped it up on the chest of drawers but she folded it up and put it away in the drawer for safe-keeping. I found all the keys to the front door in her handbag.'

She comes down for breakfast: 'I've had a terrible night. I thought I was in the wrong flat and someone would come in and say "What are YOU doing in MY room?"' She announces it in the tone of Father Bear asking Goldilocks, 'Who's been sleeping in MY bed?'

We get through Christmas Day. She and Michele have gone out to buy me a housewarming present, a radio for the kitchen as I had requested which I open with delight and mock surprise. 'Ooh, a radio! *Just* what I wanted. I can listen to music now when I cook.' Off her own bat she has also bought us all Marks and Spencer's gift vouchers. Mine is for a higher value than Michele's, we notice. For some time now I have been instated as the Good Daughter and Michele the Bad. Michele, who has spent many years in the reverse role, is relieved. The expectations are lower. My present to my mother is an appointment for a facial at Selfridges, for 27 December.

Several times as I am preparing lunch she pulls me away from the stove. 'Now this is important. I haven't bought you a housewarming present so I want you to take some money and get it yourself.'

'You've already bought me a housewarming present.'

'Have I? What is it?'

'A radio. Look, there it is.'

She examines it with uncertain eyes. 'I don't remember buying it. Are you sure?'

'Positive.'

Michele says, 'Mum, don't even think of looking at the roasting pan until *after* the gravy is made.'

After lunch, which is surprisingly good given the circumstances, though hardly worth all the effort for the actual amount of time you spend eating, my mother says, 'I'll wash up.'

'Fine with me.' It will get her out of the way for three-quarters of an hour.

She comes back a few minutes later. 'Linda, do you know you've got no sink in your kitchen?'

'What do you mean, no sink?'

'Come and have a look.'

She gestures round the room. 'Where is it?'

'There.'

'Oh, yes. I see it now.'

In the evening we all watch *Birds of a Feather Christmas Special*, the lowest common denominator.

The following morning, taking a few glasses from the living room to the kitchen, I fall down a flight of stairs. Bruises blossom across my back and legs. The pain is frightful. When I pick myself up and crawl to a chair Michele appears. 'I've got the most stinking cold,' she says. 'And Ben's ill, too.'

In the kitchen my mother looks at the turkey carcass. 'Someone's had turkey,' she says. 'I'd have liked some of that.'

A summit conference is held. 'I vote we abandon Christmas,' I propose. 'Let's just forget all about it.'

Mark says, 'The presents were lovely, the tree was lovely, the meal was lovely, the only problem was the people.'

We need one of those smart weapons that would have destroyed the guests but left the trappings of Christmas intact.

'I want to go home,' my mother says. 'I don't like it here.'

Michele makes a pretence of ringing the station to enquire about train times. We've no intention of letting her travel on her own. 'There aren't any trains to Bournemouth on Boxing Day,' she says.

'Any to Liverpool?'

'But you don't live in Liverpool?'

'Don't I?'

'Of course not.'

'Do I have a home any more?'

'Of course you do.'

'Where is it, because I can't remember?'

'It's in Bournemouth, where you moved with Dad.'

'Oh, yes, that's right. But sometimes, you know, I look round when I'm in my flat and I don't recognize where I am. Sometimes I start crying and I can't remember what I'm crying about.'

She begins another sentence then breaks off. 'I don't remember what I was talking about.' She cries again, easy tears that stop as easily, for like cigarette smoke, the memory of her sorrow has disappeared into the air.

Mark drives Michele and Ben back to Oxford, then he drives my mother to Bournemouth and then back to Oxford. He spends the whole of Boxing Day on motorways, but that was better than spending it *en famille* Grant, he said later.

I have the facial myself, a few months later.

April 1995. I go to Capri and stay in a terracotta-coloured hotel built, the management claims, on the very spot where the Emperor Tiberius once hurled his victims into the sea. Every morning I go to the deserted dining room for breakfast, come back and work on a novel, and in the afternoon I ascend by the funicular railway to the town. The island is quiet; it's the week before Easter and the first tourist arrivals from the mainland are due but they aren't there yet. The sounds are of hammering and sawing and chained beach chairs being dragged across the piazzetta. Men stand on ladders and refresh the front of hotels with new paint. The pools are empty. I do circular walks on paved paths in suede shoes and a pale lilac silk jacket, and whatever fork I take, my wanderings always end up amongst the smartest of shops, my parents' own daughter. One early afternoon my hike terminates with a manicure. I sleep soundly at night despite the smacking of waves on the beach beneath my small balcony. The Bay of Naples is right there when I part the curtains in the mornings. I buy my mother a music-box of inlaid wood which plays 'T'was on the Isle of Capri that I met her'. If Sorrento had been my mother's apotheosis of happiness, this is mine, the writer's solitary life, away from family, without responsibility. Some friends

152

who have driven from Rome to Naples take the boat over to spend the day with me. We have lunch overlooking a gorge and the blue Mediterranean spreads itself in front of us, like the best kind of dress. This is what living is cracked up to be, privileged, effortless, exquisite, what I always dreamed of when I lay on my bed all those years, improving my mind with a book. I am cut off from tragedy and tears. I dwell that week in Faery Land.

At home the new flat is full of plaster dust and builder's rubble, squalor on the grand scale. My mother rings me promptly the morning after my return.

'What are we doing for Pesach? You aren't going to leave me on my own in this flat with a box of matzoh, are you?'

'What would you like to do? Michele and Mark and Ben are in San Francisco but I could come to you.'

'I'm not staying here. I'm the only one who never goes away. I'm always here on my own.'

(Later, searching through her things, I find a scrap of paper. On it she has written: <u>People</u> TAKe <u>STRAN</u>geares IN FOR <u>YONTIF</u> I HAVe <u>NOT</u> Bean <u>OUT</u>.)

'That's not true,' I say. 'You were here at Christmas.'

'Was I? I don't remember.'

'Should I come and pick you up on the train?'

'Rubbish. I can manage on my own.'

But I don't think that she can. She doesn't know any longer that Waterloo is the terminus station. 'Why isn't it called London?' she has asked me.

There's a picture of me with pigeons on my head in Trafalgar Square, an outstretched hand filled with corn. London was the city my mother confidently navigated on annual Christmas trips. It was my mother who took me to the Tower of London where we shivered at Traitor's Gate and oohed and aahed at the Crown Jewels. At Kensington Palace she showed me the bed slept in by the teenage Princess Victoria who awoke to be told that she was a Queen. I trailed along after her to little handbag shops on Bond Street she had read about in a magazine at the hairdresser's. We did these things together, just her and me, and I never thought to wonder where my father was because I assumed that it was in the nature of men to go off in the morning alone. But it occurs to me now, as I write this, that he was seeing Sonia. Perhaps a new handbag was the price my mother extracted from him in exchange for those meetings.

Look at her now. If she takes the train by herself, will she stare out of the window and fail to recall where she is or where she is going? In transit between places, what marker will she have? How do I know she won't get off at another station, if she can't keep in her mind that London is also Waterloo? The truth is that she now has a tiny restricted planet of only a few streets to live on, frightened of venturing beyond certain well-known routes near her own home.

So I take the train to Bournemouth and walk along the road from the station to her flat, in the bosky South Coast air of a spring morning to the avenue lined with pine trees that are deceptively similar to the ones in Capri. I approach her building, a brutal up-ended matchbox a couple of hundred yards up from the sea with a petrol station in its forecourt which sells simple groceries and sweets. I ring her entryphone buzzer and she lets me in. I pass through the large empty lobby with chairs that no one sits in, vases with dusty silk flower arrangements which no one admires, come up in the small wood-panelled lift to her silent floor with its four flats. Her door is ajar.

I walk in. I call out, 'Where are you, Mum?'

'Here.'

The worst of her illness for me then and now is seeing her, sitting on the toilet, crying, struggling to put on her tights.

'I don't think I can handle myself any more.' She weeps. 'Sometimes I think I'm so brave, what I manage to do. Do you think I'm ready?'

'Ready for what?'

'To go somewhere else.'

'What sort of place are you thinking of?'

'Somewhere they'll look after me.'

'Yes,' I say. 'I think you're ready.'

I see her loneliness, her isolation from the world, the battle to make it through every day without major mishap, without getting lost or burning herself or falling in the bath or forgetting to take her tablets or turn the gas off or pay her phone bill or eat. I see the programmes marked with a cross on the television pages of her *Daily Mail*, which are her only company day after day, her television friends. The casts of all her soap operas are the ones who say goodnight to her and the presenters of the breakfast shows say good morning. They smile at her and speak to her as if she has no memory loss at all, never irritated, never complaining. They do her the honour of assuming she has as much sense in her head as they have.

As if she lived in a house that was falling down, she runs hither and thither trying to repair her roof or mend her floor, anything to stop the place from tumbling down around her ears, for she is fighting not just to manage her everyday life but to maintain her existence as a human being, a social animal with rights and responsibilities and likes and dislikes.

My family had by necessity reconstructed itself and its past for the life it would live in a new land. Cut off from the previous century, from its own line of continuity with its memory, it made itself up. All the lies and evasions and tall stories are what you must have when you are bent on self-invention. Now my mother has a similar task, that of continuously inventing for *herself* (and the rest of the world) a coherent identity and daily history. 'I'm watching a sculpture being made in Christchurch.' 'I can't stop, I'm meeting someone for coffee.' My mother presents a fictitious person for inspection, hoping it will pass muster.

This is a battle which is calling up everything she has in her. Now her old, old skills of putting on a face against the world come into the great majesty of their own. It is her capacity for deception that arms her against the destruction of her self. Only to me, for a moment, who sees her alone and vulnerable, sitting on the toilet trying to dress, does she reveal the bruising exhaustion of that daily combat.

We take the train to London. 'Would you like to live in London or Bournemouth?'

'London. Definitely. You're not making me stay in Bournemouth.'

I know why. Because of the humiliation, she who had once been a helper would now be the helped. She who had once held the hands of her old dears at the day centre would have her own clutched by her former equals.

There's no trouble that night remembering where she is but the next morning I find all my drawers and cupboards immaculately tidied. In her case, beautifully folded, are some of my clothes.

I raise again the matter of her moving on.

'I will have my own kitchen, will I? Because I'm not eating other people's food.'

'No, I don't think you would have your own kitchen.'

'I'm not going then.'

'But it's not like you cook much anyway.'

'Yes, but if I didn't have a kitchen I'd feel like I was in a home.'

'What sort of place would you like to move to?'

'Where they have a warden.'

'You mean sheltered housing.'

'That's right, sheltered housing.'

'I'm not sure if that's the right place for you.'

'Well, I'm not going into a home and that's the end of it.'

Walking along the street, she suddenly explodes like a match thrown into a box of fireworks, remembering the sheltered housing which Michele had tried to persuade her to move to a couple of years before.

'You're not sending me to Oxford, you know. I'd cut my throat rather than go to Oxford.'

'Where's the bus? I'm going. I'm getting the bus home.'

'Well, you can't. You can't get a bus from here to Bournemouth.'

She begins to sob. 'I want to go home, I want to go home. I'll get a taxi, then, you can't stop me.'

We reach my house and she goes and sits down and cries. I leave the room. I come in ten minutes later. 'Do you want a cup of tea?'

'Yes, but tell me. Have I had a row with someone? I think I've had a row but I can't remember who with. Was it Michele? Or Marina? I don't remember.' It's an excellent new tactic, this. Whatever is upsetting her, if you leave her alone for a few minutes she can't remember it.

157

The next day I mention Michele.

'Michele. Who's Michele?'

'Your daughter.'

'I've got a daughter called Michele.'

'Who lives in Oxford.'

'Who lives in Oxford.'

We are at Piccadilly Circus. 'Where are we, Mum?' I ask her.

She looks around. 'Bournemouth.'

Like Michele at Christmas I develop a violent, atrocious cold, the kind where you feel nauseous and dizzy if you stand up. The idea of taking her to Bournemouth and coming back in one very long afternoon makes me want to vomit. We go by taxi to Waterloo and I put her on the train in the care of another passenger. I come home and as soon as I think she might be back I ring. She answers without concern.

'Was the journey all right?'

'Yes. Why shouldn't it be?'

The following day she calls me. 'You've left me like a dog all over Pesach. I haven't budged from this flat for a week. I've been all alone with just a box of matzoh. What kind of daughter are you to do this to your own mother?'

'Mum, you were here, yesterday. You've been in London.'

'Don't you lie to me, you liar. I've not been out the door.'

'Don't you remember being in London? At my flat. You stayed here.'

'In Brixton?'

'No, the new flat.'

'When did you move?'

'In December.'

'And you've never bleddy invited me for a cup of tea.'

'You were here. You stayed here. You've only just got back.'

'I'm not listening to you another minute. You're telling me I'm mad.' The phone slams down at the other end.

I ring her back at once. She's crying her eyes out. 'You bitch,' she screams and the phone goes down again. This continues for the next hour.

I ring her the next morning. 'What's news?' she enquires in a calm, bright voice. 'I haven't spoken to you for ages.'

Later I understood that she wanted me to do something. When she asks me if she is 'ready' she knows she is but she cannot accept responsibility for making the decision for herself. She wants to rest now, to let go of all the burden of her life, but she needs someone to tell her what to do. So she could say, 'I was advised to. I wanted to stay in my own home but they wouldn't let me.' Then pride can be satisfied and indignity stared out. She doesn't want to be an adult any more. She longs to surrender herself back to childhood and the loving comfort of her parents' arms where everything is all right and she is safe from harm.

But Michele and I are too taken in by the advice we had received from the experts: respect the rights of the elderly; consult them; do not force them to do what they do not want. My mother's rights are allowing her to spend twenty-three hours alone, overdosed or under-medicated, and crying. Her nightmare goes on and on.

You aren't supposed to say that the old are children, it's so demeaning and patronizing. They are fully-formed adults with lives behind them. They have held jobs and brought up children of their own. When you see photographs of the frail elderly it is hard to believe that they were once the firm, confident people they show you, posed there, in command of themselves and their surroundings, intelligence sharpening their eyes. The people in the photos are like you and me. And those who showed them to you are not supposed to be the ghost of those former selves but the self they were at any moment through their lives.

I see old people in the street now and all the time I try to imagine them when they were young. In the supermarket, last summer, I was stuck behind an old lady dressed in a hot tweed coat who was bent almost double like a paper clip, her eyes forced to stare for the rest of her life at her shoes, perhaps the worst case of osteoporosis in the world. She wanted to buy a bright red pepper, the colour of fire and blood and revolution.

'How much is this pepper?' she asked the girl at the check-out.

'It's fifty pence.'

'I won't take it, then.' And she put it aside.

I thought of her at twenty, buying scent. I gave an extra coin for the pepper and ran after her and put it in her hand. 'Please don't think it's charity,' I said. And she smiled so sweetly, down at her shoes.

Perhaps she had a red dress a long time ago. Or a red ribbon. Maybe she had a sweetheart with red hair. She walked tall, once, saw the future clear as daylight, clear as a traffic light or a red rose, straight in front of her.

'Just because I'm old doesn't mean I'm stupid.'

'Just because I'm old doesn't mean I don't see, don't understand.'

So for several more months my mother is treated like an adult, left to her own failing reserves of self-invention.

October 1995. Yom Kippur, the Day of Atonement, the most important day in the Jewish year when even the least observant religious Jew should make their way to the synagogue or face the consequences. Eight days earlier is Rosh Hashanah, the New Year, when we give an account of ourselves to God, if we believe in him, or to our own private conscience if we do not. On Rosh Hashanah, we balance the accounts. In the books we can see if we have done more good in the world than harm. We submit to judgement. Then on Yom Kippur, we atone for the ill we have committed by abstaining from every morsel of food, every drop of liquid, from sunset on one day to sunset the next. And from morning to night we sit or stand in the synagogue, in prayer.

Yom Kippur is also a day of remembrance. It is the day when we recount the prayer of Yiskor that offers up our words to God for the souls of the dead. Children are ushered out and adults whose parents are both still living leave voluntarily. First there are spoken the names of the congregants who have passed away in the last twelve months. Then come the prayers for those names of the beloved of the congregation who have offered money to charity to hear them uttered aloud. Then there is our public memory of the nameless dead of the Holocaust.

Those who remain offer their own individual prayer for their dead relatives, their mother or father, husband or wife. So we cast our chain of memory down through the generations and link ourselves with all the forgotten ones of the past who have nobody left to mourn them. The synagogue is at its fullest. The old and the sick and frail will stumble there any way they can to say Yiskor. To do less is to have done nothing.

It is the most important day of the year, when my mother must pray for the souls of her dead parents, and for her brothers Abe and Harry and her sisters Miriam, Lillian and Gertie, and Gertie's only child, Martin, and for her own husband, though probably not for Sonia. I judge that she is too confused to come to London and that it will be best if I go to her.

'I will not, I will *not* stay in Bournemouth,' she shouts at me down the phone. 'This place reminds me too much of your father at this time of year. I want to come to London.'

'I'll come and get you on the train.'

In fact it was all to the good that she has decided to come to London because my long-lost cousin Sefton, who has lived in Israel for the past twenty-five years, is back in town and so I invite him to come and see my mother. 'Sefton!' she cries. 'My favourite nephew.' She remembers everything about him, who his wife is and how they married and when he had gone abroad.

I ring her just before I leave the house to remind her what time my train arrives. I explain that if she is there to meet me with her small suitcase we will only have a brief wait until the return journey.

'Yes,' she says. 'Don't worry. I've got it written down.'

I do not know if she will be there but she is, only a few minutes late, standing without any luggage. 'I've got to buy my ticket,' she says. 'I've been to the bank.' She no longer keeps money in a purse or wallet but in a small plastic bag.

'Mum, where's your case?'

She looks around. 'Where's my case? Bugger it, I don't need any clothes.'

'Of course you do. What have you brought with you?'

'Nothing.'

'Have you got your pills?'

'Yes, they're in my bag.'

'Show me.'

'Bugger off. I've got them.'

'I want to see.'

Meekly, she gives me her small handbag, the lightest of all those she owns and held across her shoulder by its strap. She's so little now. Little and old and confused. A mugger's ideal target.

There are no pills in her bag.

'We're going to go back now and pack properly.'

'Oh, do we have to?'

'Yes.'

We walk along the road to the flat. She lets us in and sits down for a few minutes with her eyes closed, exhausted, in what used to be my father's chair. Then she opens them and says: 'Well, I'm delighted you've come for the weekend. How long are you staying?'

'I'm not staying. I've come to pick you up. You're coming to London.'

She bursts into tears. 'Now you tell me. Do we have to?'

'But it was you who insisted. You said you wouldn't stay here.'

163

Her mood changes like a radio clicking to another station from sobbing violins to angry drums.

'You're not going to make me stay in Bournemouth. I'll cut my throat if I've got to stay here.'

'Well, that's good, because Sefton is coming to see us in London.'

'Who's Sefton?'

'Uncle Louis' son.'

'No, doesn't ring a bell.'

I watch her pack, a few things that don't belong to each other thrown into a small case.

'Underwear, Mum.'

'I don't need that, do I?'

In the kitchen I notice that she has a new pill dispenser from her GP, a large box divided into the days of the week. I see that pills have been taken from it at random.

We go back to the station and get on to the train. The orange signal lights inside the tunnel at Waterloo catch her eye as we approach the platform. 'Oooh,' she says, 'isn't it beautiful? Like fairyland.'

As we walk towards the tube I see a newspaper placard announcing that O. J. Simpson has been found not guilty. 'I'm just stopping to buy a paper, Mum.'

'Why, anything interesting in it?'

'The verdict on O. J. Simpson,' I tell her, knowing that she won't know what I'm talking about.

'Well, I think he did it, don't you? I've been addicted to the trial.' Thus my mother, who doesn't know what day of the week it is, or what's up and what's down, has for many months been following one of the most complex criminal cases of the century.

I go in to see her as she is getting ready for bed. She is

standing with her nightdress on over her clothes.

'Mum! What are you dressed like that for? Are you cold?'

'No. Why?'

'You've got your nightie on over your clothes. You don't do that.'

She looks down, uncertainly. 'Don't you?'

The following morning we travel in the rain by taxi to the synagogue. She gives out little cries and runs to embrace people, complete strangers as it turns out. They see my embarrassment. I see the look of pitying understanding in their eyes. I hate their pity. She does not follow the service.

On each seat is the congregation's community magazine. It contains an article about a nursing home adjacent to the synagogue. It is called Charles Clore House after the famous Jewish philanthropist who had once owned Selfridges, exactly the kind of man my parents admired and longed to be like themselves.

She reads it over and over again. 'Do you think I'm ready?' she asks.

'Shush. Don't talk so loud. Whisper. Remember where you are.'

'Why? Where am I?'

My mother's diabetes rules out fasting so I take her for lunch where she has a bowl of soup and a sandwich. Someone I know comes in and I see him start to come over to speak to us but I shake my head. Her voice is so loud though she isn't deaf, she smiles so brightly at people she does not know and they all, without exception, say, 'Oh, she's so sweet.'

'I must give you some money,' she offers.

'What for?'

'For the pictures.'

'What pictures?'

'Where we've just been. We've been to the pictures. I can't remember what the film was but I know we've been. Have I told you I've been diagnosed with a memory loss?'

And it is then that I think, 'That's it. This has gone far enough. She's got to go into a home whether she likes it or not. I've got to do something.'

I see then that the mother, in whose eyes I was a failed daughter, is gone. That I am never going to win the great argument with her about the kind of daughter she expects me to be for my adversary has left the field. In her place is a bewildered infant who the world insists on treating as an adult with no one to protect her. My mother, my child.

After half a lifetime of being an inadequate, undutiful daughter, now I am to take on a role I have refused elsewhere, that of a parent. It is up to me to do what I think is best for her, to tell her how she can and cannot behave, to protect her from danger, make sure she is properly housed and fed, to find her the best attention money can buy. I fought her for my freedom and independence. I thought I had won. I hadn't, of course. Now I am to become my mother's guardian, as tied to her as if she was my baby.

My cousin Sefton comes for lunch and as soon as he walks into the room my mother runs to greet him. Despite the fact that he's been absent for quarter of a century, the visual recognition portion of her brain is intact. 'You're as handsome as you ever were,' she tells him. 'My favourite nephew.'

We look at old photographs.

'Who's that?' she asks, pointing to a picture of his father.

'That's my father.'

'Who is your father?'

'Louis.'

'But you're Louis.'

'No, I'm Sefton.'

'How am I related to you?'

'I'm your nephew.'

'So who is your father?'

'Louis.'

'That's right. How's your wife? She was very beautiful, you know. She used to be a beauty queen.' It's true, she had been.

Why can she remember Anne, met perhaps two or three times and not since the 1960s? Why can she whisper to me when he was out of the room, 'His wife isn't Jewish, you know?'

And why is it, as we wave goodbye to Sefton, that she turns to me and smiles and says, 'He's lovely. Who is he?'

I take her back to Bournemouth on a packed train. I watch her lips moving as she tries to capture the thoughts that drift through her mind like fast clouds. A woman opposite us is watching her too. She looks at me and I see in her face what she thinks: 'The poor bloody daughter, having to look after her.' Perhaps she believes I am one of those selfless, dedicated women who love their mothers so much they would *never* put her in a home. I stare back at her, eyeball to eyeball. I send out a telepathic message. I'm not what you think. This situation is not as you imagine. I *am* going to put her in a home.

'Mum,' I say. 'Show me your chequebook.' She hands it

over. On the day she left Bournemouth she had withdrawn two lots of £30. She only had £30 when she met me at the station. Thumbing back through the stubs, I see that on various days she has withdrawn multiple amounts of money. I imagine that she had gone to the bank, written a cheque, then forgotten later that she had been and returned to get more. But what has happened to these sums?

She rings me the next morning. She's crying.

'I've left my chequebook at your house. Will you send it back to me?'

'No, you definitely haven't left it here because I was looking at it on the train and you put it back in your bag yourself.'

'*I haven't got it.* Why won't you listen to me?'

'Honestly, Mum, I promise you that you have got your chequebook. It is there.'

'It *isn't.* Why are you doing this to me? I've got no money for food. I'm hungry and I've got no money. Please, please send me my chequebook.'

'I can't, I haven't got it. If you need money, can't you ask Fay to lend you some until Monday when the banks open?'

'Why should I tell her my business? Send me my chequebook.'

'I can't, I've told you. I haven't got it.'

The familiar routine begins. The phone slammed down then a minute or two later rings again.

'Linda, it's Mum. I can't find my chequebook. Have you got it?'

'No, we just had this conversation.'

'When?'

'Two minutes ago.'

'We didn't.'

'Yes we did.'

'Well, never mind that. I want you to send me my chequebook.'

'I can't. I haven't got it.'

'Please, please, I'm so hungry.'

It goes on for two days. The phone calls every hour or so as if they had never occurred before. I go out for a while. My cleaner says, 'Linda, I was cleaning your office and there was the most terrible message on the answering machine. Whoever it was was in the most terrible distress. I didn't know what to do. It was something about a chequebook.' The last call comes at twenty-past midnight on Saturday, the latest my mother has ever phoned me. The first begins at ten to eight the next morning.

In the evening people come to dinner. It's early October and unusually warm. The last of the first phase of redecorating is over and I am free to entertain, to be gracious, to lay my marble table with my canteen of cutlery and place there the cut-glass tumblers that I had stolen from my father's cocktail cabinet. To be on the safe side I put the answering machine on. The phone rings and everyone goes quiet as my mother's demented voice forms a faint but audible back-drop to the Delia Smith beef casserole which we eat in defiance of threats to our own future sanity, just before the BSE scare went ballistic. 'I'm hungry, I've got no money for food. Why won't you help me?'

First thing on Monday morning I ring my mother's bank. I don't think anyone has been so pleased to hear my voice as that young clerk who, it turns out, deals with my mother's account, sees her each morning, bewildered and afraid as she tries to control the bills that came in and need paying, get money, not lose it, remember that she had it.

The following weekend she rings me again.

'My Visa bill has come and there's something wrong on it.'

'What?'

'It says here I bought something at a sports shop in Oxford. That can't be right.'

I tell her I will ring her right back. I call Michele who tells me that the last time our mother came to stay she bought Ben a pair of trainers. That will be it.

I speak to my mother again and tell her that she had bought her grandson some shoes when she came to visit him.

'Rubbish. I don't remember that. Anyway, what would I be doing in Oxford?'

'Because that's where Michele lives.'

'Don't give me that baloney. I'm not completely daft, you know. Michele lives in Bournemouth.'

'No, that's where you live.'

'Me? I live in Liverpool.'

'No you don't, you live in Bournemouth.'

'Since when?'

'About thirteen years. You moved there with Dad.'

'That's completely wrong because Dad only died very recently, a few months ago. Anyway, never mind that, what I'm really ringing about is this Visa bill I've just got. There's something on here about a sports shop in Oxford. I've never been there in my life.'

'You bought shoes for Ben there.'

'Why?'

'Because that's where he lives.'

'No he doesn't. They live in London. Will you or will you not ring Visa for me and sort this out?'

'I can't. There isn't anything to sort out. It's correct.'

And down goes the phone with a crash. It rings again a minute or two later and so it goes on all weekend every hour or so, until at last she slept and forgot about it forever.

It is a coincidence that at the very moment I make the unilateral decision that my mother is to be taken from her home, I receive two phone calls on succeeding days from the home help agency and the doctor's office.

The first of these, from the agency, informs me that she keeps ringing to complain that her 'helper' has not arrived, when the woman has only just left. 'Your mother doesn't recognize her from one week to the next,' the administrator says. 'We've told her not to go on a bus because we think she'll forget to get off and end up miles away. She's a lovely lady, your mother, but we're really worried about her and we're not sure if we can help any more.'

The nurse at the surgery says: 'She's coming in every day – two or three times a day – to tell us that she hasn't got her pills. We've put a new system in place, all she has to do is take the pills in the compartment for the right day but she doesn't know what day it is. We've told her to look in her morning paper to check, but she can't even remember to do that. Ideally someone would have to come in three times a day, morning, evening and bedtime, to give her her medication but we don't have the staff. She can't go on the way she is. I'm afraid to say she's now the most difficult patient on our list.' I am comforted by these reports for it seems that there are indeed objective criteria for madness and that my mother has met them in the professional eyes of others.

As it happens, it is an autumn of exceptionally heavy foreign travel for me – I will go to Iran and spend two long weeks sweating under a headscarf and chador, reporting on that country's ludicrous attempts to build itself a tourist trade. I will go to Istanbul to interview Alvin Toffler, the author of *Future Shock*. Then as a consolation prize for the Iranian adventure my newspaper is sending me on a five-day tour of the five-star hotels of Andalucia in southern Spain. The day after I come back I am to accompany my nephew Ben on a long weekend in Venice.

The burden falls on Michele. It's not an easy time for her. After twelve years she and Mark have separated and the circumstances have not been amicable. Ben is immobilized in frozen grief about the departure of his daddy and the arrival of the new woman in his life *and* her two children, those unknown girls who will live with his father as he will not. He is just meeting another new person too, one who will, in a couple of months, be coming to live in his house and whom his mum will marry the following summer. The centrifugal force that held our family together is slowing down and we are all, in some way, falling.

Now once one has made the frightful and guilt-inducing decision that one is to remove one's mother from all that she holds most dear and familiar, be it for her own good, it would seem an easy bureaucratic step for her shortly to find herself surrendered to the comfort of strangers. This could not be further from the truth.

First, where is she to go? What we were looking for was something along the lines of Bayview Retirement Home, an establishment in which a current television sitcom, *Waiting for God*, was fictionally set. Like Bayview, it would be full of feisty types, always going on strike and talking back to the staff, good old feminist bags and harmless eccentrics because the mood of the times is to recognize the continuation of personality into old age; that courageous, brave, intelligent people do not find these qualities eliminated by wrinkled skin and thinning hair, and the desires that burned in them at twenty are still there, fifty, sixty, even seventy years later, if a little ashy around the edges. But oh, their hearts are bright and inside themselves they are still young, as my mother once told me how she felt twenty-two and did not know who this stranger was who looked out at her from the mirror.

If my mother had not been Jewish the following events would have taken place. We would have trailed around many homes, examined the dried flower arrangements and the antique clocks, walked among the gardens, inspected the kitchens, then demanded to see the books. We would have observed whether or not the inmates sat in a drugged stupor. We would have sniffed for the smell of unmopped urine. Our eyes would have been sharp for bed-sores. We would have sized up the matron and asked ourselves whether or not we thought she was a lying cow. We would have wanted to know what her qualifications were and what the training was for the care workers. Someone who had been employed in such a place had told me that one day, when a couple of patients died just before the afternoon shift, a member of staff was rung and told not to come in, that was how tight they shaved their budgets. Later I would get a letter from a very old lady whose husband's centenarian father was in a home. At Christmas the owner, drunk, came round to everyone's rooms and physically forced liquor down their throats. 'Be happy for once in your lives, you miserable old buggers,' he shouted at them.

As I have been writing this book the owners of two private Buckinghamshire homes for the mentally handicapped were convicted of physical and mental abuse of the vulnerable people they were supposed to be looking after. Who, in what has been described as a 'ten-year reign of terror' were slapped, had their hair pulled, were forced to eat meals in the pouring rain, were denied toilet paper, toothpaste and soap. It took six years for relatives of the residents to obtain justice. During that time the homes were inspected twice a year by the local authority.

A private home for the elderly in Lincolnshire was abruptly closed down and the residents moved after allegations of abuse which have resulted in an investigation by police and the health authority. The owner of a Yorkshire nursing home was sentenced to four years' imprisonment for indecent assault after forcing oral sex on elderly residents, abuse which went on for nine years. Council-run children's homes across the country have been run by paedophile rings.

We know also that you could inspect and demand and poke your nose in all you like and it wouldn't make any difference because when it came down to it, hardly anywhere actually accepts people with dementia and the longer you leave it, the less choice there is. 'No incontinents' is the 'No coloureds, Jews or dogs' sign of the world of residential care.

None of this is to be our fate, however, for the simple reason that my mother is able to fall into the hands of her own community. There is something called Jewish Care, an entire social work organization dealing with all aspects of dependency – the elderly, the disabled, orphans, the unemployed, the blind, the mad and Holocaust survivors. The public face of the organization, its fund-raising face, is the actress Maureen Lipman. It has a ferociously impressive list of the great and the good on its board of trustees and none of these are the sort to have in their vocabulary the timid words: 'I thought something might be the matter but I didn't like to say anything.' Following in the footsteps of my Uncle Louis' saviour on the battlefield, who talked all night, they are the kind all too ready to open their mouths to criticize and complain. What more could anyone want?

A social worker tells Michele that when any of her clients need to go into a home she would ask them if they were Jewish because a Jewish home was the very best kind. 'Are you sure you're not Jewish?' she would enquire urgently. 'Think. Think. Even a Jewish grandmother. I know you're black and from Jamaica but are you absolutely sure . . . ?'

What is involved is a pincer manoeuvre. First comes the call to Jewish Care. Can they take her? Can they take her *now*? No, they can't. First, there is a waiting list, an *enormous* waiting list. Second, she will have to be assessed by one of their own teams. Third, if we are unable to afford the fees, around £1600 a month, then she will have to be funded by Dorset Social Services who, as she has assets of over £16,000 in the form of the ownership of her home, will eventually demand that it be sold in order to pay them back. But here is the catch – under the 1990 NHS and Community Care Act, which came into force in 1993, the local authority will only provide funding if their social services department thinks she *needs* to be in a care home. And Jewish Care will not even accept my mother's application to get on to the waiting list until they have received Dorset's assessment.

But how hard could that be to obtain when she is so obviously at risk and in need and all the other words that

bureaucracies use to describe the frail, mad woman my
mother is, with so little grip on reality?

We turn to Pat Tennuci, the social worker who had guided
us into the hands of Bettercare, the home-help agency, a
couple of years before. Ringing Pat, like talking to the
Harley Street doctor, always seems to me like stepping out of
our own lives into a calmer, more rational place where there
are reasons for things, other than that we are rotten daughters. She's the one person down there in Bournemouth who
I feel I can address in a common language, who doesn't have
anything to say about daughters who went to university and
never came back, other than the fact that she probably did it
herself, now I think about it. She's on our side.

So it is a very nasty shock when she goes to see my
mother and rings me up to report back that my mother
does not need residential care. She is supportable in the
community. Anyway, she doesn't want to go into a home. I
imagine how my mother would have summoned all her
resources to present her best self to the world.

'Do you bathe regularly?'

'Of course, every day.'

'And do you eat a proper meal?'

'Never miss.'

'Are you careful to stick to your diabetic diet?'

'I've never cheated once.'

'And your medication?'

'All under control.'

When I call my mother to ask her about the visit she
says, 'Nobody's stepped over the door for a week.'

I argue with Pat until I'm blue in the face. I don't accept
her judgement at all, because having mentally and emotionally

arrived at the decision that she's going to have to be put away, I want it over and done with and what I do not want to have to face is a corrosive, toxic decline into madness with me and Michele pulled up and down to Bournemouth like yo-yos at every fresh crisis. I get the doctor to send Pat a letter, the first in a correspondence which begins that October. He writes:

Mrs Grant is a patient at our practice. She has a high level of confusion although she maintains an excellent facade. Her insight into her memory failure is less good than it was and she is unable to handle her own medication, despite the best efforts of the District Nurse in supplying her with a box for daily dispensing. She constantly rings the surgery requesting more pills and has a great deal of difficulty remembering which day of the week it is. I gather that her daughter, Linda Grant, is arranging for her to have a place in one of the Jewish Care organizations in London. I would be grateful if arrangements for this could be expedited as soon as possible.

So Pat says she'll go back.

Pat writes to me again on 10 November.

Dear Linda
I have now visited your mother again with a colleague who is an Approved Mental Health Social Worker. She has confirmed my assessment that your mother does not meet our criteria for funding in residential care as she is supportable in the community. We accept that she does have some short-

term memory loss and that she presents as better than she actually is . . . The reason for her current agitation seems to be the break-up of your sister's marriage and also recent events in Israel have caused her a great deal of distress.

She does not really want to consider residential care particularly in a Jewish home as she feels her links with the Jewish community are not strong, the only reason she has been agreeing to this has been to please you and your sister. Both my colleague and I feel that she would be better remaining in Bournemouth with a supportive package of care in her own home. The arrangement with Bettercare seems to be working well, but if you wish to consider other arrangements for supporting her at home please let me know.

If you still feel that you want your mother nearer to you the best course of action would be for you to put the flat on the market and when it is sold look for alternative accommodation in an area nearer to you.

I am sorry that we cannot help from a financial angle at the present time as I know that your mother is a great anxiety to both you and your sister but I can assure you that she is being very well cared for by Bettercare and that I will monitor the situation closely over the next few months.

The dogma is this: Social Services comply with what the elderly client wants. What does my mother want? It depends on which sense of herself is in the ascendant at any given moment and with each of these there is no memory of there being another self that wanted something else. What does the self I had come across crying on the toilet want? And the one which holds her head high and says, never tell other people your business? Or the one that announces she is going to meet a friend at the pictures when she had almost no friends left and she can no longer follow the plot of a film?

Michele and I do all our reading between the lines. Our mother does not feel a strong connection to the Jewish community because she has voluntarily severed her links with it, out of shame. I suppose she could have been upset about the assassination of Yitzak Rabin, the Prime Minister of Israel, but the tears of her grief for him would have mingled with those for the misery of her life. When she cried while she watched TV and Rabin's murder came on the news, did she think, 'This is why I am sad'?

'Why am I so depressed?' she sobs.

The answer must have come to her: 'Because of what's happened in Israel.'

Michele had asked whether she should tell her that she and Mark and had split up.

I thought she should. I told her it would give Mum something to think about, a point of connection with our lives. On the other hand, my mother has a habit of turning other people's sorrows into conspicuous burdens for herself: 'And that's another thing that's happened to me,' was how she described her best friend's husband death.

She rings me one morning and says, 'I've just had a dream that Michele and Mark separated. Or was it a dream?'

Michele tells me later that she had broken the news the night before. This is our mother's way of referring to the event which she thought I might not have known about myself and it reminds me of the cleverness of her duplicity. It does give her something to think about and she retains the

sequential memory for many months, though sometimes
she speaks about it as if it were happening, say, to the daughter of one of her friends, a bit of juicy gossip.

'How do you think the child is taking it?' she asks me, not
remembering, I suspect, that 'the child' is her grandson.

She eliminates Mark as ruthlessly from her mind as dicta-
tors airbrush out of photographs the old comrades, now
denounced, they once marched with. Yet sometimes she
gets to the heart of things. When she meets Michele's new
boyfriend, the one she is to marry and for which event we
would some months later go shopping, she says: 'He's not as
good-looking as the other one, but he's more intelligent.'
Which pretty well sums up the situation.

I send Pat two letters. The first is three single-spaced typed
pages, a long roar of anger. I write:

> What [my mother] wants, as she has told my sister
> and me many hundreds of times, is for us to move to
> Bournemouth. I used to take her for lunch at Beales
> but gave up because she would lean over and say to
> the people at the next table that she was the only
> person she knew who had no family in the same
> town and what did they think of daughters who
> refused to be near their mother . . . You ask if we
> wish to consider 'other arrangements for supporting
> her at home'. Like what? What she needs is someone
> to come in three times a day, morning, lunchtime and
> bedtime, to administer her medication. She needs to
> have someone to make sure she has eaten a proper
> meal. Are you prepared to fund that? . . . I believe
> that two things might happen if she went into

residential care: one is that she would be dead within six months, the other is that her quality of life would improve, she would be properly medicated and fed, have company and regular visits from family, no longer be at risk of getting on a bus and not knowing where she is. To be honest, either of those options would be better than the living death she is inhabiting at the moment, a prey to innumerable terrors about a life that is slipping out of her control, lonely, and as I told you leaving messages on my answering machine begging me to help her.

Pat tells me that dealing with her medication is the doctor's responsibility. The nurse at the practice, on the other hand, says they have no resources for out-of-hours care; it's Social Services' responsibility. So we ride on our little carousel, round and round in circles.

Now Michele and I marshal all our contacts. We speak to friends who were social workers who advise us to request a case conference which our mother will also attend so we can thrash the whole thing out in person and she will not be able to play us off against each other.

I write to Pat again. I tell her that the nurse at the doctor's practice had gasped when I had told her of the decision.

Pat replies that she was going to suggest a case conference anyway:

Your mother has been visited and assessed by the Consultant Psychogeriatrician and they do not consider there is any need for their on-going involvement at the present time as they do not consider your mother's confusion at such a level. As I

am sure you will understand I have to take into
account their professional opinion.

 . . . [Your mother's] wishes must become a prime
consideration in the assessment. Your comments in
your second paragraph about your mother's wish for
you to return to Bournemouth to care for her is very
significant in that I feel that she is exerting emotional
blackmail on you and your sister.

I fully understand that there are problems with her
medication, but this is very much a matter for her GP
and the Community Nurses to resolve and not our
Department.

Yes, we are prepared to assist with the funding for
support in the Community, either through our own
Home Care Department or Bettercare. This is what I
meant by 'other arrangements'. I would not be happy
to change an arrangement that seems to be working
reasonably well, therefore we can consider funding an
assessed programme of care through Bettercare.

One of the social and political themes of the 1980s and
1990s in both Britain and America was Care in the
Community, the name of an official policy in the years of
Margaret Thatcher's and John Major's Conservative admin-
istrations. It had begun in the Reagan years when the great
state mental hospitals were closed down and the inmates,
some incarcerated for lifetimes against their will, often for a
long-forgotten crime against society such as promiscuity or
homosexuality, were released into the tender solicitude of
the streets where we tourists could see many of them in
New York, sleeping in doorways or on top of heating vents
on icy days. I observed a man once on the subway, a terrible

hulk of human being in a thick orange down jacket, the gift of a charity, maybe. From behind I could see his shoulder moving rhythmically up and down. As I got off at my station I noticed that he was masturbating.

When Britain followed Reagan's lead, the poor mad people also took to the streets where they were ripped off for their pills and their bit of dole money by sturdier beggars.

The community did not care for them as it did not care for my mother. What was this community? It was neighbours and family and kind strangers. Not all of my mother's friends deserted her, not by any means. I knew how much they worried, but in her block of flats, many were old themselves, with their own cares and concerns and physical and mental discomforts. There were many broken hearts under that roof, a lot of which you could mend through surgery or pacemakers and others which were only to be borne. Forty, even fifty years of married life, and a woman comes back home from the hospital with her husband's pyjamas neatly wrapped in a brown paper parcel. 'I gave them a man,' my mother said 'and they gave me back his watch and his slippers.'

As long as my mother stayed put, in her flat, she lived in institutionalized care in her own home, except that the care wasn't twenty-four hours a day. Did she remember, fifteen minutes after her visitor had left, that she had ever had company? We thought not.

So we rage and write letters and make angry phone calls and insist and rant. 'You can't just put your mother in a home to suit you, you know,' was the tacit message we hear from the authorities.

In the end, however, my mother rescues herself.

The start of the end of my mother's life begins with a phone call early one morning from the home help, who we are now paying to come in every day. She says that my mother is not well, that the doctor thinks she might have had another minor heart attack and they are waiting for the ambulance to take her to hospital. She tells me not to worry, but there always has to be one of us who will drop everything and this time it is Michele who takes the day off work and drives from Oxford to Bournemouth to see her.

In the hospital Mum says to Michele, 'Come upstairs, I'll make you a cup of tea, I've got a kitchen upstairs.'

Where does she think she is? She thinks she might be in a hotel. Or she imagines she is still at home, though the evidence of her own eyes should have told her otherwise. This is a new confusion. Removed from the familiar surroundings of her own flat and the shop at the petrol station in the forecourt of her building, where, I suspect, most of her groceries are bought now, her brain no longer seems able to take in new information, assess it and make a judgement about what it contains. She looks at the hospital beds, the nurses in their uniforms, the doctors in their white coats, the sick people in their night clothes, and all these visual clues tell her nothing. Or perhaps they do, for a moment, and she understands, but then she turns her head away – looking down at the copy of *Hello* magazine Michele has brought her – and forgets what she knows.

The staff sister, however, understands exactly what *she* sees. After only a few minutes' evaluation she has decided that it is absolutely out of the question for our mother to go home. Under the hospital's own guidelines they are not prepared to discharge her back to her solitary flat and a paid visitor for only an hour a day. On the other hand, they need the bed; the heart attack is what? Perhaps only a particularly heavy bout of angina. Or another of those tiny strokes that continue to afflict her. Or has the whole incident been a superbly acted performance, a cry for help from a woman abandoned and deserted? For it is true: despite the best intentions of her daughters, we neglected her during that last year. We did not travel to Bournemouth every weekend and sit in her flat listening to the diminishing round of her conversation. We stayed at home not because we didn't care about her, but because it was unpleasant to be there. I could have gone more often but I didn't. That last visit to London, at Yom Kippur, I noticed that I spent much of the time sipping orange juice, heavily diluted with vodka. On my return train journey after taking her back, I bought two miniature vodka bottles, the equivalent of two doubles, and had consumed both not long after the train passed through Southampton. It was the stress, the irritation, the constant biting of my tongue that did me in and made me dread the thought of being with her. An hour was bad enough, but a day was a forever and a whole weekend required another day to recover from it. And anyway, a day wasn't enough for her.

'Why are you only coming for the day?' she would

demand. 'Can't you stay for the weekend? You leave me like
a dog on my own. I'm the only one who . . .'

I was always hearing of people who gave up their careers
to look after their elderly relatives, particularly childless
daughters who some families breed and rear precisely so that
one day they will be available to perform the task of caring
for their parents in their old age. But if I had given up my
work, it wasn't clear to me how, without an income, I would
have been able to support us both. I suppose I could have
sold my flat or hers and lived off the proceeds, but within six
months I would have been an alcoholic and bankrupt three
or four years later for neither of our properties was worth
that much. Of all the scenarios for our mother's future, this
was one that Michele and I *never* considered. And however
badly others may think we behaved – those people who
love their relatives and would not dream of putting them in
a home – looking after her ourselves fell into the same category of the unimaginable as sharing all our secrets with
her, having her as our best friend. The intimacy simply
wasn't there to begin with.

As for Michele, could she have gone more often, when
she worked in London all week and the weekends were the
only extended time she had to be with her son? Should she
have taken him with her and exposed an eleven-year-old
child whose life had been fractured anyway to the evidence
of further disintegration in his grandmother's mind? For him
she could be nothing *but* Grandma, the person who made
him chicken soup. He did not need or want her to be
anyone else.

In the hospital, she cannot go home and she cannot stay,
blocking a bed needed for someone who has something the
matter with them, or at least something which the doctors

have a cure for. Without a nursing home place, her destination, they tell Michele, is a secure psychiatric unit. It is the very worst possible scenario, a terrifying regime where she will share her meals and her television programmes and her examination of that morning's *Daily Mail* with schizophrenics and manic depressives. 'It's not the sort of place you would want her to go to at all,' the nurse says.

Michele rings Pat Tennuci and manages to persuade her to come back for a third assessment. How will our mother present herself to Pat, we wonder. Will she tell her that she has everything under control: her food, her medication, her memory of how to navigate the route from front door to shops? And so is Michele to remind her that once back home – though she isn't going, anyway – she would be picking up the phone to whichever daughter's number was first to hand, crying, saying, 'I can't cope any more'?

That night in the hospital Michele sits by our mother's bed and gives her what she calls 'a really hard talking to', perhaps the hardest she has ever had in her life. She tells her, 'Unless you say you can't cope you will *have* to cope, you will have to go back home on your own.' Then our mother starts crying and says what we have suspected for so long is the truth; she tells it like it is, at last: 'I don't want to go back to that flat,' she weeps. 'I never want to go back to that flat again as long as I live.'

Her own home had become a prison, a torture chamber.

Michele says to her, 'You have got to tell the truth about how you feel to the social worker.'

But shrinking away from the cold comfort of reality, our mother slips back into her old world, the one in which appearances are all you have, and all you are – and perhaps, too, with the old immigrant instinctive distrust of the authorities, she replies, 'I don't want the social worker to know my business.'

Michele sleeps that night in our mother's flat and when she comes back the following morning, walking into the hospital through a long corridor leading out to the main entrance, she sees our mother fully-dressed with her hand-bag, shuffling along. She understands that if she hadn't happened to have turned up, at that moment, then the patient would have walked out. The hospital is miles from the centre of town, off a motorway. How far would she have wandered? Into the traffic? Or out beyond the navigable pavements into the terrifying anonymity of the frozen fields, to die like her ancestors in the forest? Michele can see now why they were saying she needed secure accommodation. Unless they'd strapped her to the bed she would escape.

Michele asks her what she is doing. She doesn't know. Michele takes her arm and leads her back to the ward.

When Pat arrives for the meeting Mum bursts into tears and says, 'Don't make me go back to that flat, don't make me go back to that flat.'

Has she remembered her instructions? What, out of the previous evening's conversation, had lodged itself in her head? Has Michele managed to convey to her the enduring significance of her own misery so that she can recall it? Or has she known all along that the moment would one day come in which she would have to stop playing games, and it had arrived?

When Michele rings me to tell of these events of the morn-ing she says something so funny that both of us collapse with laughter; in the middle of this domestic tragedy we are laughing so hard we can't speak. For what our mother has said has unwittingly revealed how totally remote she is from reality. And no one in the world but Michele and I could understand how completely off-base this thing is.

Michele says: 'We were sitting in this room in the hospital and Mum announced, "Your father made this furniture, you know." This was a man who needed to hire in a team of specialists to put up a cup hook. I can remember Mum saying, "I need a cup hook here" and Dad saying, "No, you need professionals, you need a Black and Decker." I tried to tell Pat that but I don't think she quite understood the enormity of it. I guess everybody has their personal test of whether you've totally lost it and that would be hers. For you it would be "Can we go for a hike up a mountain?" and then we'd know, "It's time to lock her up." You'd just have to say, "Where are my hiking boots?" and that would be it. When I start to wonder if you're still supportable in the community I'm going to ask, "Would you like to go for a hike, Linda?" And if you said yes we would know that the men in white coats would be coming for you.'

I say, 'Well, you know what an animal lover you are, yours would be, "Where's my little kitten?"'

Later we played the Alzheimer's Game, as we came to call it, with many of our friends. People came up with marvellously self-perceptive suggestions. One was, 'I don't care what I wear, as long as I'm comfortable.' Or 'The biggest mistake I ever made was to leave Nuneaton and come down to London to go to art school in the 1960s.' Or, 'I just mind my own business. People can lead their own lives, I'm not going to interfere.'

That remark – about the man who believed that manual labour was something the *goyim* did because they were too ignorant to improve themselves with a book – more than anything else is what makes us realize that our mother's mind, which has been beating like wings on the surface of reality, sometimes brushing it, sometimes not, is moving off to a place we do not know or recognize. She's stopped making sense altogether. What is she thinking of? I have tried and tried but I cannot get to the bottom of it. I could see how someone who didn't know us might reason that perhaps my father was an enthusiastic amateur carpenter and she had extrapolated a whole business concern from that, but of course he was nothing of the kind. The remark could be sane but it isn't, it is insane. My father making furniture has no bearing on anything at all. Though there again, I think now, given our family, I would not be in the slightest bit surprised to discover that all along my father had had a sideline in supplying furniture to the National Health Service, which for whatever dark reason, he had declined to inform his daughters about. Perhaps the hospital furniture fell into the same obscure portion of his private life that included our sister Sonia.

Now it is my turn to relieve Michele and go to Bournemouth, clutching a copy of *Hello* magazine which I am not then aware that Michele has already bought her and which is nowhere in evidence. It doesn't matter. She seizes mine eagerly, thirsty for celebrity gossip which goes in one ear and out the other: 'Princess Diana went on television and told the world that she'd been seeing another feller . . . Have you seen this, Linda? Princess Diana, you'll never guess what . . . Well, I never knew, Princess Diana . . .'

For the first time I notice her displaying the symptoms of paranoia that are so common in dementias. 'They've stolen my coat,' she tells me. 'Where's my coat?' She screams at the nice Australian nurses who try to soothe her. They are bitches, they are all against her. It turns out she had not been wearing a coat when she was admitted.

I go to Social Services for a meeting with Pat, our first face-to-face, and understand at once that she is an intelligent woman whose hands are tied by the system, particularly that aspect of it which insists that the demented elderly are best left where they are, to be cared for by the community. We talk for ages. She's delighted at this resolution. Then I go back to the flat to find some clean nightdresses. The ones that are there are completely awful, torn nylon diaphanous garments from the early 1960s. Michele had noticed in the hospital how her dressing-gown was filthy, covered in stains. I can't believe how old the food in the fridge is.

When she had the first heart attack I had rented a portable television for her bedroom and now I go down to the show-room to sign the forms for cancellation. There's a rain-storm and I run, soaking wet, into Marks and Spencer's. I purchase the finest nightgowns money could buy as well as a quilted cream lace bag of toiletries. I want her to walk through the doors of wherever she is to go with her head held high, dressed as well as she has ever looked in her life, right down to the incidentals of the bathroom sink. When she enters Bayview Retirement Home or its clone, the other residents will see the mother *we* had known: the one for whom how you looked was who you are.

I go off to Spain and – not without guilt on my part and resentment on hers – leave Michele to it. Leave her to phone calls from our mother in hospital claiming that she has been kidnapped by the nurses and that Michele must come and get her at once.

Pat Tenucci's new assessment is that our mother has gone

from not needing residential care at all to being an emergency case. But events need to be synchronized; ideally she should be transferred straight to the place where she will permanently remain in order to avoid the gathering confusion and paranoia that a change of scene seems to entail. But Jewish Care only makes its decision to allocate places at a special meeting, held every Tuesday morning, several days away. Until they have received the formal assessment from Pat she is not even on their books, so whatever they decide we do not have the option of going to inspect the homes they run.

Now there is a three-day wait between her expulsion from hospital and the future place at which she will be accepted. Because Michele is there, on the spot, the hospital enters into a piece of blackmail: either our mother goes home with her or they will discharge her into the secure psychiatric unit. So of course Michele says she'll take her, what else can she do? She is subsequently told that the number one rule when dealing with elderly and confused people is that there are not supposed to be interim gaps, they're supposed to go directly where they're going to end up because it causes such problems and the hospital should have kept her. But then again, because Jewish Care isn't a Bournemouth Social Services place, this complicates matters.

Before bringing our mother back to Oxford Michele has to go to the flat to get some things for her. She doesn't want to take her there, she doesn't want her to think she is returning, so she leaves her at the hospital. At the flat she puts into a suitcase enough clothes to last the next few weeks and she takes the rented television back to the showroom and in the middle of all this has to deal with our mother's friend Fay who wants her to give her a lift to Asda. In the flat Michele notices that there are hundreds of chequebooks and about twenty Visa cards. She goes into the bank to make the arrangements to put the account into their joint names so that she can sign cheques for the bills that will continue to arrive until the phone, gas and electricity are disconnected. She sees a woman called Sara who says that our mother had been coming in every day to draw out money or cry that she had lost her chequebook or Visa card and they are very, very pleased to see a relative. Michele wonders what they are thinking. Is it, 'How could they have let that poor old woman manage on her own for so long?' Then she goes back to the hospital and picks her up and takes her back home to Oxford.

Now they wait, wait through stonewalling discussions with Jewish Care who continue to insist that there is nothing to be done until Tuesday. What is going on in the mind of the object of all this attention and activity? She seems to know – or rather remember, for knowing and remembering, for her, aren't the same thing at all – that she is going to a home and keeps asking, 'When am I leaving?' Michele tries to find distractions for her, they go shopping, they go to the pictures, they do anything to keep her mind off what is happening. And there is Ben who is beginning to find the presence of his mad grandma disturbing, and it is Michele's task to try to keep these two disturbed people apart.

Finally on the Tuesday she receives a phone call from Jewish Care. They've got a place. Michele says, 'Great, when can she come?' And they reply, 'You can bring her now if you like.'

She's sitting in the living room. Michele goes in and says, 'We've got the place and it's really nice and it's near Linda, in London.'

When she sees the future close in on her our mother cries out, 'I'm not going,' and runs off down the street. She shoots out of the house, she must have been running because Michele has to run herself, and only at the end of the road can she catch her. Michele is frightened and angry. She shouts at her, dragging her back into the house and then our mother starts crying and says, 'I'm sorry, I'm sorry, I'm sorry.'

Michele feels bad, she feels really guilty, but then our mother slips back into 'I don't want to go' and she keeps slipping between the two polarities of 'I don't want to go' and 'When are we going?' . . . 'I don't want to go' . . . 'Let's go.' Which, as Michele points out later, probably describes her state of mind. 'Thinking about it now,' she told me, 'it's a totally normal thing. Whenever I move house I think, I don't want to go, and then, I want to be there.'

When she said this I remembered the early morning of the day I moved from Brixton, from the flat I had lived in for nine years. You could see it was going to be a very cold, very bright day. The sun was coming up and as I looked out of the kitchen window a fox ran across the frosty grass, through a gap in the neighbour's fence, and vanished. And I, who had been sick with worry in case the deal fell through and I would lose the place I had coveted for so many months, asked myself, 'Why am I leaving here? What have I done?'

By now it's mid-afternoon, Ben is home from school. Michele and Mum are both exhausted. Michele decides to get in the car and go. But when she imagines the journey she pictures a sudden tantrum, the door opened and a frail body jumping out on to the motorway. She needs another adult to restrain her if necessary and she will have to take Ben anyway because she can't leave him on his own. So she phones Mark, pulls him out of a meeting and tells him that he has to come with her, for whatever his faults, he has always been a calming influence on our mother, and to his credit he drops everything and comes straight over, though he and Michele aren't even living together any more.

In the back of the car our mother is quiet, not hysterical but seething. At about six in the evening they arrive. It is a dark, cold, miserable night, early December. The main office is closed and the residents are about to eat. The four of them, Mum, Michele, Mark and Ben, stand on the doorstep ringing and banging for about ten minutes. The place is almost deserted for the head of the home, whose responsibility it is to oversee the admission of new residents, has taken most of them off to the theatre, so there is hardly anybody there, just a skeleton staff and those who are so frail they can't attend. It's a care worker who finally answers the door and lets them in and who will handle the admission procedures.

They walk into a place which has hard floors instead of carpets, where everybody is decrepit and seems to be over ninety. It smells of what these places smell of — disinfectant and institutional meals and air freshener battling to combat the stink of urine and decaying flesh. Michele looks round and instead of grandfather clocks, antiques and pot pourri, she sees death's waiting room.

She says, 'This is no good, they've chosen the wrong place, she can't possibly stay here.' Mark thinks the same and they tell this to the care worker who, looking at our mother in her smart clothes, with her unlined complexion (a result of a lifetime's dedication to expensive face creams) thinks they are right. Appearances, it seems, *are* everything.

'But the funny thing was,' Michele told me later, 'that though Mum didn't like it, she wanted to stay, I think she felt safe and she certainly preferred it to going back to Oxford.'

In the end they agree that she will remain overnight and that they will come back in the morning. Michele, Mark and Ben turn their back upon the home and on our mother. As finding her on the toilet, her tights around her ankles, was the worst moment for me, this is the depths for my sister: 'I was so upset, I was hysterical, sobbing my heart out. I felt – I don't know, what did I feel? In a way it was like the final goodbye to a real mother. It was at that point that she became a patient. It felt like that we had crossed a big line and it felt wrong but I also knew that there was nothing else we could do. And then we drove back to Oxford, stopping for a pizza on the way because Ben was hungry.'

The next day Michele returns to London. She goes to the offices of Jewish Care in Golders Green and in the spirit of a family used to demanding the best and only ever seeing the Top Man, insists on an audience with John Bridgewater, who is head of Residential Services, and destined to become an important figure in our lives. Michele is cross and convinced that this individual, with all his training and certificates and experience, doesn't understand what our mother's problems and needs are at all and if only he did, then somehow a new and better place would be found for her, that fantasy home which still exists in our imaginations where everything can be made all right. For we fervently believed, then, that there was a tip-top solution to our mother's problems and we did not accept that there was only the best of a bad job.

Michele tells him, 'You don't understand, she's very active, she's much better than you think she is.'

He replies, 'I am convinced that this is the right place for your mother and if you don't agree then take her home with you.'

Shaken by this unattractive offer, Michele stays. They talk some more. Michele sees that he realizes that she isn't stupid and she realizes that he isn't stupid, and they go on talking. She is with him for an hour and a half. At one point the fire alarm goes off and they walk down the road and, standing on the pavement, carry on deciding our mother's future as the cars roar by carrying their cargo of Orthodox Jews in black hats and sidelocks, an alien culture to us. John Bridgewater apologizes and says that he gets a lot of people coming in who are in denial about their relatives and he had thought that this was the case with us. Michele is impressed by him. She thinks he's very good. But she still isn't convinced.

She tells him, 'Our diagnosis is that she needs a lot of distraction and the place where you have put her doesn't seem to provide it.'

So he says that he will come to the home right there and then and see her.

They drive through north London. They enter the place of the old, old people. Our mother, instead of being busy in her kitchen or watching daytime television, or watering her plants, or browsing in the shops, is sitting in a chair in a row and the first time Michele sees her like this – in a row, as old people are placed – is a shock.

She's one of them, but she isn't. She's ignoring the other residents, as if by acknowledging their existence she will become part of their society. John Bridgewater sits next to her while she tries to get him to agree that she's ready to return to her flat.

'Stay here for a couple of weeks and I'll come back and see you,' he says to her.

She looks him in the eye and says, 'When?'

Then Iola Samuels, the head of the home, whom Michele now meets for the first time, tries. She tells her that she's going to be there as a live-in helper and our mother takes to this idea. Perhaps it gives her a way of imagining herself into such a set-up, allows her to see for the first time what she's doing there. Or maybe she knows all too well, but Iola has given her a chance to surrender to her care without loss of face.

Observing the staff, usually the chief concern in such places, Michele finds that she isn't worried about them at all, she's very impressed, with Iola in particular. It's the other residents that bother her. They're so old, death is in their eyes. She can't see how our mother will have anything in common with them.

The problem, and it will take her a little time to work this out, is that it's not about who our mother is but who we want her to be. For despite our two lifetimes of complaining about her, we loathe the idea that she is finally going to be someone else, not a mother at all. 'You look at her,' Michele says, 'and think "I don't want her to be that person sitting in a row," but she didn't seem to have any sense of being unhappy about it. She had already lost her freedom long ago.'

What we did to our mother that day was more than the simple act of putting her in a home, for we were no longer who we once were to each other. Who was she? The mother who had once bought our school uniforms and sewed our Locke's name-tapes into the collars was gone. How were we related to her, as she would one day ask me herself?

Two years later, my friend Ruth Picardie, a journalist, died of cancer at the age of thirty-three, leaving two-year-old twins behind her. The carcinoma which began in her breasts would invade her lymphatic system, her liver, her bones and her brain. For a while she went mad. They had to put her in a hospice to keep her away from her bewildered children. Sometimes the tumour in her brain made her forget that she had cancer though at the end that illusion retreated. Her husband, Matt Seaton, wrote of her final weeks:

> The survivors have their guilt, the dying a justifiable anger. Since I now found myself making decisions for her, with only her grudging consent, I was often her gaoler. I wrote a series of long, self-pitying e-mails to a faraway friend. She had the courage to tell me what I knew already: that I had probably had as much love now from Ruth as I was going to have . . . like Eurydice, she was lost to the underworld, and the true meaning of dying is its absolute loneliness.

Like Matt and Ruth, my mother and her daughters had a new relationship now in which the habits and customs and expectations of the old life no longer made any sense. Like Matt, we were our mother's gaolers. Like him, we felt guilty. Like Ruth, my mother would never lose her rage at the place to which she had been delivered. She wanted to be still in the world, the land of the living, but like Eurydice – like Ruth – she belonged with the dying, abandoned in the twilight zone, and we could not go there with her even if we had wanted to.

When I arrive home after my foreign travels my mother is on the phone straight away and I suppose she must have been trying all that time, in the home's phone box with her clutch of coins, always reaching the disembodied voice of my answering machine.

'I've been here a week and they've made a new woman of me,' she says. 'I'm ready to go home now.'

'I know, it's because you're eating properly and not having to worry about whether or not you've taken your medicine.'

'Yes, and now I can go back to Bournemouth. I miss my flat, it was beautiful.'

I say, 'Don't you remember how unhappy you were? How you rang me up and you cried and you cried?'

'Yes, but now I'm better.'

'Only because you've got people looking after you.'

'Yes, but you're forgetting that Bournemouth was very new to me. I've only been there a few months.'

'You moved to Bournemouth in 1981.'

'Rubbish.'

'It's true.'

'I've only just lost your father.'

'That was in 1983.'

'What year are we in now?'

'1995.'

'That can't be right.'

'It is.'

'I want to go home.'

'Mum, I don't think you should.'

'Have I got to stay here for the rest of my life?' she cries.

I am silent. I do not have the heart to tell her the truth, to inflict that terrible sentence on her. She hears my silence and understands it.

'You bitch,' she says.

The phone is slammed down then rung again. 'Well, Michele thinks . . .' I say.

'Her? She's worse than you. You're both the same, you bitches.'

And so it goes until I telephone the office and ask them not to let her ring me any more. Then she falls out of the habit, and it stops, for once and for all, those terrible calls. We move on to something else.

The home where Jewish Care had placed her is familiar to me for it is a minute or two's walk from an office where I used to work. Years later, I still passed it regularly on the bus and had seen the decrepit wrecks that sit in the window, staring out at the iron railings of the small park across the road, where they could watch young men and women playing tennis or mothers taking their children to school or nursery. It had been a Jewish area once, but now the synagogue was gone and its congregation long moved away. In their place are professionals who like a well-built Georgian, or at a pinch, Victorian house, close to the city. It's the northern boundary of Tony Blair's Islington, and further up the road is gangland, a heavy-duty neighbourhood of guns and drug deals, all these elements co-existing on one bus route. All her life she had wanted to live in London and here she is, but in her dreams she has a place in Mayfair and can step out of her front door to shop. She would have liked Hampstead, too, or even Richmond, anywhere smart and elegant. Islington is hard to explain to her. Like Hackney it does not fulfil her criteria for a fashionable address though at that moment it could not have been more modish, a year and a bit before the General Election when Blair and Gordon Brown were still dining together in Upper Street's restaurants.

According to a plaque in the entrance, on the site of my mother's new residence there had originally been a home for illegitimate babies run by the London County Council but during the war it was taken over to house poor Jews who had been bombed out of their houses. Then it became an old people's home and in 1967 the building was demolished and a four-storey brick structure replaced it, in the faceless style of the architecture of that period. It lacked a garden, perhaps because of the proximity of the park, perhaps because Jews are not considered great nature lovers.

In front is a small patio on to which kind relatives place pots of flowers every summer and chairs can be dragged out so the residents can be even closer to the rush of traffic. Its clientele is not drawn from Golders Green or Finchley or Hendon, the traditional Jewish London suburbs, but Stamford Hill and Hackney and Finsbury Park itself. There are homes where the Ginsbergs would have comfortably lived out their twilight hours and there are homes for the Hafts. This is definitely a place for the poorer, smaller, more working-class branch of my family.

Inside it is not at all as I expected. Stubbornly, like Michele, I persist in thinking of dried flower arrangements and ticking grandfather clocks of polished walnut. But graciousness is missing, as well as eccentric old dears. The floors are hard and uncarpeted – easy to mop after an 'accident' – the walls covered in a maroon vinyl. It's institutional. Like a small hospital. Once you're through the doors there's a lobby with chairs and a coffee table. In the next few months I would come to know by sight the men and women who sat there: the half-deaf man in a wheelchair who reads all day because it's too much of a trial for anyone to endure a shouted conversation with him. He's a widower, with no children. His visitors are his home help and a former employee. And there's the gentle, elderly man always impeccably dressed in a Homburg hat. He's a Holocaust survivor, my mother tells me later, and suffering from advanced Alzheimer's Disease. Jewish Care had a particular problem with demented victims of the Shoah, for what is it to live in the past when the time of your youth and childhood is the memory of Auschwitz, not plaiting posies in a field, your lungs full of the smell of grass and flowers? There was a man in another of their homes who had to be carried screaming to the showers, mistaking his wash for a final march to the gas chamber.

To the left of this entrance way are bedrooms. To the right another large L-shaped open-plan room with the kitchens in part of it. There are chairs arranged in rows and a number of vinyl-topped tables to which the inmates shuffle a few feet for their meals. There's a large television. There is also, off the main entrance, a small TV room where, I later find out, the men gather to watch sport or the racing and place their bets. And that is it. This is the tiny prison in which my mother is going to spend the rest of her life.

The staff don't wear twin-sets but uniforms. I had imagined

she was to be tended by suburban ladies with time on their hands, which is utter nonsense when you think about it for more than a minute, such women being in the prime of their lives and at the peak of their careers; for volunteering is in sad decline now that practically everyone seeks paid work. Anyway, looking after old people is itself a skilled job, not something you could leave to the WRVS. Apart from the head of home, Iola, and the administrator in the office, the staff are all black, one generation of immigrants being cared for by the next generation, from another part of the world altogether.

What strikes me then, as it had Michele, is the other residents. They are so very, *very* old. The women wear those floral sacks that my mother, a few months later, was to ignore completely on our shopping expedition at John Lewis and below the hems of their skirts their legs are chapped and scaly. Their thin hair is brushed but neither set nor styled. Femininity has drained out of them long ago. I see them sit like shapeless bags in their seats and stare into their limitless future of chair and meal and television. On Sunday they would receive their visitors who would sit by them and hold their hands. And there is my mother in *her* chair amongst them. What crime have we perpetrated, bringing her to this terrible place?

She doesn't see me and I don't go out of my way to attract her attention. A meeting has been arranged with John Bridgewater and Iola. Michele arrives and we go into the office. John Bridgewater turns out to be a red-haired, freckled man with a boozer's nose. He's almost flamboyantly, in-your-face not Jewish, a man who likes a pint and his game of golf, quiet-spoken, introverted, tending to mordant

ironies. I like him very much. He had started out in psychiatric nursing, was seconded to the Home Office for a
while and worked with disturbed adolescents at a youth
treatment centre, then he went to a psychotherapy centre
and finally to a local authority where he stayed for fifteen
years.

'But I always had a feel for the sort of people who were in
institutions and I had a very practical approach,' he would
later tell me. 'I have supreme confidence that I can touch
what matters in that type of person. I don't regard it as an
intellectual process, it's like having an ear for music or an eye
for colour. I just know when to engage with people like that
and when to back off and I find it very difficult to cope with
do-gooding.'

Iola isn't Jewish but her husband is. They both work for
Jewish Care, running homes. She's charismatic. People look
up when she walks through the room. The two of them take
Michele and me step by step through a door marked reality.

John has already met my mother for a second time and
done some kind of assessment. 'I don't know what it says for
our relationship with the Royal Family in this country,' he
says, 'but your mother didn't seem to have much difficulty
remembering seeing Princess Diana giving that interview on
television recently.'

'Looking at her now,' he tells us, 'I'm not sure I would
have put her here. She looks out of place.' But then he
begins to tell us things about dementia we don't know, don't
understand. He explains that he's against the current grain of
things, against every fashion in the care of the elderly, how
you must keep them in the community for as long as possible, how they need to stay in their own environment. He
describes going into sheltered housing where elderly ladies

are found to be keeping their own excrement in biscuit tins. He talks of the terror and the loneliness out there 'in the community'. He explains why the people in the home are so very old, why the average age of residents has gone up to ninety. The policy of care in the community has meant that it is almost impossible for elderly people to get their local authority to pay for them to go into a home until they are so frail, so incapacitated, that they are nearly dead.

Still we urge him to place her elsewhere, a home where she will have friends like herself, can go out shopping with them, can pretend she has a normal life.

'There is somewhere she could go,' he tells us, 'where there is a group of women who go out, like you have described, but I have met your mother and her mind is very damaged. She would be ostracized by those women and do you think that would make her feel worse or better?'

He reminds us that *this* home has, upstairs on the second floor, its own Alzheimer's unit, and when our mother reaches such a state as to be incontinent, unable to feed her-self, no longer able to assimilate the memory of strangers, she will not have to move out. The staff who care for her now will care for her then and she will be to them not just another patient, but someone who they themselves have memories of in better days. She will be the Rose they had known once, who went on outings and had her hair done and her nails manicured, all services provided free of charge at the home for those residents who could still appreciate them.

So we have to confront the truth about our mother. That appearances are not always the thing. That the Jaeger suits and the new nightdresses count for nothing, for lying deep beneath the surface is a woman who, in her own way, is just like the ruined bodies that sit outside the office, staring into oblivion, and unless death intervenes first, will become one of those unseen residents of the floor above.

Still we doubt. Can she have her own furniture? Can she have her own phone? John laughs when he hears this. 'So you want her ringing you up at all times of the day and night, do you?' he says. As for her own furniture, it's a classic mistake. 'This is not what she needs, she's better off with new things. You have had this idea that you wanted her to have her own home within a safe environment but she's beyond that.

'Your mother does not deal in the past or in the present but in the here and now, and I deal entirely in the here and now, in fact very small sections of the here and now. And most of the trouble for people with dementia comes about because of people's unreasonable expectations. The typical thing is that a carer gets Mrs So and So out of bed and says, "I'll get your slippers." Totally unreasonable expectation. Mrs So and So can't remember what's been said, so she feels anxious. What was five minutes for the carer is a lifetime for her. So she gets up to get them herself, falls down and fractures her hip. How was that problem created? Because of a totally unrealistic expectation. Your mother has to live in the here and now. The important thing is *this* moment. If she's touched, even for a few seconds, she feels happy. And I train my staff to touch the people here, to help them feel okay just for now.'

He then begins to talk about the work of Irving Goffman, the American psychologist who wrote a book called *Asylums* about the workings of closed social systems.

'Goffman described closed institutions. Most people work in one place, live in another and have recreation in another.

And most of our living experiences are done as an individual or as a couple. In institutions all those functions are altogether under one roof and that has a number of consequences. One is an institutionalization, people give up any sense of self and become lethargic and depressed, and the other is that people develop pecking orders – they devise systems to distinguish them from the others and that includes the staff with their keys. How do you monitor what goes on in an institution if it's closed? I characterize it like a spinning top with the string attached to head office. When you go in the dynamic is at a certain stage but the whole thing is moving. You see it in the morning, when the day staff are arriving and then later when the volunteers are here running activities, but at night it's somewhere different again.

'The other thing about residential life is that whatever comes in gets absorbed into the whole process. Local authorities have failed miserably with children's homes because they've tried to apply employment practices and systems that don't understand that. If you've got someone who decides to do something insensitive and cruel to a resident you can't go through the process of having three trade union reps involved. I'm quite convinced that in Jewish Care the lowest thing that could happen, I'm in touch with it. There's nothing bad that could happen that is beyond my imagination and I can live with my imagination. You never really know but it's as ventilated as any situation can be.

'With Jewish homes the community is much more a part of them. You have all sorts of people going in. The visitors are not just relatives but the next generation down. It has its disadvantages but in terms of institutional abuse the links in the chain go from the bottom to the top of the community. I could insult a lady in a home and I get a phone call from

Israel the following morning. That's important in terms of the kind of potential power the residents exercise. It doesn't stop some dim care assistant in the middle of the night losing her temper and snapping at someone but it does offer a great deal of protection in keeping the whole thing steady.'

As we are absorbing all of this we get up and go to see our mother. In her capacity as 'helper', as appointed by Iola, she is polishing the candle-sticks for the Friday night service which brings in the Sabbath, invoking the prayer she herself had said every week of my life, her head covered, her eyes closed, her hands moving over the brightness of the flames, saying the *brocha*.

Her face is that of an orphan child's, as she rubs her cloth over the brass and silver.

'Do you remember me?' John Bridgewater asks her, sitting down at the next chair.

She looks at his face. 'Have we met before?'

'Yes, an hour ago.'

'Well, we may have done and you are familiar but I don't recognize you.'

'How's the food?'

She screws up her mouth. 'It's what you'd expect.'

'I'd like you to stay here for a while.'

She examines him again and sizes him up. She can see he is the Top Man. She's going to have to draw on all her reserves of energy and cunning to win him over.

'I have a flat, you know, in Bournemouth. Don't you think I'm ready?'

'Ready?'

'Ready to go back. They've made a new woman of me, here. I'm right as rain. I want to go back.'

'I think you should try it here for a couple of weeks.'

'I want to go now.'

'I'd like you to stay. But I'll come and see you again.'

'When?'

'In a couple of weeks.'

'Why not tomorrow?'

'I'd like you to spend some time here.'

'I want to go home.'

'I'll come and see you again.'

'When?'

Behind us the kitchen staff are preparing lunch.

'Would you like your daughters to stay and have lunch with you?'

'NO.' She turns away, her face bitter and beaten.

Back in the office, John says, 'She had us on the ropes there, she had us on the ropes.'

I say that I'll come back the next day and the day after. I will not allow her to feel as if she is abandoned. But Iola tells me I'm wrong. 'Stay away,' she says. 'Stay away.' Every time she sees me I would hinder her acceptance of her present state. 'Let her settle in.' Let her adapt to the life she must lead.

Michele leaves to go to work. I return to the big room. She's finishing lunch, meekly eating food I know she doesn't like.

'Show me your room, Mum.'

And to my surprise, she takes me. We get in the lift and she presses the button for the third floor. Slowly, crankily, like the old people it carries, it wheezes upwards.

We step out into a large hallway and to one side is a lounge. 'This is where we hold the Shabbos service,' she

211

says, pointing to the prayer books and the sacred cloths of velvet that cover the scrolls.

Along the corridor is her little place. She takes me straight to it, as if this were home. The floors are the same grey vinyl as everywhere else. She has a narrow, single hospital bed with a gold coverlet. She has a sink. She has a wardrobe and two chests of drawers. And this is her life now, this is what we have reduced her to. The ormolu clocks, the showy reproduction furniture, the walnut dining room table, the boxes and boxes of china in patterns she had collected since the 1950s, the silver plated cutlery, the pots and pans she had received as a wedding present, manufactured before the war when steel and aluminium had not been pressed into military service, everything down to the 'little black knife' as she always called it, which she used to pare vegetables – all gone. She's down to this.

It's my turn to go, leaving her there, in the institution.

I ring the home every day and then every other day.
'How is she?'

'Not too bad. She's settling in, she is settling.'

I'm divided. Of course I want her to 'settle' but better still would be if she rose to her feet and said with utter coherence, 'I don't belong in this place, let's go shopping,' and then be restored to the world as I once knew her. For the more she settles, the more I have to accept finally that the diagnosis is correct and that despite the Jaeger jersey suits in her wardrobe, my mother belongs in that crepuscular realm between life and death. But which mother would I get back? The depressed menopausal one? The mother of my childhood, more intent on coffee mornings than reading a child a story? The gay, carefree girl of her own adolescence, who wasn't a mother to anyone? Who is the real Rose Grant? I have only known her for a section of her life. She didn't enter the world as Mum. John Bridgewater says: 'People have a view that during the lifespan from birth to death there's a point where we become an optimum human being, a grownup. But it's not true. It's a cycle and you and your mother and your sister are all meeting at different points. She wasn't just a mother, she was a daughter and a wife as you and your sister are not only daughters but mothers and wives also.'

★

The next time I go, there's a Chanukah party – our festival of light in the darkness at the time of the solstice, the darkest moment of the year when the sun is in exile and we despair that it will ever return. Seven candles are lit, one for each day of the week, and an eighth, representing no day but the eternal, infinity which exists outside time. It is dementia's candle.

The home has hired an entertainer, a bold, upbeat woman who comes in and belts out show numbers in answer to which there is some feeble singing-along. The chairs in the big room are arranged for an audience. A tea is spread in the hall for the relatives, bagels with cream cheese prepared by the black kitchen staff.

I sit beside my mother. She's repeatedly rummaging in her handbag, looking for something she can't find. She begins to cry.

'I don't know what to do,' she weeps, 'I can't find my keys. I don't know where they are and I can't go home.'

I see for a moment the dreadful strain of her old way of life. I remember that for years she had been repeatedly looking in her bag, as if she had lost something but could not remember what it was, and her search was as much to recognize this thing that had gone missing – which was, of course, her own memory, her life – as to find an object she had mislaid.

'But you are home, Mum. You live here now.'

'NO, I DO NOT,' she shouts in that Daddy Bear voice she had used when she thought she was sleeping in someone else's room. 'I'm a helper here but it's a tiring day and they let me spend the night, you know. I've got my own bedroom so I don't have to make the journey. Would you like to see it?'

'I have done, already.'

'How come? You haven't been here before.'

'Yes, I have.'

'When?'

'A week ago.'

'Did you? I don't remember.'

Iola comes over and takes my mother's hand, raising her from her chair, and leads her on to the dance floor, where she twirls her around and around as in the days when my parents had gone to dinner dances, my father with a band of braided satin down the trousers of his dinner suit, my mother in cocktail dress and pearls. Everyone applauds and my mother returns, pink and laughing, to her seat.

'She's the owner,' she tells me, pointing to Iola. 'It's her business, this hotel, you know.'

Am I to put her right? Shall I return her to reality, convincing her that she is not a volunteer at an old people's home, nor a guest at some establishment on the South Coast? Of course not. I let her think what she likes. Would it be kind to treat her like an adult, someone with the right to control over their existence? Should I act and speak with the honesty and authenticity I so deplored the absence of when I was growing up? Shall I refuse to collude with her in the new myths she is manufacturing, as we all invent myths to make sense of the world we live in and render it bearable? For without these legends of good and bad gods and heroic deeds and miracles what have you got? What my mother faces now. Small flickers of consciousness in the blackness. Some distraction.

When the entertainment is over, the guests are sent out to enjoy their refreshments. My mother is not allowed to accompany me. She is seated with the residents at their vinyl-topped tables, segregated from her daughter. I think this rude but how can the lame stand, with glasses and plates and napkins in their hands, making afternoon-tea-party conversation? On the other hand, why can't we be in with them?

She has already made a friend. Her name is Rose, too. She's very old. She's one of the chapped-leg women of that place. My mother sits and holds her hand. I don't have any idea if Rose has any objection to these attentions. 'She's a very nice woman, your mother,' she tells me. But she will die a month or so later and my mother sees that this is the way things are going to go in this place – you make a pal and she dies. She turns her attention to the staff instead.

That was the first visit, when my mother stopped being my mother and became someone else, one of those individuals who are defined by the term Old Person. It wasn't just that she was in an institution but that the place itself was outside the world, in a hinterland between death and life.

'They won't let me go out on my own,' she tells me, this time and on every single subsequent visit. 'I'm the only one who . . .'

The second time I visit she demands to be taken out and so we go to her room and she removes her slippers and puts on her street shoes and coat and she smiles at the staff as we walk through the doors.

She clenches hold of my arm as we pass over the zebra crossing. She's a slow walker, one of her legs stumbles and she limps a little, the product of an old, minor stroke we had hardly been aware of, for she didn't mention it. We go into the park. It is going to be a very hard, cold winter. She does not see the bare trees or women walking their children or

the empty tennis courts or the closed shutters of the little
wooden house that in the summer will open to serve tea and
biscuits and toast and even egg and chips. She does not see
the white majesty of the Georgian terraces.

'They won't let me go out on my own, you know . . . I'm
the only one . . . Other people can go out but not me . . .
Got four walls to look at . . . Have I told you that they won't
let me go out on my own and *I* am the *only* one who isn't
allowed out . . . I hate it, I hate it, I hate it . . . I want to go
home to Liverpool, my flat was beautiful . . . what have you
done with my flat? Have you sold it? Is it still there? . . . I
want to go home to my flat in Liverpool with my contemporaries, my childhood friends . . . Gertie and Maime . . .
they're all still in Bournemouth, you know . . . They won't
let me out on my own. I'm the only one . . . If I went back
to my flat in Bournemouth Auntie Milly can look after me
or I can go and live with her . . . I've had a bereavement. I'm
only like this because your father's just died . . . Dad, Dad,
where are you? . . . He only died in the summer and it's too
soon, I came too soon . . . Where am I? These shops are
better than in Bournemouth . . . What time's the train
back? . . . They won't let me out, you know, I'm the only
one, the others, they can all go out, but not me . . . What
shop is this? Oh, it's Marks and Spencer, they've got some
lovely things here. That cardigan would look nice on you,
Linda, why don't you try it on. Me? Well, see if they've got
it in my size. I don't know, what do you think? Or do you
prefer the navy? It's smart, isn't it? Be lovely for when I go to
the day centre. Well, if you insist, but I'll pay you back . . .
Why have we got to go home? I'm enjoying myself and
where's home? I can't remember where I live . . . I don't live
in London, do I? I've always wanted to live in London but I

live in Bournemouth with your Auntie Mill. . . .You bitch, you bitch, you're as bad as your sister, the pair of you, taking me back to that place . . . I hate it, I hate it, I hate it . . . I'm the only one who isn't allowed to go out . . . The others go out, but not me . . .'

I still see us, in my mind's eye, walking down Upper Street, me half-dragging my mother who alternates between conversation and sobs and screams, stumbling and howling on to the platform of the crowded bus as we turn our way homewards. Drying her eyes as we walk towards the home. 'I don't want *them* to see me like this. I don't want them to know.'

She smiles a bright, artificial smile as a care worker opens the door for us, who tells me as I leave, 'See, she's settling.'

In Marks and Spencer's my mother became, for a brief moment, a proper person again, her identity reformed itself around the undamaged, coherent centre of the part of the brain which controls our urge to shop. I have not been able to locate this area on any diagrams but I know it must exist. My mother could not take part in a conversation or follow the sequential narrative of a book or a film but she could go shopping – that trivial, materialistic activity in which we enslave ourselves to consumerism, the basest, most acquisitive part of ourselves in the ascendant over the spiritual. When she shopped she existed in the here and now of that engagement with dresses and cardigans and shoes and hats and handbags. Her fractured life slipped away for a moment and she was whole once more.

Over the course of the winter, my mother does 'settle', that is, she sinks into a bitter acceptance of her fate. Every time I go to see her it's the same thing: 'I go to bed and cry. I wake up and I cry,' she tells me. 'I pray to God that I won't wake up in the morning but he doesn't listen to me. Why won't he listen to me?'

When I pass on the bus, I see her, her chair facing the window and the traffic and the park. She's always staring out, talking to no one, like a prisoner who longs for the outside world but has forgotten how to escape. If she isn't there, then she's at the table eating her meals.

I long to find out more about the society of the home, this total institution, but it's difficult. I am never allowed to pass any visit with her in the lounge, for the moment she sees me she jumps up and walks quickly to the lift. 'Come upstairs,' she says. She sits on the bed, I sit in the room's only chair.

'Are we going out?' she demands.

If we aren't, there's the devil to pay, as she cries and stamps her foot and shouts at me. So we always do. I have a small number of excursions which she enjoys. They are: to the garden centre in Muswell Hill for tea; to Kenwood, the famous house on the edge of Hampstead Heath for tea; to

Highgate Village for tea and a look at the shops; to Marks and Spencer's in Islington followed by a cup of tea; to Brent Cross shopping centre to look at the shops and have a cup of tea; occasionally to the West End where there are so many shops that often we do not even get round to the tea.

On these expeditions, I notice that she has stopped walking with a limp. She tells me herself that she has been having physiotherapy – a staff member takes her through her exercises every morning. Her skin is blooming, her cheeks filled out. A combination of regular meals, proper medication and the falling away of all anxiety about her keys and her chequebook and her credit card and the phone bill has restored her to excellent physical health. Far from being dead within six months, it now looks like she can go on for years and years.

I had thought, early on, that if her physical condition were improved, perhaps there might be some small reversal in her mental state. In fact it's the other way round. The struggle to maintain even the most marginal grip on day-to-day life created the illusion of her being more capable than she really was. With responsibility removed from her, she actually seems a little worse, more childlike.

The staff, who are they, Mum? 'Our parents,' she replies.

As I've said, they are almost all black. They come from the Caribbean and from Africa. I'm not sure what she is going to make of this. Though we were a Conservative-voting family, my parents surprised me in my teens by a passionate loathing of apartheid – my mother boycotted the goods of two countries, Germany and South Africa, with positive discrimination in favour of Israeli products. When the South African president, Verwoerd, was assassinated in 1966, and this item came on the news, my mother said, in a loud, emphatic voice, 'GOOD.'

My father surprised me even more by saying, 'Yes, but it will be someone worse next.'

They weren't anti-racists of a liberal, left-wing, intellectual type. My father liked the *idea* of communism, which he had been exposed to as a young man in America during the ascendancy of the Party there under the influence of the recently deceased John Reed. He liked communism's grandiosity and even more than this, that it was something you could argue about for hours on end. But he was a pragmatist. As a businessman he voted in the business interest. The Labour Party to him meant trade unions (which you should be for if you were a worker and against if you were a boss) and a kind of simple Christian socialism that had nothing whatsoever to do with his love of abundance and ostentatious display. On race, my parents made a simple equation between the Mosleyite anti-Semites – the ones who had written to my father with the threat of extinction – and the National Front and saw that they were exactly the same thing. Had they been American they would have been life-long Democrats. They adored President Kennedy – 'He'll be good for the coloured people,' my mother said, when he was elected.

It was one thing, however, to have a view about the segregation struggle in the Southern States, quite another to be dressed and undressed and told off and cuddled by a race other than your own, when you have lived an entire life within the closed walls of your own community, never even having had a non-Jewish friend.

There is racism in the home. I know because my mother tells me. She gives a fastidious shiver of distaste as she

221

recounts it. The staff seem to take it in good part, under-standing that some of it speaks from the heart of illness and dementia and that in another life, another time, it would have been different. Provocatively, my mother puts her arms around the cool young black chef and kisses him to show that *she* is different from the rest. It's another means by which she can distinguish herself in her own mind from those she finds herself amongst. 'I'm better than you,' the kiss announces to the other residents.

I talk to John Bridgewater, fascinated by his take on this cultural collision. 'Here we have a group of Jewish elders being looked after by non-Jewish people,' he says. 'What does it all mean? There are clear reasons why there are no Jewish care workers. Unlike the Irish who came to Britain looking for accommodation in advance, there isn't the tradi-tion here of Jewish care work, nor of nursing. There is left-wing field social work emanating from the East End but residential work there isn't. There are Israeli social workers, but not in this country. We do a lot of training with the staff about the Jewish way of life. When I came here if someone had said to me what's your culture I would have said, "I live in Harold Wood, I like James Cagney films and that's it." But the more I get into Jewish culture, it doesn't make me more Jewish, I discover myself, I discover my own culture. There's a home we have on the South Coast and after a very difficult meeting there I went straight to a pub and had a bacon sandwich, though we hadn't been eating meat at home for a couple of years.

'With demented people what they need is contact all the time and I think staff distance themselves because they're frightened of making a mistake. Not being Jewish it's a fairly dangerous exercise to make contact with the relatives. You run the risk of tripping up on some prejudice you didn't know you held, some distant echo from the past, some attitude. I can chat with your mother about her grandson's bar-mitzvah but I can only do it by asking questions, so it's a totally different conversation. I can only start to relate to her by acknowledging the differences. At important times such as festivals, families can't make themselves available so on Friday evenings you can have this strange phenomenon of non-Jewish staff lighting the candles and trying to carry the residents through the experience that doesn't mean anything to them themselves. It's those sort of issues that are problematic.'

My conversations with John Bridgewater make me realize that in the home it's non-Jews who are the transmitters of memory and of our culture. The link has been broken with the past, there's a gap in recollection and it's filled in by words and rituals learned by rote. It forces me to wonder what it means to be Jewish. It's not exactly a racial thing, nor is it confined to religion. I'm Jewish because my mother is. That is how Jewish identity is transmitted, matriarchally. Sometimes I look at my face in the mirror, at my pale skin and hazel eyes and I know that my distant ancestors didn't come from the Middle East. All those centuries hanging round Eastern Europe – I'm a Slav, I can see that. Those memories we resurrect on the feast of Passover of our days of slavery in the land of Egypt, are they personal memories or just as parroted as the ones the Jamaicans and the Ghanaians say when they light the Sabbath candles for the old Jews, who watch the flames and try to remember where they've seen something like them before?

As our mother 'settles', Michele and I remain unsettled. Although we think John Bridgewater a wise and clever man, we still resist the idea that this is the right place for her. We retain, in a corner of our minds, the hope that there's some other home which would be just perfect, where all the misery will drop away from her and she'll be happy.

First, we go to a prominent Jewish institution in south London, one which is raved about as 'state of the art', the best of any kind in the whole of Europe, it's said. It's a fifteen-minute walk from the tube station. When we arrive there are security guards on the door. Have we an appointment? We have. In the lobby, we're encouraged: we see smartly dressed women making their way out for a little shopping. We're shown round. It's enormous. The facilities are out of this world – the art room is superbly equipped, there's an in-house hairdresser's shop. It reminds me of a small university campus.

Then we are shown the dementia unit. It's a distinct area of the building with its own dining room and television. This is where she will be, one small cell in a giant hive.

We leave and go and have a cup of coffee at a pâtisserie near Clapham Common. Michele is the first to express her doubts. Of course we are impressed, it knocks spots off the place she's in, there'll be no shortage of distraction. And yet the sheer size of it puts us off. She'll never be able to find her way round, it's just too big, and although she'll come to no harm if she gets lost inside the building, confined to the dementia unit, will she have any more freedom than she has already? Is it not the case that what it provides is a form of segregation, an apartheid separating the mad and the sane? Michele thinks that what Mum needs is intimacy, that the very smallness of her current home surrounds her with care.

And those smart ladies in the lobby. What will they have to do with her? Are they going to be her friends? Of course not.

She's nagging away about going back to Liverpool. She wants to be in Stapely, the old age home where my grandfather spent his last years. It is astoundingly inconvenient for us, for in order to visit we'll have to undertake a 250-mile journey. We point this out. 'But Marina will look after me,' she says, referring to her niece. Also, she argues, 'if I'm in Liverpool I'll be with my contemporaries.' She's talking about her childhood friends, Gertie and Mamie and Jean. I somehow doubt that any of these will be popping in every day, but certainly they would come to visit *sometimes*. And it also stands to reason that currently in the home there must be people who she already knows, if not her friends, at least acquaintances. We take the view that we should at least go and see Stapely, for if that really is *the* place for her, then we must find a way of making it work for us.

Marina is lukewarm about the suggestion. First, she wants to make it completely clear that she has no intention of being dragooned by my mother into the role of carer. She's well aware of her capacity to use her. Plus she visited her own mother-in-law at Stapely until she died and she doesn't want to have to go through that again. We're glad she's taken this stand. We're as keen as she is to stamp out any idea in our mother's mind that there is some ideal substitute daughter out there. There's some other objection as well, but she's being reticent.

It's strange being back in Liverpool. I'd forgotten how beautiful the suburbs where I grew up still are. We drive past the low red sandstone walls of Calderstones Park and glimpse the green carpet of grass, the stands of trees and further off, not visible from the road but vivid in my imagination, the large eighteenth-century house in the centre, protected by a ha-ha, where they used to sell – and for all I know, still do – Mivvis and choc ices and teas and sticky buns. I spent so much of my childhood in the park, climbing over the wall instead of walking round to the gate. I remembered the cold winter of 1963 when people went tobogganing down a slope on home-made sledges or even tea-trays and there's a picture of Michele, aged around four, in a red duffel coat, bending over in the snow with her little bottom in the air. I remembered how when I was at nursery school on the other side of the park we would go for walks, little boys and girls holding hands in twos in a crocodile, led by our teacher. And in the park we would thread individual florets from rhododendrons on a stick and a girl showed me how to blow into a blade of grass to make it squeak.

I take Michele to the house we lived in before she was born. 'Along here, now turn, turn again' – the topographical memory perfectly preserved though I haven't been there since 1959. In my day the front garden had a rockery made of glittery white stones and there were the flowerbeds in which I planted flowers made of paper that I'd learned to make from *Picturebook* on children's television, and I recall how heartbroken I was when they did not turn into real flowers and grow but became sodden pulp in the rain and were removed by the gardener. We peer through the windows and Michele remarks on how old-fashioned the furniture is, with antimacassars on the armchairs, and she suggests that the very same people that our parents had sold the house to in 1959, the year of her birth, might well be living there still.

We take Ben to Forthlin Road to see the house where
Paul McCartney lived and where I used to hang about outside after school, in the hope that he would be there and
invite me in and I'd marry him.

We drive down to Otterspool where the Mersey narrows
before widening out to the sea and listen to the seagulls
which were the sound of my growing up, that and the
foghorns on the ships on the river which are still in my
dreams. If my mother returns to Liverpool, my life will loop
like a figure of eight back on itself and I will have to come to
terms once more with the city I left at nineteen, the city that
is my teens and childhood. Here in Liverpool my mother
will also be more herself, she will exist, as she has not done
for so many years, in the context of her old friends and her
own beginnings. She will be replanted back in the earth she
came from, a wandering Jew no more.

Then we drive back, through Penny Lane past the chemist
where I once bought her out of my pocket money a bottle
of perfume called Manhattan that cost 6s 6d and came in a
cylindrical cardboard container with a design of night-time
Manhattan in silver against a black sky. We pass W. H. Smith
where I used to go to buy books from their children's section
to take home and read, lying on the bed, improving my
mind. We pass the bus shelter featured in the Beatles' song,
Penny Lane and the barber's and the Trustee Savings Bank.
So many memories imprinted on my mind in indelible ink,
the ones I'll be left with when everything else is gone: 'I
wrote a book about my mother, you say? I don't remember.
But I do remember queuing for the children's matinee at the
Gaumont cinema on Allerton Road and buying a pyramid-
shaped ice lolly called a Jubbly. You tore open a corner of the
wrapper with your teeth and sucked out the orange flavour

until the heat of your mouth melted the ice. If it was an "A" rated picture which you could only see if you were accompanied by an adult, then me and my friend Sara Davis would ask a grown-up to take us in and sometimes, if it was a man, he'd want to sit next to us and buy us something from the ice-cream ladies' tray, which was kind, don't you think? Have I told you I've been diagnosed with a memory loss?'

We come out of the home an hour later and go back to Marina's. 'Well?' she says. 'What did you think?'

Michele says that we're not sure.

Marina tells us that Stapely isn't what it was, it's run down. She talks of a doctor who has just died there, I was at school with his daughter, she reminds me. Well, he was covered in bed-sores, crying.

'They just don't seem very professional,' Michele says.

In the event, they reject our mother. 'In my opinion she might go mad and have to be taken to a psychiatric hospital,' the head of the home informs me.

I tell Iola this. 'But that's rubbish,' she says.

So our mother is going to have to stay where she is, a wandering Jew to the end. She'd always wanted to live in London, where it was smart and the best shops and addresses were to be found and celebrities prowled the streets in search of autograph hunters like herself. As Truman Capote remarked, there's nothing so disappointing as answered prayers.

S pring comes. A reprieve. Leaves unfurl on the trees in the park and she notices it for the first time.

'Linda! Have you seen? There's a park over the road. We've just been there and had tea!'

We walk across and she shows me the wooden building, closed during the winter, which now serves hot drinks and toast and clumsy slices of cake. She gestures round, her eyes shining. 'Have you seen our lovely park?'

Everything is on a roll. Iola is wonderful, a Florence Nightingale, a mother to her. She's won a nightie in a contest for the most tidy room, and she keeps it neatly folded in a drawer. '*I* won it. The others were jealous. I heard them talking, but *I* had the best room. I had to go up and collect it in front of everyone.'

'Who gave it to you?'

'Our parents, of course.'

But it's only a reprieve, a pause. I start to keep, then abandon, a diary.

19 May 1996
Haven't been to see Mum for two weeks. Can't remember why I didn't go last weekend, the weekend is a blank, in fact, apart

from Tricia's party in the evening. I spend about forty-five minutes procrastinating round at Susan's first. Quick journey. Big sign outside advertising a jumble sale from 10 to 2. I've just missed it. Lots of activity but Mum sitting in her chair reading You *magazine. The usual smiles but she grabs my wrist in her bricklayer's grip and tells me to come upstairs. She's angry. We run into Iola by the lift as Mum is beginning to explain something about her newspaper delivery, the paper not coming. With Iola, however, she's sweetness and light, 'Oh no, nothing the matter,' she tells her. 'Why didn't you say anything about the newspaper?' I ask. 'Why should I tell her my business?' she replies.*

Upstairs in her room it's the usual thing. No sign of that plant I bought her at the garden centre, and I'm not going to ask or else she'll start in on how the staff are all stealing from her, that business of them stealing her knickers – she's hiding them in the sleeves of her coat, no wonder she can't find them when she goes looking.

'I hate it, I loathe it, I loathe the Londoners, they're horrible, horrible. If you don't do something I'll take an overdose.'

Today it's Bournemouth that is the lost paradise. She was so happy there, had so many friends, she says. She has had a short letter from Betty from the League which might have set this off, one of those 'Do you remember the lovely times we used to have' letters which fails to admit that these lovely times fell off very sharply as soon as Mum had her heart attack. But now Iola is horrible, two-faced. Everything is horrible.

I give her the Blue Grass gift set I bought her in Edinburgh and she's really thrilled. I thought the scent might come back to her because she used to wear it, years ago. She doesn't recognize it, though she does cry out at the name Elizabeth

Arden. She sprays some on. I remember the scent and want to concentrate on it because it brings back my childhood, but she won't. Nothing is as important as her unhappiness and anger.

She does, however, remember that I've been on TV, without my raising it. Everyone was queuing up to watch, she says. Or were they?

We go out for a walk along Aberdeen Park which is much grander than I had expected with a huge building called the Foreign Mission Club, perhaps a pied-à-terre for missionaries when they are home on leave. I try to explain this to Mum. She really is impressed and views her building from the side for the first time, identifying her room, but like the blustery day itself, she alternatively rages and smiles, sunshine and showers. The houses give out to an odd smart piece of suburbia, inter-war semis with wisteria round the doors and I don't believe I'm in London at all, at least not Highbury. Another time this might have served to reinforce where she is, but though she raves about the neighbourhood, she's still harking on Bournemouth.

To the café in the park for tea and an extraordinary dialogue with a small child holding a pink lolly-ice arrangement. 'Have you got a lolly-ice?' she cries. 'Yes,' the boy replies, pointing at the display, 'it's this.' 'Well, aren't you clever,' Mum says, 'because you've chosen the best one.' She runs over to a pram and the child's exhausted-looking parents. She tells the couple that this is the best time of their lives. 'Is it?' they ask doubtfully. Don't remember her ever being so engaged or engaging with me at that age. We walk back. She's saying something about Dad and his children. I get the impression that he boasted to others about our achievements – going to university – but what he really wanted was for us to get married. Or is that just her talking?

How animated and coherent she is in anger. She invents friends and the conversations they have with each other. 'Come back to Bournemouth,' these imaginary people say. She refers to me as a niece again.

I am getting pissed off. We have been over this same ground so often. 'So what's your answer?' she cries. 'What have you got to say?' There is no answer, I tell her, the tears are part of her 'condition'. She thinks about it but says no, she doesn't believe me.

Back to the home. We go downstairs. She introduces me, once more, to the man who sits reading. He's on M. M. Kaye now. I like him. He has an escape. Then into the TV room to meet her other friend, also male, but asleep. Interesting how it's all the men that she likes, perhaps because they're younger than the women, not able to look after themselves when their wives die, or at least not expected to be able to. Is she flirting with them? Notice how long her hair is, almost to her shoulders, and wonder when she last had it done.

Before I go, she says, 'Forgive me but if I can't cry to my own children, who can I cry to?' Who indeed? I leave, chastened.

If my job is to attempt to maintain weekly visits, then Michele, in Oxford, is left to deal with the finances. These pertain to the matter of Social Security and its complex calculations of how much pension she should be receiving and where it is to be sent; the various bills owing on the flat; the demands by Dorset Social Services that the flat should be sold. Michele's visits are less frequent than mine for she lives further away. She isn't sure if her mother knows exactly who she is any more, an idea I resist. Of course she knows Michele. Or is she just someone she recognizes? Whenever Mum introduces me to anyone now, it is as a niece or a sister, never as a daughter. The niece is Marina, the girl she had grown up with. Reverting to her childhood, she is sloughing off later recollections. As her sisters Miriam and Gertie and Lillian had looked after her when she was the youngest child, so I'm now someone who looks after her. I'm a sister, she reasons, I must be.

What does she retain? She knows that Michele is getting married. She remembers this from visit to visit, but only when I remind her.

At the wedding itself, in her £209 outfit, she tells anyone who will listen, 'It's my niece that's getting married, you know.' Someone remarks that in this she reveals how entirely

233

she has now repudiated the idea of herself as a mother. Except for the odd business of her saccharine sweetness when she sees a child.

She runs up and bends over: 'Hello, hello,' she tinkles in an ickle-baby voice.

I don't think it's that she feels a new sense of maternity that she didn't possess before. I think she relates to children as if she were part of their own tribe, people who have other people looking after them, called parents.

Iola, with whom she had formed a real bond, Iola – who one night came to her room where she was in bed and gave her a goodnight kiss before she left to go home, as my grand-mother and aunts must once have kissed my mother goodnight – has left, gone to become head of a spanking-new place in Finchley. To my mother, who is heartbroken, she is 'selling the business'. Who will the new owners be, she asks.

She wants to go with her. Perhaps she should? We have another meeting with John Bridgewater. He thinks not. He says that the residents of the new home will include far more people with dementia, she'll be worse off than before.

The new head starts, Fionnuala Baiden, from Northern Ireland. My mother likes her too, but Iola has given her the kind of warmth and intimacy that so few people in this life can offer strangers.

While the wedding is a success the aftermath is a disaster. A week later she has forgotten it.

'Don't you remember? The wedding. You were there, and Marina came and Jonathan and Lynne and Sefton.'

'Who are Jonathan, Lynne and Sefton?'

'Oh, never mind.'

'I'm very unhappy here. I want to go back to

Bournemouth. I hate the Londoners, loathe them, they're horrible. I don't know anyone here. I've got nothing, I'm a nobody.'

A nobody. It's true. With her own past ripped away from her, and not just in her own mind, who is she? Who are any of us without a history? Buddhists long to move into a state beyond time, they want to rest in the moment. My mother has achieved this without any of the meditation and what state of transcendental bliss has it brought her?

At the wedding she was a somebody again, people knew who she was. She's forgotten the event itself, but the memory lingers of a single day in which she felt herself to be whole, an actor in a wider world. Then they all went away and she was brought back here, to her anonymity, to being Rose, from Liverpool, whom no one knows or remembers as a child or teenager or young mother. She's only Rose, who repeats herself, who has a daughter who comes in and takes her away for a few hours. That's another kind of prison we've put her in, not just the one with locked doors.

But she is so angry, so aggressive – she took me by the shoulders and pushed me out of her room, once, when I told her I didn't have time to take her out. I want something to be done. What Michele and I are after is a chemical solution. How about Prozac, the happy drug?

At this time, also, we need power of attorney. Consulting a solicitor, we find that this can only be obtained if she is judged by a doctor to be sufficiently *compos mentis* to be able voluntarily to grant it. If not, the care will have to be referred to the Court of Protection.

I make an appointment with the home's GP.

Just before the meeting I say: 'Now Mum, we want to get

power of attorney over your affairs so you won't have to worry about your finances any more.'

'Yes,' she says.

'For example, one of the things Michele is dealing with at the moment is Dorset Social Services who want us to sell your flat so we can pay back the money we owe them. But we don't want to sell just now because house prices are going up and anyway, there's a move by the residents to buy out the freehold on the whole building and that would add some value to your flat.'

'Oh, I'm past dealing with all that,' she says. 'You handle it.'

'That's just it, so we can, we have to have power of attorney and we're about to go down and have a meeting with the doctor to discuss it.'

In the office, the GP, an energetic, intelligent young woman, takes my mother through a set of standard questions they always give sufferers of dementia.

'Do you know what the date is?'

'No.'

'Do you know what day of the week it is?'

'No.'

'Do you know the name of the Leader of the Opposition?'

'No.'

'Do you know the name of the Prime Minister?'

'No.'

'Do you know the name of this place where you live?'

'No.'

'Do you know where it is?'

'No.'

Oh shit, I think, this is surely going to have to go to the Court of Protection.

'Do you know how to make a cup of tea?'

'Do you mean with tea bags or a strainer?'

'Your daughters want to have power of attorney over your affairs. That means you wouldn't have control any more. What do you think of that?'

'Well, I think it's a good idea,' my mother says, 'because someone wants to sell my flat and we don't want to because the house prices are going up and we'll get more for it. And we want to buy out the freehold, so that will make it worth more as well. I can't handle all that. I totally trust my daughters, they'll look after me.'

'I think your mother is *compos mentis* in her own way,' the GP says to me. 'Don't you?'

After the meeting we have a talk about her aggression. 'That's the emotional incontinence,' she says. 'It's a standard aspect of Multi-Infarct Dementia.'

'Isn't there any medication she could take?'

'I could consider one of the sisters of Prozac.'

'*One of the what?*'

'The sisters of Prozac. Not Prozac itself, but a drug in that family.'

And so she is prescribed something and it seems to work. The rages stop for a time. The Prozac Sisters and the Grant Sisters are the best of friends.

Why was it that my mother did not know where she was or what day it was or who the Prime Minister was, when she was able to recall the conversation I had had with her earlier, which contained what to many would be complex issues concerning property?

I concluded that she simply did not need the information about the date and place – why should she? She had no appointments. She never had to find her way back there. As for the name of the Prime Minister, what bearing did the government's disputes over entry into the European Exchange Rate Mechanism have on her chair and her place at the lunch table and her excursions to Marks and Spencer's? None.

With only so much room in her memory, she jettisoned anything she didn't need in order to retain what she considered to be important. Mention doctors or lawyers and her old immigrant's brain went on full alert. The authorities. You had to deal with them. You had to give them the right answer or who knows what ugly decisions they might make, not in your favour?

13 October 1996

The Sarah Tankel Gala Fête. One of the few jumble sales in the world with a police presence in case of terrorist attack. A swarm of grey-clad Chinese nuns attend, also some sharp-eyed, rapacious pensioners, not Jewish. One wins on the raffle and is offered a choice of the collection of supermarket wines. What's this? she asks, picking up a bottle of Calvados. It's spirits, the organizer says. Very strong. I'll have it then, she replies. The prizes are: a Goodman's hi-fi, won by someone in St John's Wood, to the meagre and disgruntled applause of the poorer folk of Finsbury Park; a three-hour taxi tour of London – sounds like hell; and a Teasmade.

Mum has now been on a sister of Prozac for two weeks. They have cut the dose in half because she has become 'very quiet', Fionnuala says. Not with me, she isn't. She chatters and jabbers. Far from being more confused, she is more alert. She seems able to follow, from visit to visit, the saga of my kitchen and bathroom being done up and even offers some quite useful advice on the purchase of a new cooker. We're back in territory she understands.

239

Back in the home she says, 'I loathe this,' as we sit amongst her fellow-inmates. 'They're waiting to die. Some of them are wrong in the head. I was frightened of them when I first came but then I got used to it.'

Go in to see Fionnuala. Realize I haven't taken in a word she's saying having noticed a video-tape on her shelf called Sex and Alzheimer's. 'What's that about?' She starts to tell me stories that make my jaw drop – finding roll-on deodorants inside the bed, even inside incontinence pants. I am completely baffled. 'What are they there for?' Masturbation, apparently. Sex, she says, is the last instinct to go.

February 1997

Back from New York with the picture frame Barbara's mother gave me. What to do with it? Give it to Mum, that would be ideal. Hand it to her, wrapped up in its bag from a gift shop on Madison Avenue. Opens it, she's thrilled, perhaps even more so with the bag, like a toddler who spends Christmas Day playing with the wrappings of her present.

'It's gorgeous, it's gorgeous, where did you get it? I'm going to put it here.' She removes from its place a picture which I bought her and Dad for their twenty-fifth wedding anniversary. It had hung on the wall in the house in Liverpool and the flat in Bournemouth. She takes this picture and walks across to the other side of the room with it, props it up on a chest of drawers. 'It's gorgeous,' she says, 'Where did you get it? I've never had anything so nice before.' In a matter of seconds she has forgotten the existence of the new picture frame and

has transferred the idea in her head that she has some-
thing new to the picture she's lived with since 1971.
That means her short-term memory is now only seconds
long.

April 1997. My cousin Stewart, the London taxi driver, rings to invite my mother and me to a Seder night – the meal of the Passover, what Christians know as Christ's Last Supper. For us Jews it is the most political of all our festivals, when we remember how we were slaves in the land of Egypt and how the Pharaoh slaughtered the first-born, except for Moses who led us out of our exile across the Red Sea, whose waters God parted for us before our wandering in the wilderness for forty years. We eat symbolic foods: spring onions representing bitter herbs – the bitterness of our hearts as we sang in our chains; boiled eggs in salt water are our hardships and our tears; a mess of cinnamon and nuts and honey is the mortar we used to bind together the bricks of the Pyramids. The Seders of my teens were during the civil rights years and the arrest of Nelson Mandela and the Six Day War, so my father never lost the opportunity to deliver a declamatory speech about the world's evils.

'Your nephew Stewart has invited us for Seder night,' I say, as she sits on her little bed after the usual 'Any news?'

She leaps across the room like an elderly fairy and claps her hands. 'Eeeee,' she cries. Then, 'Who's Stewart, if you don't mind me asking?'

'He's Marina's brother.'

'He's Marina's brother,' she repeats.

'You remember your older brother Abe, who went to live in London?'

'Ye-es,' she replies but she doubts it.

'And remember how his first wife, Marina's mother, died and he remarried?'

'He remarried.'

'And his second wife was a Holocaust survivor? And she had two children, Stewart and Lorna.'

'Stewart and Lorna, Stewart and Lorna. He was my favourite.' She has said this about Sefton, favourite now seems to be an attribute of nephews. 'And I was his favourite aunt.' Somehow, I doubt this. 'I haven't seen him since he was a little boy, you know.'

'Of course you have. You saw him at Nathan's funeral.'

'Who's Nathan?'

'Marina's husband.'

'Marina had a husband called Nathan. No. Blank. Have I told you I've been diagnosed with a memory loss?'

'Yes, you have. Anyway, as I was saying, Stewart has invited us for Seder night.'

'Who's Stewart?'

'Marina's brother.'

'Marina has a brother called Stewart.'

'Yes, whose mother Betty was in Auschwitz.'

'That's right. And where does Stewart live?'

'Redbridge.'

'Where's that?'

'North London, well, Essex really.'

'Oh! Who lives in Redbridge?'

' Stewart.'

'And who's Stewart, again?'

So this goes on for some time longer, as she puts on her coat and changes out of her slippers into her shoes and we descend in the lift and she reminds me, as ever, 'Have you told the office we're going out? Because they won't allow me out on my own, you know.' And we're still engaged in the circles of conversation that get smaller and tighter until they are like a noose round our necks as we oscillate between who is Stewart and where is Redbridge.

We get off the bus at Muswell Hill Broadway and when my mother sees the shops and all the bustling, social life of the streets she stops up short, takes her handbag from her shoulder and gets out her lipstick. I reach into my own bag and give her a powder compact for its mirror. So she stands in a tiny moment of sanity and awareness, applying her Christian Dior lipstick, the one my sister had bought her for the wedding, looking at her reflection in my Clinique mirror. She's an elderly girl or even, as the day wears on, an old, old four-year-old, but with cosmetics in her hands she is, for a few seconds, a woman again.

We pass a shoe shop where the new, square-toed shoes are in the window. 'I prefer square toes,' she says. 'There's more room for the feet. I wouldn't go back to points now.'

We enter Marks and Spencer's where I buy a packet of fishcakes and some broccoli. She looks at everything but I don't think she knows any more what it is she sees. From moment to moment the whole world seems to change for her. Almost anything causes her immense delight.

'Look at that beautiful bus shelter,' she exclaims.

And 'I love looking at that tree.' She points down the road. I can't see a tree.

'Where?'

'That tree that goes up.'

At the end of the road there's a church and its spire.

'Do you mean the spire of the church?'

'That's the word, the spire.' Trees, spires, both things that go up.

She's talking a long inconsequential stream of nonsense, of phrases begun but not remembered past the first few words, in which Stewart and Betty appear in incongruous contexts, helping her bathe or being her old schoolfriend. Every few moments there's a question and my own monologue is no less uncommunicative. 'Yes. No. That's right. Yes, yes. No, I don't. Probably.' I know how these curt replies wound her, I can see it in her face. What a cow, people must think when they overhear us. I see them looking at me. You don't know the half of it, I want to say. You don't know you're born if you've never had to put up with this.

We walk down the hill and over the little graffiti-covered bridge that leads into the park of Alexandra Palace. 'Ooh, this is beautiful,' my mother says as we push through the desolate crisp packets and crushed cans of Tango.

It's an unusually early spring, the sun is warm on our faces and the trees already clothed in a modish green. Cherry blossoms hang as heavy as fruit from the branches. My mother tells me she has never seen a cherry tree before. The long avenue off which our road in Liverpool led was lined with flowering cherries.

'I'd love to come here on a summer's day when the leaves are on the trees,' she says.

We walk past a man rocking his child in a pushchair, couples coupling on the grass, a ragged football match interrupted by one of the players getting a call on his mobile phone. 'Tell her you're playing football,' his team-members shout.

We continue on the path down through the trees to the road.

'Oh, no,' my mother says, grimacing. 'Oh, dear.'

'What's wrong?'

'This road is full of clocks.'

'Clocks?'

'Yes, clocks that take you home.'

'Do you mean buses?'

'That's it. I meant buses.'

Clocks do take us home, of course. Ticking away to our deaths.

We go to the garden centre for a cup of tea. When I return to the table, I notice there's something in her mouth. 'What are you eating, Mum?'

'Lovely sweet.'

'Where did you get that?' She points at a bowl with sugar cubes in it.

At the next table two men are in conversation, perhaps a father-in-law and son-in-law, for the younger man is talking about his own father.

'It can't go on much longer,' he says. 'He's going to have to go into a home, he can't live by himself. Do you know what he's started to do now? He's feeding all the stray cats on the street. Feeding cats! My father! When we lived on the farm he hated animals, always told us not to go near them. Now he's feeding cats.'

On the bus on the way back she suddenly says, 'When is Stewart calling for us?'

I mean to write all this down as soon as I get home because I feel that it has been a momentous day, that she is now definitely worse, another step down the stair, another branch lopped from the tree. Instead I take off my coat and pour a glass of whisky from a small bottle I have had for a year because I don't much like those brown drinks. I can't wait for the ceremony of the corkscrew which wine, so healthy for the vascular system, such a warder-off of silent strokes, would involve.

I did not take her to Redbridge. She was wandering now in her own wilderness. How lonely it was in that desolate place with only death as the Promised Land.

Time goes on without her. Great events more or less pass her by, first the General Election then something altogether more momentous. I go to pick her up for our Sunday expedition. I say, 'Did you watch Princess Diana's funeral yesterday?'

We're standing at the bus-stop. I watch her face. She is floating about in the deep emptiness of her mind to try to find something. Out of the corner of her eye she catches sight of a recollection and reaches out for it.

'Yes. We all watched it together, they put all the chairs out and the helpers watched it too.'

'It's sad, isn't it?'

'Why?'

'Those two boys.'

'Oh yes, that's right, she's got children, hasn't she?'

I've bought a small, cheap bunch of freesias for I think she might like to go to Kensington Palace to do what so many tens of thousands of others have done already, lay flowers at the gates, the millions and millions of blooms that scent the air, the children's teddies, the boy's football shirt nailed to a tree with messages from all his family. I hope that an event of such magnitude will bring her back to the world, make her feel part if it.

Knightsbridge is chock-a-bloc. It will take an age to struggle down to the Palace. I decide that we can lay the flowers in front of the window of Harrods instead, where the twin photographs of Diana and Dodi al Fayed, framed by white lilies, make a tableau for an enormous crowd up in London for the weekend, for the funeral. I think it's nice for my mother that for once a department store has become a proper shrine.

She puts the flowers down and we read some of the cards and messages, me hanging on to her arm like grim death so she isn't swallowed up in the crowd.

Then we walk up to Harvey Nichols for a cup of tea.

'Those poor boys,' she says. 'Left without a mother.'

'I know, it's awful isn't it?'

'Do you think she'll remarry?'

'She's dead.'

'That's right. I saw her sons walk behind the coffin. Terrible. Do you think she'll remarry?'

It's November 1997. Ben reaches thirteen years of age and religious law demands that he will go through the ordeal of the bar-mitzvah – reading in front of an assembled congregation of relatives, friends and strangers a portion of the Torah *in Hebrew*, a language which he has so far shown no inclination to master; at the end of which there will be a sit-down lunch at a restaurant for seventy and he will be a man, daubed in hair gel and CK One, his feet aching to be out of their leather prisons and into trainers. Eighty years before, in 1917, the year of the Russian Revolution, his grandfather went through the same ritual. And his great-grandfather 110 years ago in 1887, the time of the Tsar.

Neither of these events can have entailed such a nightmare

in the compilation of the guest list, for while Michele and I are determined that it is to be a family affair, a reuniting of the Hafts and the Ginsbergs, over the years my mother has managed to fall out with so many of them that few remain who do not incur blinding rages when their names are mentioned: 'That bitch? You haven't invited her, have you? I'm not coming if she's invited.'

My cousin Joy, who lives in Birmingham, alone has managed to live up to her name and to pass sixty-odd years without once having caused my mother a moment's offence, evidence of a nature so sweet that if we were Catholics we would apply immediately for her canonization. But even Joy, unbeknownst to her, is capable of inspiring in my mother a sudden frisson of temper, for the lapses in her memory cause her to imagine a whole new set of slights.

'Is Joy married yet?'

'Of course she is.'

'The bitch. She never even invited me to the wedding.'

'Yes she did.'

'Well, I don't remember.'

'I'm not surprised, she must have got married forty years ago.'

'Forty years! But she's still a teenager.'

'No she isn't. She must be around sixty.'

'Don't give me that baloney. She's just a girl.'

'Now look here, do you agree that Joy is older than me?'

'Yes, years older.'

'Well I'm forty-six, so how could she be a teenager?'

There is a silence. She glimpses, for a moment, the extent of her confusion.

'That's right. She must be about sixty. And she got

249

married years ago and never invited me to the wedding.'

'Yes she did. I've seen pictures of you and Dad in the wedding photos.'

Her silence now is angry. She believes that she is being lied to, humoured. I'm one of her enemies. She knows what I say is nonsense for it does not tally with her own recollections and increasingly now, she is forgetting what she used to remember, that she has 'a memory loss'.

This conversation takes place in the taxi on our way to Temple Fortune in north London where we are going to buy Ben a *tallis* and *yarmulke*, the prayer shawl and skull cap he must wear in worship, now that he is to be a man. I remember my father's, kept in a maroon velvet bag in a safe place – the cupboard next to the television. I remember the men walking along our road to the synagogue on high days and holidays, each with their velvet bag, so sensuous and feminine a fabric for those hard-bitten yet sentimental old Jews, with their tumblers of whisky and suits covered with cigar ash.

When I arrive at the home, I tell my mother to put her coat on, for winter has come early, frost is on the trees in the park, it's cold and I'm wearing myself a Max Mara coat, which my mother recognizes at once as brand-new and extremely expensive.

'However much you paid for it, and it must have cost a fortune by the look of it, it was worth every penny,' she says. Everything dwindles but this, her fashion sense.

She comes back down from her room without her own coat, having forgotten what it was I sent her up for.

'Where's your coat?'

'I don't need it, it's not cold,' she says. It isn't, in the home, which keeps its heating cranked up all year round.

'It is. Go upstairs and get a coat.'

'You'll feel the cold later,' Fionnuala says.

She stamps her foot. 'I'm not going if you make me wear a coat.'

'Okay.'

Seeing the growing gap between her own sense of reality and that of other people, she trusts her own instincts.

Now, in the taxi, she shivers. 'Why is it cold?' she asks me.

We find a Jewish bookshop and go inside. It sells all kinds of Jewish paraphernalia: *menorahs*, the eight-branched candlesticks used for Chanukah; Shabbos candle-sticks, lit by women on Friday nights at the setting of the sun; silver goblets over which men say the blessing for wine; the special silver cup we fill and place on the table at the Passover service, leaving the front door open so that the Prophet Elijah – or the Angel Gabriel, depending on which family you grew up in and to which legend they subscribed – could pass invisibly into the house and sip from the cup and we excited children believed our father when he cried: 'Look! The level in the cup is lower. Elijah has come.'

At the far end on the wall are mounted glass-fronted drawers, like in an old-fashioned draper's. Folded inside them are white woollen *tallit*, each with twelve fringes. There are two types of *tallis*, the old-fashioned kind worn by my grandfather, indeed brought with him from Poland, voluminous, black striped items in which the wearer was virtually wrapped from head to foot. Oddly, these have come back into fashion having been supplanted, from the 1950s, by a smaller, scarf-like number, striped blue, possibly to represent the colours of the Israeli flag, and cooler in the heat of our new country.

I choose a blue, scarf-sized *tallis* for Ben, and a blue velvet *yarmulke* and a blue velvet bag embroidered in silver to keep them in. If he manages not to lose it, he will have this *tallis* for the whole of his life. He will wear it at his mother's funeral. And at the bar-mitzvah of his own son, if his desire to pay lip service to the traditions of our family survives into the new millennium. Reborn for the twentieth century, who will we be in the next? I don't know. It is not a question for me to have the answer to for I am, like my parents, this century's child.

After handing over £49, we leave the shop and over the road I notice a sign announcing in orange neon the presence of Hot Salt Beef within. The restaurant is called the Catskills. We go in, sit down and order matzos, pickled cucumber, salt beef and latkes for me, Vienna sausages and chips for my mother, which we finish with glasses of lemon tea. I like it in there. A fat man in shirt-sleeves marches up and down inspecting the food on the tables, though whether he is affirming that people have the right order or checking to ensure that they have left not a morsel behind, in contravention of the First Convention of Jewish Dietary Laws – thou shalt eat too much – I don't know.

The woman owner comes over to our table and asks us if we enjoyed our meal. We have, very much. 'Come back,' she tells us. We will. She asks where we are from. I tell her that originally we lived in Liverpool. 'I had an aunt who married a Northerner,' she says. And mentions a name. 'Do you know her?'

My mother says, 'She ran a chip shop.'

'That's right,' the woman says.

Outside, my mother shivers in the cold air. 'I'm freezing,' she says. 'Why is it so cold?'

'I told you to put your coat on but you wouldn't listen. You said, "I'm not coming if I've got to wear a coat." '

'I wish my mother was still alive. She would have *made* me put my coat on.'

On the bus, we return to the difficult matter of the guest list. I tell her that a couple of her old friends from Liverpool have been invited. She does not recognize the name of one of them, whom she has known since she was a child. The other, she does.

'I'm glad Maime is coming. Because I'm going to tell her I want to go to Liverpool and she's going to take me back with her and look after me.'

There is nothing at all to say to this. I remain silent.

'Is there any reason why you don't seem to care whether or not I'm happy?' she asks, in a calm, accusing voice.

The bus stops. Passengers get off and new ones get on. 'I like the colour of that woman's coat,' I say. 'What do you think?'

Then we are into a discussion of coats and the moment has passed, forgotten. The rest of the journey home is confined to the elimination of all the relatives invited to the bar-mitzvah, the presence of any one of whom will prevent her from attending. '*That* bitch. If she's coming I'm . . .'

Talking to Fionnuala later, about the coat, I tell her how she'd complained about the cold.

'What that was about was loss of face. She'd gone upstairs to put her coat on and had forgotten it, so when you said to her, "You've forgotten your coat," she had to brazen it out, saying she didn't need a coat. You'd reminded her about her short-term memory.'

'So I should have just pretended that she hadn't been up there to get a coat at all?'

I'm beginning to think that these people who surround my mother every day know what they're talking about.

★

A couple of friends, Fran and Graham, have agreed to drive me and my mother to Oxford early on the Saturday morning, for there is no possibility that she can go the night before and sleep in a strange bedroom after all this time. I have arranged: that the navy suit bought for the wedding is sent to the dry cleaners and its drooping hem mended; that her hair is shampooed and set the day before and combed out in the morning; that her nails are polished; that her Christian Dior lipstick is applied; that she be given a Valium or something to keep her from falling into rages, but this request is ignored.

Fran and Graham arrive at my house half an hour early. 'I had a dream on Thursday night,' Fran says, 'that I arrived at the bar-mitzvah and I realized that I'd forgotten to pick up you and your mother and I was sneaking around trying to avoid Michele because I thought she'd never speak to me again.'

'She never would speak to you again,' I tell her.

'No, I wouldn't,' Michele says, when I recount this story later.

When we arrive my mother is upstairs on the second floor, the Alzheimer's Unit, having her hair-do touched up.

'Go up,' a care worker suggests.

I get out of the lift into that locked world. The doors to the stairs won't open, the lift buttons can only be operated by a key. I glimpse into a long room full of people being fed with spoons. I look quickly away.

Along the corridor there is a mini hairdressing salon with sink and hairdryer. My mother's head is bent as a member of staff entwines her fine grey hair round curlers. 'She's not ready yet,' the woman advises me.

'Hi, Mum,' I say. 'I'm here.'

But she doesn't reply. Because she can't see me, she doesn't register my presence. She seems to rely heavily on visual recognition. Normally, if more than one person was talking, she'd say, 'What? What's that? What are you saying? Don't leave me out.' But I think that was an aspect of paranoia rather than keen hearing, her brain intent on protecting itself by zeroing in on information it thought it might need, making a sweep of the surrounding area. But here, lulled by careful hands about her head, she feels safe. So she ignores any noises there might be in the room.

I go back downstairs and we sit in the lobby waiting. There's a board detailing the week's activities. For example, there's touch therapy, which involves someone bringing in a dog for the residents to pat. I assume my mother stays in her room for that session. Michele and I have learned from her to flinch when a dog comes near us, baring its fangs in a red, dripping, hairy mouth. Yuck.

'Apparently she takes part in the quiz nights,' I say.

'WHAT?'

'I know, I know. Beats me, too.'

She emerges ten minutes later, looking young and exquisite. 'Doesn't your mother look *well*,' Fran says, a remark that would be repeated by many others during the course of the afternoon.

We bowl along the M4 in bright sunshine, the autumn leaves showing all the glory of tree trauma touched by early frost.

'Would we like some soothing music, do you think?' Fran asks.

'What a good idea.'

So she puts on Classic FM and soon my mother is

humming and smiling. We drive over Magdalen Bridge on to the High but she doesn't recognize it.

'I've never been to Oxford in my life,' she says.

We've made good time, only a few guests have arrived. A woman in a purple suit looks uncertainly at me. It's my cousin Joy whom I haven't seen since I was a teenager, together with her husband Bunny – 'How do you get a name like Bunny?' I ask him.

'It was Bernard, then Bernie, and to a Yiddisher grand-mother it's Bunny,' he tells me. His father, who wasn't Jewish, ran boxing gyms around the time of the First World War, when there were any number of prominent Jewish boxers. He married the sister of one of the kids who came there and converted to Judaism. Bunny himself, after serving in the Navy during the Second World War, worked all his life in the film distribution business until he retired. Shaina can't make it, Joy tells us, she's ill. I'm sorry not to see her but a major scene has been avoided. Also my mother's two old friends from Liverpool, Maime and Gertie, have not been able to attend and why should they, at their age? Oxford is a long way away. But my mother doesn't remem-ber that they were supposed to be coming, anyway, so she doesn't miss them.

And here's Nopov, who at thirty-eight I still can't help thinking of as snotty-nosed little Dave Kaye, the kid who years ago hung around our house playing with Michele after school. Later, he got rid of his father's anglicized name and reverted to the original one. Nopov has put on weight since I saw him last but it suits him. With his slicked-back black hair and olive skin, he used to look like a Californian rock star, but now he bears a closer resemblance to a Mafia boss.

Give him a double-breasted suit and a Homburg hat and he could have been inserted with ease into that photo of the Ginsbergs taken in 1950 in my Auntie Tilly's garden.

Nopov knows my mother of old and goes to speak to her. 'It's like trying to tune in Channel Five,' he says when he comes back. 'And when you do find it, all you get is repeats.'

Having told me over and over again what a lovely person Joy is, confronted with her actual presence, she's saying, 'Joy? Joy? Who are you again? You're whose daughter? Who's Gertie?'

My cousin Marina arrives with her son Jonathan and daughter-in-law Lynne. Her brother Stewart, Auntie Betty's son, arrives. That's it for relatives, the Hafts and the Ginsbergs are each represented. The rest of the hall fills with old friends of Michele and Mark, Mark's mother and his two brothers, a few people from the media, journalists and producers and executives.

Despite a large, shifting population of Jewish academics and students, the permanent synagogue-attending numbers are too small to sustain more than one congregation, so the Orthodox United Synagogue lot – the denomination I was brought up in – have to share the building with the Liberals, the most radical arm of modern Judaism, the hall being screened off into two halves. Ben is to be bar-mitzvahed in a Liberal service and has spent several months of study with his Hebrew teacher, Tony, who isn't a rabbi but will lead the service. Tony has said to Michele that she can pretty well design it herself, so as well as reading aloud in Hebrew his portion – from the Torah, which is the Five Books of Moses, from Genesis to Deuteronomy – Ben is to give a short talk on social responsibility, based on discussions he and Tony have had about why so few Gentiles helped Jews during the

Holocaust and the lessons that we ought to learn from this. I am to read from the Haftarah, which is a passage from the Prophets designated to accompany the Torah portion. Michele will read the Covenant, the promise God made to the Jews anointing us as the Chosen People which the Liberal text finds embarrassingly unegalitarian and attempts to tone down – tricky this, because nothing could be more clearly spelt out in black and white in the original, it being a founding tenet of the faith, so that jettisoning it is rather like Christians dumping the Resurrection. Finally Michele will read a later extract discussing the relationship between parents and children.

But in the most ground-breaking departure of them all – topping even the participation of we two women in the service – Mark and John, Michele's husband, are together to remove the sacred scrolls from the *aron kodesh*, the ark in which they are kept, remove the silver caps from the wooden columns around which the sacred word is wrapped, undress it from its velvet robes embroidered with sacred text, bring it to the *bimah* – the raised platform on which the activities of the service take place – and, in Mark's case, raise it aloft for everyone to see this Torah, the books which are what, in the end, make us Jews, not Christians.

Mark and John are terrified that they'll drop it and that it will fall to the floor or rip in two. I discover in myself an ancient, atavistic reaction. I don't want these two *goys* handling what isn't rightfully theirs, let alone that triumphant gesture in which we show what it is that is ours, what we think God gave us, what makes us different. It's not that I actually believe any of this ancient mumbo-jumbo. I know there's no supernatural being out there who could care less about whether or not we eat pork or whether we resist the

coveting of our neighbour's ox. But as I think back to my
father and my grandfather and my great-grandfather each in
his turn holding up the scrolls, my heart says, 'This is about
us, not about you.' It isn't rational but that's what I feel.

The family members who are to participate sit in one
row, at the side. My mother and the rest of the Hafts sit
behind. The service goes well, it goes swimmingly. Ben is
dressed in cream Versace jeans, a small checked jacket,
slightly too big, bought a few days before, a pale lilac shirt
and two-tone purple tie: the whole ensemble finished off
with Kickers, *tallis* and *yarmulke*. He holds the silver pointer
and moves it from right to left along the dense, square letters
of the text.

Michele and I sit together willing him not to make a mistake. We've spent thirteen years waiting for this.

At this precise moment, the most important in the service,
the one at which Ben marks his passage from childhood to
manhood and re-enacts the Covenant made back in Biblical
time between God and the Jews, made for all future generations so that time fast-forwards and backwards like a film
shown at dazzling speed – I hear a whispered argument in
the row behind: '*Disgusting*. I've a good mind to get up and
walk out and show them what I think.'

'Oh, live and let live.'

'So you condone it? How *dare* you?'

This is the business of the Gentiles and the Torah that she's
objecting to. She has managed to spoil the moment for her
daughters. What else is new?

I talk to Marina for a few minutes.

'You remember Mum when she was young,' I say. 'What
was she like?'

'Oh, I was so naïve, I thought she was wonderful. She was spoilt rotten, being the youngest. She had things nobody else had. You'd go out shopping with her and she'd say, "No, don't get that, get this," and I'd listen to her. After I got married and I had two little children, she'd ring me up and say, "Come and meet me in town," and I'd tell her I couldn't, I was busy. But she wouldn't take no for an answer. And the things she made me say to Auntie Miriam! I wish she was alive now, so I could apologize. It was like she put a gun in my hands. But I'm not like that any more. I've grown up. I'm not naïve any more.'

John drives my mother back to London and I accompany them, in case she forgets who he is and is frightened. She falls asleep almost at once and only wakes up five minutes from home. 'Are we there yet?' she asks.

She walks groggily from the car into the building, hardly aware of our presence. She does not say goodbye or thank us for the lift or kiss me on the cheek or talk about the lovely occasion. It must be odd to fall asleep in Oxford and wake up again back in prison. Besides, it's been a long, long day.

'She's like a shell,' Michele had said a couple of weeks earlier. 'With bits of her rattling around inside.'

John and I return to Oxford. Joy and Bunny are there for dinner. We reminisce about the Ginsbergs, mentioning matters I have had to draw a veil over here, for fear of offending the living or the memories of the beloved dead: 'Came home from work and found her husband in bed with another man . . . a baby by an American GI but he never came back for her because he was married, of course, and she insisted on having it so they sent her away to . . . no, they'd got over the trouble with income tax by then . . . was it embezzlement? I know he was in Israel on the run . . .'

Ben is falling asleep at the table. It has been a long thirteen years for him. His head droops, jerking up in surprise when he hears the business about the homosexual husband. But then he goes and lies down on the sofa and perhaps one day he too will say, 'When I was a child they used to talk about our family but I didn't listen. I didn't ask. I thought it was boring. Who cared about those dead old people when it was 1997, Oasis was in the charts and I fancied Posh Spice? It's too late now. I left it too late to ask.'

After my mother has been in the home for over a year I go to see John Bridgewater. Her days of rage have died down since the summer and the sisters of Prozac have done their quiet chemical magic. When I return with her from our afternoons out she would smile grimly as we entered, turn, look at the comatose figures around her and say, 'Back to the dungeon.' This is as settled as she's going to be. Fionnuala has her sorted: 'Your mother is a snob,' she tells me. 'She would be best off if she was somewhere where there were other people she could compete with over having the nicest clothes and the most successful children but unfortunately there isn't anyone else like that here, they're all a bit more down to earth. It's a characteristic of people with Multi-Infarct Dementia that they try to cover up their difficulties but that passes after a time. Your mother has kept it up longer than most. Were appearances important to her earlier in her life?'

The headquarters of Jewish Care are in Golders Green. There's an Iraqi–Jewish falafel bar over the road where I go for a quick ethnic bite before our meeting. Golders Green is an alien world, full of the dutiful Jewish daughters my mother had never been, who still shaved their heads and wore wigs in ritual observance. The children as white as

sheets from too much study. There's a small pub and it's difficult to imagine who its clientele might be. I feel like an
anti-Semite among such concentrated Hasidism. And they
look at me, not registering me as Jewish, which according to
their stringent application of the Torah, I'm not, even with
a kosher falafel inside me.

I feel more at home in John Bridgewater's office, more
English than Jewish. We share a common language, common
intellectual references. His boozer's nose seems to direct itself
down the pub to cigarette smoke and pints and women with
too-short skirts.

I tell him how things have been over the past few months,
how, all over the autumn, my mother and I have sustained a
kind of relationship over the saga of the kitchen. How could
she be all that bad, I say, for when she sees me she recognizes
me?

'I thought your mother was not typical in that she presented so well, which masked a lot of her difficulties. There
are certain areas of her that are well intact. But I suspect that
her memory is much worse than you allow. Are you quite
clear that she does know who you are? There's no possibility that she confuses you with her sister? How do you know
she recognizes you?'

'Well, when I appear I'm someone she recognizes.'

'That's different. You say she recognizes you, then when I
challenge you you say she recognizes me as someone she
knows, and there's a whole big difference between the two.'

'Yes, it's true that she refers to me as her niece, her daughter or her sister. But is it the word that she has the problem
with?'

'It might be, but you may be a composite of all of those
people.'

'She knows I'm not the one who has the son.'

'Your mother's grossly demented, there's no doubt about that, the software in the computer is all muddled up and sometimes she might be able to put it together, other times she might not. But in the here and now the main thing for her is getting through the day, that piece of time, without feeling bad, without feeling anxious or distressed in any way. If she's uncomfortable and really can't figure out what's happening then that's a problem. If you give her reference points like a kitchen it doesn't matter whether she can remember the conversation or not.

'You make assumptions about her all the time because without them we can't get through the day. We can't keep checking out with people all the time that this or that is true. You asked me earlier if I had read a book and I nodded, I hadn't but I did that to move it on and I think that demented people at every level are doing that sort of thing all the time.'

'It doesn't help with my feeling that I've abandoned her to the wolves,' I say. I tell him how I pass on the bus and see her sitting, staring out at freedom or perhaps at nothing.

'Look, if I take your mother out and stick her in the middle of Leyton High Road she will disintegrate in front of our eyes because she won't be able to cope, so we put something around her that enables her to function in the here and now and why should you try and hang on to her when you're at work and she's in that place, provided you've checked out that we're not beating her or starving her? If your mother was a tightrope-walker all her life and had had one leg amputated, would you allow her to carry on as a tightrope-walker? No one in their right mind would. So to allow her to be left on the wire would be to subject her to obscene cruelty because she would be up there terrified, alone and anxious.'

264

'Yes, but' (and this is to be very much a conversation of yes buts, which psychotherapists, I believe, call denial), 'because of the way she presents herself she cons me into thinking she can do more than she can. And I have absolute power over her which is all very well for a child but not for a grown adult.'

'Why do you not see it in terms of love rather than respect and control? You don't allow a two-year-old to fall because you love it.'

But do I love my mother? This is not something I am going to discuss with John Bridgewater. I will collude in the public convention that children love their parents and none more reservedly so than when they are cast into the role of 'carer'. But at least it's true that I care what happens to her.

I tell him about the conversations we had when she told me she wanted to go back to Bournemouth. 'I now know that the way she behaves, the crying, for example, is a product of chemical changes which are taking place in her brain, but if she tells me she's unhappy, am I to tell her that the emotion is somehow not real? Am I talking to a person or a set of symptoms? As a human being doesn't she deserve recognition for her emotional state even though it is induced by mental deterioration? She requires that I respond to her as an adult. I can try to talk her out of this Bournemouth business or I can ignore it, which she won't allow. Where does that leave me?'

'One alternative is to confront her with the reality, the other is to ignore it. But there is a middle way. Think of a girl rabbiting on about some boyfriend and it's all going to be different this time and you know it's always going to end up like this. So because you want to get through the evening without arguments, you're not going to confront her with reality, or your sense of what reality is, but neither are you going to totally ignore it, so you've got to engage with it in some way which isn't upsetting for her or you.

'It's like listening to adolescent daughters with all their gumph and they're going to chew you out, but you know there's light at the end of the tunnel because you live for that day when they're going to see things differently. The distressing thing about dementia is that there isn't that light at the end of the tunnel and you're stuck at that point. I've got a daughter of twenty-four who was obnoxious for a long time, so self-opinionated. Now it's as if some calm adult has come out of that and she's a different person. If I were to be demented we wouldn't be able to continue our journey because we wouldn't be able to resolve it. *You* can't resolve those issues. You can't resolve the past and you can't resolve the future.'

'When I see her asleep in the chair perhaps I should accept that that's where she needs to be, at some kind of ease. But that's not what I see in her face, I see only misery.'

'Is there anything you can do to change that? There probably isn't. What you're dealing with is the rhetoric of distress. The probability is that when you're not there she's not quite as acutely in touch with that distress because it's her encounter with you that triggers it. So you're stuck with that.'

'I just don't know what's going on in her head.'

'She will forget her good experiences and she will forget her bad experiences. What she will have is a feeling and our job is to try and make a situation in which she's got more good feelings than bad because you can't hold on to two contradictory feelings at the same time. You could wreck your life, you could move in with her, move into the next room, doing everything a dutiful daughter should. But it still won't hold her in the night. You have to trust that it's not that terrible. You have to let her go – when you let a five-year-old child go in the playground you identify with that distress but in the end you have to let it go. What else is there? So in a way she's got to be allowed to be as she is. Our job is to not make it worse.'

'Part of the problem I have in assessing her state of mind is that her personality is not the same as it was twenty years ago and I don't just mean memory. I think I'm seeing sides of her that she never actually showed me or maybe I'm seeing sides of her that existed in the past and then fell away in her middle years.' I tell him about the sweet cooing person my mother became when she saw a child.

'Where is personality rooted, where is the soul? Let's get really heavy on this. Where does our sense of self come from? If a person is brain-damaged, you get a man, some reasonable father and husband, and he has a head injury and he comes out wicked and bad-tempered, he's got no insight, his personality is never the same. When he goes to heaven does he go as Mr Pre Bump On The Head or Mr Post Bump On The Head? And it's a very profound question about who we are and where our sense of self comes from. People have a view that during the lifespan from birth to death there's a point where we become an optimum human being, a grown-up. But there isn't, it's a cycle. Why should you expect your mother to be someone you know and can relate to when she only related to you for a certain number of years in her life? She was a wife, a daughter but now a great big thing has cut through her mind and how can you synchronize with that?'

'When I go with her on these outings it would appear to

the rest of the world that we're close, but it's actually a relationship I have constructed to deal with this brand-new individual who has vestiges of her old personality. And I have to make up a personality for myself as well.'

'Do you not think that we reconstruct each other anyway? You have a mind's eye view of yourself and other people and in order to survive we rehearse what we're going to say, we visualize almost instinctively and automatically. The trouble with dementia is that it cuts across all of those constructs. How do you relate to people when you are re-inventing yourself and the situation almost as you go along? That's what your mother does. How else could she do it? In a way your mother is dead and in a way she's not dead. But you're equally dead because you're not the child she carried through to whatever point. So how do you hang on to whatever sense you have of who that person really was, is and should be about, so that you don't just stick them in a box somewhere and forget about it *and* at the same time recognize the reality that you have to let go? You just have to let go. And people find it extraordinarily difficult with dementia because they're letting go of themselves as well. You can't finish the story, you can't resolve whatever it was and you can't bury it, you can't let it go.

'Without memory there's chaos. Without memory we don't exist. When a member of the family starts to lose their memory it turns everything up because not only are they losing their recall of you, your recall of them is challenged. It's almost a challenge to your own existence. If you live in the memory of someone else and their memory starts to fade, where are you? It's a strange thing and people find it extremely worrying, upsetting and the natural way of dealing with that is some sort of denial, and I remember when your sister came to see me that first day, she was so angry, so upset because somehow it was too frightening, if her mother was that bad, it's almost like you don't exist yourself.

'If your mother can't remember you, on what basis do you relate to your mother, or if she's not sure if you're her sister or her daughter? It's like being thrown out to sea. So the whole thing about memory is that it's not just one member of a family losing their memory. And for the Jewish community it's even more complex because while all cultures are to do with memory, none more so than the Jewish community in which everything is about what was.

'Let her be, as she is now. Let her be. If she was in her full and right senses would she be worried about you all the time? But you would be living a life aside from her fantasies and anxieties. Why can't you let her be, the same way? Let her be for the day.'

Without memory, what is left of our family? When Michele went to clear out the flat she found in our mother's many cupboards and wardrobes one of Britain's most important collections of carrier bags, a history of post-war shopping which we must get round to donating to the V&A one of these days. She'd thrown nothing out. Each bag, once the purchase had been removed, was carefully folded and put away in the spirit of make-do-and-mend that characterizes those who spent any portion of their adult lives during the war years, when the Ministry of Information terrorized housewives with the spectre of the Squander Bug, portrayed in cartoons crawling across the dead bodies of our boys on the battlefield who would still be warm and fighting if only those at home had saved string.

They came from everywhere, the bags: from the now defunct Bon Marché, incorporated decades before into the Liverpool branch of John Lewis; from Cripps on Bold Street, the city's smartest store, and from Hendersons, second poshest, neither of which survived the recession of the 1980s; from Lucinda Byre, a 'boutique' in which I had a Saturday job when I was fifteen, and from Coopers, the delicatessen. It was fitting that carrier bags were what she had left behind

her; not a book or a musical composition or a painting but
the marvellous ephemera of our times.

But also in the flat, interleaved with the carrier bags, inside
them or folded in their midst, was our documentary history,
the part that exists in black and white, official papers and
personal letters, not just my parents' private lives, but my
own too, hundreds and hundreds of pages. Michele took
everything away and I searched through them myself later. I
transferred everything into four red box files and on 19
November 1997 I picked up the fragile papers in my fingers
and I read.

From the 1940s, that terrible decade, is a communication
from my mother's brother Harold, dated 28 September 1940
and sent from Hadrian's Camp, Carlisle. He writes it to Dear
Father, Mother & Rose, so my mother was wrong and my
grandfather did not die before the war.

As regards when I will be home I cant say the exact
time. . . . If Fanny is in Liverpool, & hasn't bothered
to call, bugger her. I wont bother writing to Abish.
Five of us here in B Company are Jewish. 2 of us
from Lpool & the others from Manchester. We all go
to see the Jewish minister, that's what he is called
here, every fortnight on Wed. dinner time. He is not
much good, the real english kind, all services in
english & most of the fellows don't know what he is
talking about most of the time. All he seems to do is
take your name and number every time he comes. We
were supposed to be vaccinated and have another
inoculation today, but they haven't bothered, so I
suppose they will do it next weekend. They always do

it on Saturday because they have to give you 48 hours off duty every time they inoculate you & we are supposed to be off on Sat afternoon and Sunday (I said supposed to be). You do more work then, than you do during the week. The food is not as bad now, as I complained to the officer when he came round one day, & I had a good complaint, as I was on the sick list for a week after eating one of their meals and had a doctors note to prove it to the officer. It's the fact that some of the fellows in the cookhouse are swines. The food is good, its the mess they make of it that's the trouble. Did I tell you about the fish they gave us one day? One each. You would be glad to get it in Liverpool. When we started to eat it, we found it hadnt been opened or cleaned. They just cut the heads off and then boiled them as they were. They give you good potatoes here, they have more eyes than a hundred men. . . .

In the same envelope as that letter is a photograph of the first, temporary marker in the shape of a six-pointed Star of David (amongst a field of crosses) which they put on his grave, the dug earth still a fresh, damp mound out of the Italian land. The place is the Sangro River cemetery, Plot 14, Row B, Grave 22. Here lies H. Haft. Regimental number 3460673. 50/R Royal Tank Regiment. Died 21.12.43. There's another picture, this time in colour, taken many years later by persons unknown – perhaps my mother, for my parents went on a holiday to Rimini once – of a stone monument, an inscription I can't read, and scrubby Adriatic flowers growing at the foot of the stone.

Curious about this unknown man, dead at thirty-one

without wife or children, I ring the Royal Tank Regiment. 'If he went in in 1940 when he was twenty-nine, he would have been a volunteer rather than conscripted,' a Mr D. Fletcher, the librarian at the Tank Museum in Dorset, enthusiastically told me. 'He'd have thought, "Things are looking interesting."' Ah yes, that devil-may-care language of prangs and whizz-bangs that the British so love using when they come close to trauma. Maybe my uncle did join up in this gung-ho spirit but I suspect that for him, like all Jews, the Second World War was a deeply personal business.

'He'd have had a good war,' Mr Fletcher continued. 'First

in a Valentine then a Sherman. The 50th were in the desert right through from Alamein to Tunis, then to Sicily and into Italy. The operation on the Sangro started in October. According to the war diary on 27 November his CO, a man called Russell, returned after being wounded and two days later he was killed. Your uncle would have been a driver or a loader. He could have been killed by an anti-tank gun. Or it was considered to be fair game that as you leapt out you would be machine gunned. Or you might be standing outside with a cigarette and be shot. If he'd survived to the January he would have moved over to the other side of Italy and become operational under the Americans. Not a bad war at all.'

So now I know. Personally, I'd like him to have died peacefully, having a smoke.

Later, there's an undated cutting from the letters page of the *Liverpool Echo* in which Maurice Drabin of the Bayshore Men's Golfer's Club, Miami Beach, Florida, writes:

Just looking through my set of old pictures, I came across this one of a bunch of the lads. We were walking down Lord Street in 1922 and one of us noticed that we were all wearing the same kind of snap-brimmed hat. It seems that a George Raft movie had been shown a week or two previously and this was the style. Thought it might make an interesting item.

They stand, nine of them, in two rows, done up as gangsters. Young immigrant boys, trying to look like Americans in those days when all your style came from across the

Atlantic – so what's new? Reading the names, I recognize almost all of them: Jake Ostrin – didn't I play with his daughter when I was a child? Lauri de Freese, a friend of my father's. Maurice Gravo. Maurice Drabin, who got lucky and really became an American. C. Miller. Alec Bernstein. Issy Ginsberg – it's my uncle, that's why the cutting was kept. Maurice Cordova – Michele had a friend called Alison Cordova, was Maurice her grandfather? Dave (Docker) Skulnick. Was he really a docker or just built like one? And was this Docker the older brother of my mother's boyfriend, killed in the war?

Something is wrong with Maurice Drabin's memory, it's faulty; if the year this photograph was taken really was 1922 it can't have been a George Raft picture they'd just seen. He never played a gangster in the silents and that style of hat didn't come into vogue until the 1930s. Raft's big break was *Scarface* in 1932. Perhaps 1922 was just a misprint and Maurice meant 1932 all along.

No letter of reunion would have come to him from his long-lost pal Issy, one of the lads. Here's a document from the Corporation of Liverpool showing that in 1947 Jack Bloomberg (I remember him, a kosher butcher) had paid £3 for a plot at Lowerhouse Lane Cemetery in which was to be interred Leslie Israel Ginsberg.

And here's a typewritten letter dated 4 July 1951, from an address in Ormskirk, Lancashire.

Dear Rose
On Mother's behalf, Joyce's and of course for myself I wish to thank you for your kind letter. It was a dreadful shock for us, and yet we have been expecting such a thing to happen for so many years, he was such

275

a delicate person, and down the years steadily more
so. We little thought that my dear gentle daddy's
death would be considered National news, but he was
so highly thought of, and had done such valuable
work for servicemen that his passing was broadcast,
and a fitting tribute paid. He had a military funeral,
which was attended by all sorts of people and we have
received literally hundreds of messages. All this is little
consolation, but it satisfies us to know that his great
work has not gone unnoticed.

I feel that you will be pleased to hear that Sonia has
passed her scholarship, and will attend the Grammar
school with Elka, starting in September. I did know
you had a baby daughter, and have already wished her
every happiness and good health since the day she was
born but had no heart to write to you.

You see it is futile to go into all the old arguments
for and against, but the fact remains that both myself
and the children, as far as the Ginsbergs are
concerned, are definitely unwanted, and I also know
that the reason being they are afraid I might ask for
something. Well my dear they need have no fears on
that score, I intend to stay away from them all. They
cannot dig up any more lies and inventions about me.

If and or, when any of them should ever wish to
see me for any reason whatsoever, they always know
where to find me. Family quarrels are odious and
usually petty and mean, but in my affair the most
striking thing is that there is no quarrel, merely a
coldness, which until the final break was covered with
a treacly smarmyness, which is worse.

However I did not write to say this, except that I

want you to understand why I have not written or
attempted to see you, as you already know this is
hardly your fault, but I do like to hear the truth, and I
think it is despicable of women, to say nothing about
a man who will lie about a woman for his own ends.

I can honestly say that I wish you all nothing but
the best of good health and good fortune, but
however anybody may or may not have liked it, I was
after all Les's wife, mother of his children, and by the
indisputable ties of blood they will remain so. A thing
which even the mighty Ginsbergs cannot sever,
however much they may wish to.

The children send their love. Mother and Joyce,
Billy and myself wish you the best. Kisses for baby
Linda.

Yours

Mollie

Who was Mollie, this child of such a respected figure that
his death was national news? My uncle Issy's wife. Why had
the Ginsbergs ostracized her? Because she wasn't Jewish.
Because their beloved brother, the best-looking of them all,
who had stood once in the middle of the front row to have
his picture taken in a snap-brimmed American hat, like
George Raft wore, had stepped outside the tribe, had dis-
obeyed the oath which the family had taken, to be Jews for
all time, the Covenant they re-enacted with God at their
bar-mitzvahs. Poor Issy, born a generation too early, before
these days when tolerant people say, 'Live and let live.' In my
mother Mollie apparently found that tolerance, one sister-in-
law writing to the other, though my mother had not spoken
to her own sister Lillian after she had married out of the

faith, and would she have continued to adore her beloved
brother Harry if he had survived the war and married his
sweetheart? Who sent his mother a letter on the news of his
death, expecting sympathy and the sharing of grief and
instead found only a stony heart?

Poor Mollie, too. At least she remarried, and in a grand
irony for two decades from the 1960s was the matron of
Stapely, the old people's home where my grandfather spent
his final years and which would one day turn my mother
down flat on the grounds that she was dangerous and mad.
What happened to Mollie's clever daughters Elka and
Sonia – two Sonias fathered by the Ginsberg boys, as it
turned out? I don't know. No one does. They must be in
their sixties now, married women with grandchildren of
their own and married names to live under; glad, I'm sure, to
have discarded Ginsberg as soon as they could. There was a
son, too. He was called David and became a pharmacist, I
believe. I dare say I could just pick up the phone, get his
number from Directory Enquiries and speak to him.
Apologize for what my family did to him and his sisters.
Perhaps one day I will.

Does he know that his father was in prison during the
war, on charges connected with the Black Market? A nice
husband for the high-born Mollie, this Jewish scoundrel
who didn't just dress like a gangster but behaved like one.
Does David know the family story that he picked up some
infection there and could, one supposes, be said to have died
of prison fever?

Now it really is the 1950s and the sun is shining. Known and
unknown people are sending telegrams to congratulate my
parents on the birth first of one, then two daughters. Here's

the details from Sykes, Waterhouse & Co of their new home at 1 Williton Road, of my childhood bedroom sized 13′2 × 12′2′ and of the '<u>FRONT LOUNGE</u> (15′2 × 12′) with bay window extension, expensive modern tiled grate and two side windows', the 'bright <u>MORNINGROOM</u> (11′4 × 8′10′)', from the ceiling of which my bunny rabbit once hung, quietly steaming in the room's warmth, by the ears. I miss my bunny. I miss being a child in the 1950s when everything was safe and my father came home spilling loose change from his pockets for me to catch and once I was told off, for as my mother unfolded a Madeira tablecloth in the <u>FRONT LOUNGE</u> to show off to her friends, I tried to jump into it, like a hammock. Here's a pattern for a Castle Erin Art Needlework tablecloth Design No.532 ('Belfast Castle') to be worked in Clarks Anchor Stranded Cotton, and I remember now – she really did embroider and finish it and it was placed on the solid walnut dining table beneath her spreads of meats and salads and fruit cocktail pavlova.

Here is my parents' first-ever joint passport issued in 1952 – now that my father had, in 1947, proudly become a British citizen. Here are their travels: to Belgium, Holland, Israel, France, Mallorca, and my father's one and only return to America in 1965 on a B-1 and B-2 visa, reason for visit – business consultation and to visit relatives.

Here's a little card with instructions for the use by hairdressers of Barri Cold Wave Reagent, the perm formula my father pinched from Toni. The card is decorated with an Art Deco design and lettering: 'CAUTION This preparation may cause injury particularly to the skin of some persons and is sold on the express condition that the manufacturers BROLL LABORATORIES and the immediate vendor are not liable in any circumstances for any personal injury, illness or damage resulting from its use.' Broll Laboratories was the name above my father's business. On all his documents – his wedding licence, my birth certificate, his naturalization papers and change of name deed poll – he's described as a hairdresser's sundriesman, but to himself, he was a scientist! Broll Laboratories, it said on his business card. Manufacturing Chemists.

Now it's the 1960s and the past is catching up with my family. There's a small piece of lined paper with ten lines of Hebrew writing that I can't even begin to read and under-neath, in English, 'These are the names you want to know.' They are the Hebrew names of my father's ancestors. He's taking part in the same quest that I would undertake, nearly forty years later. But the future is in their sights too, as well as the past. Another certificate shows: One tree has been planted in the name of LINDA GRANT a pupil of Allerton Hebrew classes in April 1961 in the Children's Wood. Does it grow there still? Can I visit my tree? What kind is it?

Here's my father's handwritten draft of the notice that will appear in the *Jewish Chronicle* announcing the death of my grandfather and the document which gives the dates, year on year, when he must light a *yarzheit* candle in a glass which placed on the mantelpiece in the morning room will burn for twenty-four hours in memory of Wolfe Ginsberg. Those flames that lit my childhood, so many of them, recol-lecting dead grandmothers and grandfathers, uncles who died in the war and uncles who died with rage against them because they had violated the first law of the Jewish family: the tribe above all else.

But look! It's Tuesday, 6 April 1965 and Lodge Shalom, under the jurisdiction of its Worshipful Master Esta Phillips

Cohen, is raising to the High and Sublime Degree of a
Master Mason, Brother Rose Grant. My mother, a free-
mason. Just up her street, keeping secrets. My father was one
too – in the business interest, you understand, all those din-
ners with aldermen who could nod through a planning
application, the Ginsberg way of taking on the authorities,
rubbing shoulders with the Top Man.

The 1970s arrive. Things aren't so good. A letter comes from
Ada Minion, the Lady Mayoress, saying how disappointed
they are that my parents couldn't join them at the town hall the
previous evening, 'but we do understand your difficulties at the
present time'. What difficulties were those? I don't know. I
can't remember. It sounds like an edgy time in Liverpool. On
holiday in Israel, they get a letter from Marina: 'Today the
petrol delivery men are going on strike. No sugar in the shops
now, they're on strike at Tate & Lyle. Everyone has been rush-
ing to the shops, you would think there was a war on.'

Letter from one of my mother's friends, on notepaper
from the Hotel Alexander, Lido di Jesolo, Venice:

> My Dear Rose
> I'm sorry that I did not phone you before I went
> away . . . I do hope things are much better at home
> and you are feeling a little brighter. It is very hard for
> me to write this letter without upsetting you, but you
> know that that is the last thing I want to do.

The postmark is 1971, so my mother is fifty-three, it's the
time of her menopause, the years when Michele found her
crying in the bath and a year after my father's terrible heart
attacks when she's out at work doing the books, making up

the wages bill, while he sits convalescent at home, watching
the racing, shuffling heavily to the phone to place his bets,
our money draining away down the course at Epsom,
Aintree and Uttoxeter. I notice how frightened the writer of
the letter is of giving offence – *It is very hard for me to write this
letter without upsetting you* . . . She's well aware that one wrong
word and she will join the ranks of the fallen-out-with, be
known forever as 'that bitch'.

More letters: one from my mother to me, sent from
Mallorca:

Dear Linda
Hope everything is OK & you are switching off
immersion heater locking back doors & not leaving
lights on & being extremely tidy and not leaving
anything *Personal* around. Have you given Peggy the
electric & phone bill if not you will be cut off?
  Michele is having a wonderful time she is aching
with sunburn. Please write to me.

Love Mummy x x x

And from Michele, now at university:

Dear Mum amd Dad
Well I thought I8d impress you with my typing skills
but I don't seem to have done very well so far! A
friend has lent me this typewriter for a few weeks so I
can type up some of my academic work (they tend to
view a piece of work more favourably if it's typed –
I8ll try anything).
  Last weekend was very tense ans by the end of it I
felt quite exhausted but I suppose you felt pretty

much the same. I want you to know that I felt very
hurt to hear you sufgest that I don't care about you
because any one of my close friends can tell you that
precisely the opposite is the case. I hope that some of
what was aid was only really said out of frustration
with one another and that you didn't really mean
everything. I hope that this can clear the air a little.
We both know that in some areas we are never going
to agree and I think we should try and accept that . . .

The 1980s. Everything comes unstuck. An invoice from W.
A. Hoare & Sons (Sculptors) Ltd, Boscombe, Bournemouth.
Re memorial to the late Benjamin Grant. To supplying and
erecting memorial etc. including 109 English and 36
Hebrew letters including white chippings all as contract . . .
£513.70. In a covering letter Mrs G. Cranford thanks my
mother for her custom and hopes she will 'feel able to rec-
ommend us to your friends should the occasion arise'.

A cutting from the *Manchester Jewish Telegraph* reporting
the death of my father's sister Tillie, Shaina's mother, 'after a
long illness'. It was Alzheimer's Disease. What was she left
with when she no longer knew her own daughter? The
memory of how when she was a child her father kept a
horse called Tonypandy to draw his cart, which took off at a
gallop and stopped up short at the docks? Or that they had
a cat in the bakery to keep the rats down, which her sister
Gertie once dressed up like a baby and showed it to itself in
the mirror, whereon it fled screeching away, never to be
seen again? Gertie's daughter Joy told me these stories and
they pass with her from events recollected into myth.

'She was associated with nearly every Leeds Jewish charity
and could be relied upon when large sums of money were

needed,' the report continues. 'In her younger days she was responsible for cooking Passover meals for Jewish prisoners.'

And another cutting, this time from Lynda Lee Potter's column in the *Daily Mail*, headed 'What I wish I could tell my mother', reporting on a Channel Four documentary 'in which famous daughters talk about their mothers'. Mine has underlined in red ink: '*All mothers, it seems, are obsessed about their daughters' appearance and this is probably one revelation we can all learn from. My own mother spent hours winding my hair round rags, curling tongs or the earliest home perm rollers.*'

The 1990s. Here's the card with her room number from the hotel in Sorrento on her last foreign holiday. Here's her last passport and a form headed East Dorset Health Authority Transfer of Care/Hospital to Community, dated 30.9.91: 'Treatment required: Check visit to see if managing to cope. Goes for days without eating.'

A second form from the same Health Authority: 'Appears alert and orientated most of the time but occ. vague and dis-orientated. Rarely admits to pain until Drs are around!'

Not much left now, just scraps of paper in which she has put down disjointed letters to herself. The torn-off half of a Christmas card on which she has written

Linda & Michele
Deads in
Bank
Poole
Will in
left 3 eggs
40p

★

An old piece of paper, with yellow stains. A handwritten copy of a poem. I don't recognize the writing. It's headed *For Ben* – The Jester, from *Flutter*. It's called, 'The Heavens Weep'.

> *It's midsummer day, the dawn it is bright*
> *Gone is the fear of that dark troubled night*
> *I gaze at you darling, before you're awake*
> *And gently your hand in my hands I take*
> *Two years you'll live the medicos say*
> *Tell me they're wrong, dear God I pray*
> *Yet even then the dark angel was near*
> *You answered his call without any fear*
> *The rain gently falling, the skies filled with gloom*
> *They'll lay you to rest in the earth's dark womb*
> *Slumber, beloved, your last long sleep.*
> *For lo and behold 'The heavens weep.'*

Who is Flutter? A girlfriend? More like the nickname for one of my dad's pals at the race course. It was just the kind of poem my father liked. Educated English people consider sentimentality a cheap, inferior emotion, a degradation of real feeling. Years of studying literature have taught me to despise this kind of nonsense and yet I think of it as the essence of my father's love for my mother. We're a senti-mental family, we cry easily in movies. My love for my father is also a sentimental attachment, for the man who always wore his heart on his sleeve. I think of him, now, when I hear the voice of Al Jolson but above all in the soundtrack of a film he did not live quite long enough to see, Sergio Leone's *Once Upon a Time in America*, released the year of his death, and which sums up for me his 'boyhood days' in New York, which had the best of him.

For my mother, that's another matter. Do I love her? Yes, but not in the same way as those who say 'I *love* my mother. I could never put her in a home.' For loves are like people, each is different, and they are not just the same love which finds different objects to attach to. When I was a child our Sunday morning ritual was to gather round the gramophone and listen to records, great big '78s like black dinner plates that broke when you dropped them and melted in boiling water so they could be shaped into useless and ugly ornaments, according to my comics.

All our records were on Jewish themes, all, without exception, tear-jerkers. We played one about the displaced persons of post-war Europe with its triumphant discovery of the newly emergent Jewish state:

> *Tell me where can I go*
> *There's no place I can see*
> *Where to go, where to go*
> *Every door is closed to me*
> *To the left, to the right*
> *It's the same in every land*
> *There is nowhere to go*
> *And it's me who should know*
> *Won't you please understand?*

But the loudest sobbing was reserved for Sophie Tucker's rendition of 'Yiddisher Momma', sung in both Yiddish and English, my parents joining in in their first language, Michele and I in ours. It wasn't a song of the Old World but the new one, as the lead-in makes clear: 'My fancy takes me to a humble East Side tenement . . .' And so it went on, oozing schmaltz:

Mein Yiddisher Momma, I need her more than ever now
Mein Yiddisher Momma, I long to kiss her wrinkled brow
I long to take her hand in mine
As in days gone by
And ask her to forgive me for
Those things I did that made her cry.

And so on. What always made us laugh, in this song, laughing through our tears, were these lines, when we all looked up at my mother whose capacity to match navy would be preserved long after she could distinguish the difference between her daughter and her long dead sisters:

> *How few were her pleasures*
> *She never cared for fashion styles*
> *Her jewels and her treasures*
> *She found them in her baby's eyes.*

As if.

As old now as she was then, I find that I can love my mother when we shop together, when we lose ourselves and the past and future in a department store – nothing that belongs to time of any significance except the rise or fall of the season's hemlines or its shades or the width of lapels or the colour of lipstick. So we shop together, outside time, mother and daughter united each in our purposeful quest to do what we have always done, and which to her goes on making sense: 'That would suit you, Mum.'

'Have you seen the price of this?'

'I know, but it's a Joseph.'

'Oh well, that explains it.'

So we find our common ground.

Apart from the documents, which tell their own version of the truth, out of context, as always, what is left? What I know is that as long as I live I will remember my parents and that the memories I have of them will be transmitted to the next generation, until they erode away into myth, nothing but stories, and when they do they will exist in another kind of recollection.

What is memory? So many things. Here's a description of the brain:

Soft as porridge and wrinkled like fingertips after a long, hot bath, the average human brain contains some 100 billion neurons, as the nerve cells that conduct the chemical and electrical traffic inside our bodies is known. Surrounding the billions of brain cells are at least 10 trillion synapses, the tiny gaps between neurons through which messages are transmitted from one cell to another. At any given moment millions of impulses are streaking through the neurons and synapses in our skulls, kindling this elaborate neural network into a flurry of signalling activity. The resulting barrage of neural firing forms the biochemical basis for all our perceptions, thoughts, emotions – and memories.

There are many metaphors for the memory – we used to think of it as a great warehouse, then a filing system, then a computer with its hard and floppy drives. When people say they have recovered long-suppressed memories of the past, when they remember their father sexually abusing them, for example, the images play themselves through their minds as if a long-lost video-tape had been found. But memory isn't like any of these things. Above all, it isn't a place, a store-house or a machine for recording events. What the scientists think now is that it's 'an intricate and ever shifting net of firing neurons and crackling synapses, distributed throughout the brain'. It's a labyrinth, 'the twistings and turnings of which rearrange themselves completely each time something is recalled'.

Fifty years ago the American psychologist Karl Lashley conducted an experiment with rats which he taught to negotiate successfully complex mazes. Incrementally removing thin slices of their cerebral cortexes to try to find the memory, he discovered that whichever section of the brain he removed, the rats were still able to remember how to run the maze. As more brain was excised, their performance diminished, but there was no single region, the removal of which erased the memory of how to find their way through altogether.

Memory, says the biochemist Stephen Rose, 'is a dynamic property of the brain as a whole rather than of any one specific region. Memory resides simultaneously everywhere and nowhere in the brain.' I like this idea very much. Memory, unlike people, doesn't dig itself into the soil and claim territory, it's rootless, the Wandering Jew of our physical selves.

Memory took about a hundred million years to develop. It came into being not as a way of remembering the past, but to predict the future. Our brains evolved to help us to navigate the world safely. We remember what we consider needs remembering, the rest indiscriminately dumped and forgotten. Once, when the world was much younger, memory survived only for a lifetime. Someone was born and lived and died and everything they saw and felt was gone, for there was no language to communicate it to anyone else. Hot summer days came and went and no one remembers them. Earthquakes, tidal waves, or the sight and scent of a flower that is extinct now. All gone, irretrievably.

Animals live this way. In a future time without intensive battery farming a chicken will not be able to pass down the generations the history of how its ancestors were once kept in extermination camps. There is no chicken history for chickens themselves. If you don't have language, I'm not sure if you can remember events at all, just images and the sensation of past pain.

When I recall my bunny rabbit hanging from the ears in the kitchen or my mother remembered those incidents from the long-forgotten past – watching the food cook in the open pot on the fire in the house in Devon Street and the soot from the chimney falling down into it, she and her sisters would always agree how much better meals tasted in those days before hygienic kitchens with formica worktops, before everything went electric – what we held in our minds were eidetic memories, from the Greek for image, photographs of the past. Most of us preserve such images from childhood but the ability to see the world this way, as a series of snapshots in an album, disappears as we enter adolescence and is replaced by a sense of the past that is chronological, as if we are entering both into our own personal histories over which we now have control, and so too, public history. And history isn't the totality of everything that has happened but how we interpret the past, the meanings we give it.

Only a few people preserve the capacity into adulthood for creating new eidetic memories, those with what we call photographic memories, music-hall acts. Steven Rose writes that photographic memory can't be much of an asset because those who have it don't usually make much of a success of their lives. To be able to synthesize and generalize from past events and to be able to forget them is what we need to survive, he says. So my mother retains what *she* considers to be important, such as the visual skills required to match navy, the imperative to look young, particularly on your daughter's wedding day, and the importance of always holding out for the best price on property.

Perhaps eidetic memory is a holdover from a pre-linguistic state and children lose it as they acquire the capacity to speak. When speech arrived, with it came the power to transmit memories from the past into the distant future after death, so a man or a woman could, like Ulysses and Penelope, achieve a kind of immortality, could aspire to be gods. Memories were woven into stories and songs, personal memory became collective memory and most of human history is the part which pre-dates writing, when the oral tradition was all one had.

Poets were the preservers of memory, of the origins of the tribe and their epic battles, their victories and their defeats. To be a poet was to commit prodigious acts of memory. They told their stories in verse and song because we remember things more easily through rhythm, like those tunes you listened to as a teenager the words of which you can sing correctly, all the way through, as soon as the first notes are played (where would karaoke machines be without this capacity?). For music creates structures of language that resemble the rhythms of our blood and heart and pulse.

But some things do not readily turn themselves into stories – the names of a general's troops, his battle orders, his route through the great forests of Northern Europe. Before writing became commonplace, the memory had to be trained by mnemotechnic systems which were called even then artificial memory. A man who was to deliver a speech would in preparation imagine a house or a temple and he placed in different rooms the various parts of his recitation so that when he stood up before his audience he had only to visit each room in turn and find within it his arguments. The longer the speech, the grander the mansion he built in his mind with its many columns and chambers and ante-chambers in which to keep the sub-clauses of his disquisition.

Up to the beginning of the twentieth century in Europe and America people who could not read relied on memory. Millennia went by before there were shopping lists. Illiterate Vermont countrymen took down in their heads the shopping of isolated farm wives and brought back their orders correct to every necessity.

Now the world is full of artificial memory: books, newspapers, films, television programmes, video-tapes, computer memory. The storage capacity of technology is illimitable. It mocks us with all we have forgotten. And we understand too the importance of forgetting lest we go mad with all there is to remember. When a Dorset village was the extent of your world, what you had to keep in mind from day to day formed a coherent, unfragmented whole: the names of the members of the tribe you called your family and the names of the crops and animals and wild things your survival depended upon, the kinds of frost and sun that froze or warmed you, the road to the next village or the town with its marketplace. But not much further beyond. And like distant echoes a few details of the history of the times you lived in: Where was the war your uncle died in? And your great-grandfather? Did you remember that your village lit a beacon to warn that the Spanish Armada was on its way? Yes, but what else did you know about sixteenth-century wars with Spain? Nothing.

In my head I carry a rough but intelligible history of Europe since the Middle Ages. I can tell you what happened in places I've never even been to. I know all about the American Civil War which happened a century before I was born and the American civil rights movement which began when I was a child. I once met a man who as a schoolboy stood outside the Finland Station when Lenin returned from exile to lead the Russian Revolution, his personal memory dovetailing into my public one. I have read, I think, thousands of books. I remember the tiniest fraction of all that my brain has devoured. There is too much information in the world now for anyone to remember in the way that people used to do.

Because we do not remember everything that has ever happened to us, because we must filter and select and edit the experiences and information that enter our senses every day and transform it into a meaningful narrative, our lives are essentially stories. Starting out to find out the 'facts' about my mother, I always had to bear in mind that in the end all I was going to have was a fable.

So my mother lives in this book and elsewhere. She exists in artificial memory, as any literate person does who was alive this century: in language, in photographs, in the letters she wrote and which were written to her. But like the poets my mother is also the transmitter of oral history, of *our* history, and like the poets she has brought to our family's stories her own capacity not just to remember but to imagine. PET scans show that whether we imagine or experience something, the same portion of the brain is stimulated. Imagination and memory are inseparable. When we remember we must use the imagination, for the memory of an event is never identical with the event itself (a blessing or a curse?) and when we explore the world imaginatively we use memory, filling in the spaces with all that we have learned.

My family's story is no less a mythology than the tales of the heroes that sailed the Mediterranean and met the Cyclops and Scylla and Charybdis and fell victim to the Sirens. And whatever I set down here is no less the work of my memory and imagination. If memory is about story-telling so the talkative Ginsbergs, with their tales exaggerated or half fictionalized or made up on the spot to suit an exigency, were all Homer's in their way.

They're talking about brain transplants, now. It was in the paper yesterday. The journalist rang the Alzheimer's Disease Society, as of course you would, for who would need a replacement brain more than a victim of dementia? Just think of it, my mother's failing mind could be replaced by someone else's. But then you have to ask, if I am not my own memory, who am I?

The self isn't a little person inside the brain, it's a work-in-progress, 'a perpetually re-created neurobiological state, so continuously and consistently reconstructed that the owner never knows it's being remade'. Memory, then, is a fabrication, a re-interpretation, a new reconstruction of the

original. Yet out of these unstable foundations we still construct an identity. It's a miracle.

The week in which my mother spent her first few terrified
days in the home, I was in Venice with her grandson. I took
him to the Accademia Museum and we spent a long time sitting in front of a Tintoretto. It was a depiction of an episode
from the New Testament which neither of us was familiar
with, something to do with the Resurrection. I was trying to
get him to examine the structure of the picture and the artist's
use of colour. I was trying to train his eye in the service of his
brain. And as we were looking I thought, 'In thirty years'
time, what will he say about me? "She took me for my first
visit to Venice and she showed me a Tintoretto but she's lost
her mind now and I had to put her in a home."'

What will he know of me? He'll have an archive of the
millions of words I have written but still I will be a mystery
to him. I have many secrets he doesn't know and other
things I've never bothered to tell him.

I'll survive in his memory, as his mother and grandma
will, endlessly re-imagined and re-invented each time he
thinks or speaks of us. We're so insubstantial, creatures that
emerge from an 'ever-changing maze of neural firing for-
mations and synaptic connections', made from raw materials
in a constant state of flux.

What makes family? Genes. When I went to Lomza, to
the place my father left so long ago, I found not only a
plaque on the wall recounting the fate of those Jews who
remained when my grandfather and his children left and
Lomza was still a Jewish world, but a cemetery. The graves –
chiselled with Hebrew writing and the Lion of Judah and
some defaced by painted swastikas – crumbled in the rain

and the wind which blew across the agrarian plains. In the soil beneath, it stands to reason, lie those who share my own genetic make-up, but I don't know who they are, cannot describe their faces. They're from another time. And the family that sailed to England in the mistaken belief that they would step ashore in the New World, has also struck out in all directions like stars in the expanding universe so that I could pass my cousins on the street now, and not recognize them.

The century of the Ginsbergs and the Hafts comes to an end; they were twentieth-century inventions. My nephew goes on into the new millennium and we'll be forgotten, too. The memory of almost everything is lost in the end. My mother, my sister and me. All equal. Yet we try to buck our fortune. What memories! What stories!

Afterword

In the year that has passed since this book was written, my mother's condition continues to worsen. By the spring of 1998, she was unable to concentrate on the whole content of a short sentence. Thus we had the following exchange:

'I won't be able to come in next Sunday because I'm going to Nice for a long weekend.'

'That's marvellous! Where did you say you were going?'

'Nice.'

'How long for?'

'For a long weekend.'

'But you haven't told me where you're going yet.'

'Nice.'

'Oooh. I'd love to go there. How long will you be away?'

'For a long weekend.'

'And where did you say you were going, again?'

'Nice.'

'How long for?'

'A long weekend.'

'But where . . .?'

And so it went on.

By the summer, we stopped the outings. The further she got from the home, the more confused and disoriented she became. Even shops offered little happiness. On the day that

Arsenal won the League, when the traffic along Highbury Grove was at its heaviest, she got off the bus, tears streaming down her face.

'Please, Mum,' I said to her. 'Please don't take this out on me. It's not my fault.'

'You?' she said. 'I couldn't care less about *you*.' And turning, she ran into the oncoming traffic. I pulled her back, forcibly by the shoulders.

'Whose benefit are these expeditions for?' John Bridgewater asked me. 'Are they for you or for her? Clearly she's finding them more and more distressing. Why can't you let her be?'

But I observed that there was a gold standard of attendance by relatives to the home, which I fell far short of. There were relatives who came in every single day. How could I say I was acting out of over-burdened guilt when I only visited once a fortnight?

'This woman who's there every day, sitting with her husband,' a friend said. 'What would she be doing if he was well? She'd be sitting at home with her husband. You wouldn't be seeing your mother every day, would you? You see her more often now than when she lived in Bournemouth.'

So now I go in less often and we sit in her room while the conversation wheels in smaller and smaller circles. I sense that sometimes she is happy, a lot of the time she isn't. She is unhappy not because she is ill-treated but because she does not have what you or I would call a life.

It is becoming clear that the road my mother is travelling down now is not to a smiling, placid, tranquil place. Increasingly, she has violent mood swings of aggression, rage and paranoia as the strokes cut out the last repressive mechanisms. Her speech remains lucid but what she says no longer describes reality. I suppose that speech will go one day and all that will be left will be howls or laughter.

This is an extremely bleak prognosis and it seems a shame to end at a place so unforgiving. People have asked me if I found writing this book therapeutic. No, in the sense that I did not sit at the keyboard of my computer, making myself feel better. But after it was written, in the period in which it was being typeset, I found myself on many occasions, thinking, I wish I'd written this or, I'd like to add that. And I realized that all these amendments were about reconciliation, so perhaps there was some therapy there after all.

In July, the family went on holiday to a villa in Tuscany, an umber seventeenth-century house in the great bowl of a fragrant valley near the hill towns of Montepulciano and Cortona. We arrived late at night, when it was dark, and I woke early the next morning. I got up and walked across the grass to the pool. Something was moving on the surface. A hedgehog had fallen in and was doing comic lengths, up and down, turning when it reached the end. Unable to get out, all it could do was keep itself afloat. There were dark patches on the bottom of the pool. It had shit itself in terror. There was a net on a long pole, to clear leaves and other debris away. I picked up the pole. It was heavier than I expected. Three times the hedgehog fell off the net as I tried to lift the creature out. It sank to the bottom, then bobbed up to the top again as I prepared another rescue bid. Finally, I managed to tip it on to the grass. It lay there, paralysed in fright. But when I came back out an hour or so later, it was gone, so I suppose it recovered itself and re-adjusted to its proper domain, the darkness of the bushes, the dry rustle of olive leaves.

Even while I was watching the hedgehog, I knew that it

reminded me of my mother. Life had taken a terrible turn and thrust her into a new element. Like the hedgehog, she was exhausting her energy trying to keep going, to keep up an appearance of there being an order to things, as the hedgehog at first looked merely as though it were enjoying its early morning exercise. Like the hedgehog, she had fouled her environment, which was our family, in her terrible fear of what would become of her. Unlike the hedgehog, there was nothing at all I could do to save her.

It may seem a little rude to compare one's mother to a hedgehog (and if you have read this book you'll understand we're not exactly animal lovers) but I think about that hedgehog a lot. It's the only way I have of making sense of what has happened to us, that brave animal doing everything it could to keep itself from drowning.

Another thing that has happened since the book came out is that I have received many, many letters. At first I tried to reply to every one but the backlog got bigger and bigger until I realized that I would be spending half of every day answering them so now I have another guilt – about all the letters that people sat down and wrote and no response came. But the letters are, in some ways, the real addenda to this book because they answered the question that has been raised about this kind of genre. Why did you have to *write* about it? Why go public?

Because there is a silence, a taboo. No one knows how to feel, or what to think because the meteor of dementia that strikes families and wipes out so much is supposed to be part of the realm of privacy. What you don't talk about. What you keep to yourself.

You could have written a novel, people argued. Yes, I

could. Indeed there had been two novels already. Yet when the letters came, what the writers said was, 'What was important to me about this book was that I knew it was true.'

I don't know what this means for the future of fiction. Do we distrust the invented, the imaginary? Or will it be that, in twenty years, literary critics will recall that odd period in the closing years of the last century, when there was a fashion for what was called 'confessional' literature, and how strange a phenomenon it was, and why did it die out so quickly? Or will they think, how peculiar that when the literary memoir finally appeared, such a fuss was made of it, and how it was branded as 'confessional' as though it was new and had more in common with *The Oprah Winfrey Show* than, say, the great work of St Augustine, which is called, of course, his Confession.

There was one letter, however, which stood out from all the rest. The writer had bought this book for his wife whose own mother had suffered from dementia. But reading it himself, he recognized someone. He recalled that as a student, during the vacation, around 1961 or 1962, he had worked as a relief van-driver for a Jewish businessman in Liverpool, and carried in the back of his vehicle, 'enough peroxide to bleach the hair of the whole of the North-West'.

And how could my father have known, he asked, that for a month or two he had employed one of the original Quarrymen, a childhood friend of John Lennon who had formed a group with him back in 1957 while they were at school, and who had, of course, been at that historic meeting in that same year when Paul McCartney came to a church fete in Woolton Village and met John and joined the Quarrymen? And the rest, as they say, is history.

So now we have that one to add to our family mythology. I could have met John Lennon! It could have been me he married, not Cynthia (never mind that I was only ten or eleven at the time).

So the past goes on re-arranging itself in surprising new ways. It is not over, never finished with. It keeps returning. And always to surprise us.

November 1998
London

Acknowledgements

Those who have a relative with dementia sometimes feel they are held prisoner in a secret society with its own rules and customs and justifications and even language. Out in the world you go to work, do the shopping, have friends, go to parties, take holidays. You may feel in control, even powerful. But at home you are confronted with the dissolution of meanings. Struggling to do the right thing, hoping that there is a cure or a solution, you sink into guilt.

In December 1994 I mentioned to Roger Alton, Features Editor of the *Guardian*, that I would like to write about the difficulties we had had with Social Services in trying to get them to make what we considered the correct assessment of my mother's needs for residential care. I envisaged a careful, objective indictment of the Community Care Act. What poured out from my fingers onto the keyboard was far more personal than I had imagined. I had not planned to describe in such detail my mother's dementia. Yet how could I explain the decision we were confronted by without the detail? Shocked, I put the text away for several months.

When I came back to it, I showed it to my sister. She made a number of suggestions and agreed that I should go ahead and publish. What I anticipated, guilt doing my thinking for me, was that I would be inundated with letters from readers accusing me of being heartless, selfish, cruel. To my astonishment, the opposite was the case. Apart from two, the many letters that came – all from those with their own dementing relatives or professionals engaged in caring for them – offered nothing but support and thanks. Many told their own awful stories, often shot through with black humour – the woman who had booked a Saga holiday and who ordered a taxi from her home in Somerset to the airport in London every morning for a week. Or they were too terrible to think about – the grandmother who thought her son was her brother who had been killed in the First World War, and was so traumatized by his return from the dead that in the end he stopped visiting her and she remained, unvisited, until her own death.

My agent, Derek Johns, after reading the *Guardian* article, told me I should extend it into a book. I had been struggling for some months to write a novel based on my family. I felt that the fictional characters I was creating were in some bizarre way robbing my relatives of their own biographies. The characters were flat, inauthentic, every made-up incident an insult to my family's many, varied truths. So I agreed to go ahead. I wanted to write a paean to the Hafts and the Ginsbergs, though whether it's fiction or non-fiction, as Philip Roth has remarked, 'When a writer is born into a family, the family is finished'.

I went first to the Alzheimer's Disease Society, whose support and encouragement did much to assuage the continuing feelings of guilt. They directed me to Professor Gordon Wilcock, of Bristol University, Frenchay Hospital and Chair of the Scientific and Medical Advisory Committee of the Alzheimer's Disease Society, who took time out to meet with me and answer my many questions. In this context I would also like to thank Professor Steven Rose of the Open University for explaining some matters to do with dementia and the functions of memory.

I talked to my cousins, Marina Moss, Stewart Haft, Sefton Grant, Shaina Taylor and Joy Pond who frequently confounded me with versions of the family history which directly contradicted my own received myths. Frankie Vaughan kindly shared with me his memories of Devon Street between the wars.

The person who had the greatest influence on my thinking about dementia and the role of residential care was John Bridgewater, head of residential services at Jewish Care, whose wise and thoughtful insights into memory became the basis of how I came to understand the illness which afflicted my mother. I sent chapters to Pat Tennuci, of Dorset Social Services, who gave me permission to quote from our correspondence, and I wish to make it quite clear here that despite the restraints of the system her advice, help and guidance during my mother's last few years of liberty were at times the difference between going mad and staying slightly sane. I also want to thank the staff and volunteers of Jewish Care who enclose my mother with safety and, as their name implies, care. Particularly Iola Samuels and Fionnuala Baiden.

It was not just my mother's blood relatives who were affected by her illness. Mark Adams bore much of what is described in these pages. John Boughton came to events later but with his own history of a parent's dementia.

When the idea of this book was first mooted by my agent, Frances Coady, Publisher of Granta Books, sent him a letter of such strength and passionate belief in the enterprise that once again, I was given the courage to continue. For her unstinting support and diplomatic editorial advice when I got into endless difficulties over structure I owe her a great deal.

After the book was finished, I went to see my mother on a cold, wet day. When I said the weather was too bad to go out she flew into a rage and told me that I needn't have bothered coming for by now who I am to her is not a daughter (she can no longer remember my name), but 'the person who takes me out'. I spent some minutes in the lobby talking to a woman whose husband was a resident there. She shopped in the morning, spent every afternoon with him, went home, had a bath, took the phone off the hook and recovered. And this, she told me, was her life. 'You're a writer,' she said, accusingly, 'Why aren't you writing about all this?' And I was happy to tell her that I had.

Finally, my greatest debt is to my sister, Michele Grant, without whose permission there would have been no book. Who went through exactly what I did and whose story this is as well as mine, though each of us would tell it differently according to our own point of view. Who understood so much that I didn't. And who has the answer to a question some readers may have been asking and therefore has the last word:

'You should write a book about this, Linda.' My sister and I were into the second hour of our regular mutual therapy telephone conversations about The Mum Problem. Neither of us then knew what such a book would be like, still less the moral dilemmas we would both face in pursuing a very public airing of our family's dirty linen.

Is it right to subject your family to forensic scrutiny?

For this I must share Linda's burden of responsibility. She sought, and I gave my permission. First, because I hope that others who must live through the experience of a close, dementing relative can feel just a little bit less alone. Second, because like Linda, I am seduced by the idea that the family I had always thought of as shallow and inconsequential is actually fascinating and even significant.

But most of all I gave my permission because my sister is a writer and to suppress the impulse to write about the very core of oneself would be an unbearable waste. To examine life is a difficult choice – but for my dear sister, the only meaningful one.

THE CAST IRON SHORE

Winner of the David Higham Award
and shortlisted for the Guardian Fiction Prize 1996

Sybil Ross has been brought up by her Jewish furrier father
and style-obsessed mother as an empty-headed fashion plate.
But on the worst night of Liverpool's Blitz she uncovers a
secret that leaves her disorientated. When the war is over,
Sybil embarks on a voyage that leads her to the very edge of
America, and to a final choice.

'Grant's writing is intelligent, and she rises to lyrical
and sensual moments with grace. As it treads the fine
line between the personal and the political, Sybil's
story will stay with you. Read it, treasure it, then
wonder: Why does contemporary literature field so
few smart, courageous heroines?' Natasha Walter,
Observer

'In Sybil Ross, Grant has given us a female
protagonist to match the end of the twentieth
century.' Lisa Jardine, *New Statesman*